THE PROBLEM WITH GRACE

THE PROBLEM WITH GRACE

Reconfiguring Political Theology

Vincent W. Lloyd

STANFORD UNIVERSITY PRESS
STANFORD, CALIFORNIA

Stanford University Press
Stanford, California

Printed in the United States of America on acid-free, archival-quality paper

Library of Congress Cataloging-in-Publication Data

Lloyd, Vincent W., 1982- author.
The problem with grace : reconfiguring political theology /
Vincent W. Lloyd.
pages cm
Includes bibliographical references and index.
ISBN 978-0-8047-6883-2 (cloth : alk. paper) --
ISBN 978-0-8047-6884-9 (pbk. : alk. paper)
1. Political theology. I. Title.
BT83.59.L56 2011
261.7--dc22
                                    2010048538

Typeset by Bruce Lundquist in 11/16 Bembo

For my father

Contents

THE PROBLEM WITH GRACE

INTRODUCTION

Beyond Supersessionism

IN 1933, GRACE MULLIGAN WAS PASSING THROUGH RURAL ALABAMA when she happened upon the Manderlay plantation. A white woman of refined tastes and social conscience, Grace was traveling with her father and his posse of upmarket gangsters. The cars in their caravan slowed, and then stopped, as a black woman hailed them and asked for help. "They're going to whip him," the distraught woman cried. Grace discovered a community of African-Americans who had never been informed that slavery had been abolished decades before. As she entered the Manderlay plantation to investigate, Grace took it upon herself to inform the black residents of Manderlay that they no longer were slaves and were now free. Grace abolished the rules of the plantation, "Mam's Law" and reorganized the community into a democratic polity. She remained at Manderlay to facilitate the transition from slavery to freedom, overcoming various difficulties along the way. Her efforts paid off, and the new community reaped a bountiful harvest. But Grace's success was short-lived: the community soon imploded with suspicion, blood, and flames, viciously turning on itself and on Grace.

Lars von Trier's film *Manderlay* ends as its fictional heroine, Grace, is fleeing the plantation. Grace came to replace Law—with unanticipated, disastrous results. *Manderlay* allegorizes a structure that is pervasive but almost never acknowledged in political theory and political theology: a supersessionist logic. The world is amiss, fallen; some redemptive force, with its origins both inside and outside the world, is needed to make it right. Supersessionism within Christian theology has been forcefully criticized and largely abandoned in academic theology after the Second World War. But supersessionist logic, in many guises, remains regnant in political thought. The time to question its supremacy, and to offer an alternative, is long overdue. There is a political theology underlying much political theory, and that political theology must be reconfigured.

Political theology, understood as the discussion of religious concepts in a political context, has been stifled by a limited theological vocabulary. Political theology, as well as adjunct discourses such as theories of secularization, has focused on shifts between "immanent" and "transcendent" conceptions of God, noting how these correlate with different political structures. The requisite fix to the fallen world comes either from outside (in sovereign God or sovereign king) or from within. Such political theology reduces theology to the practice of pointing outside or pointing inside. Reducing the richness of theological tradition to two vague gestures leads directly into the trap of discarding Law in favor of Grace, for it focuses on modes of redemption rather than modes of living and acting, religiously or politically.

I take religious language seriously, and I do so in a way that retains the rich legacy of Jewish and Christian reflection on and refinement of religious concepts without subordinating those concepts to an overarching theological narrative. We gain something of value when concepts like tradition, liturgy, and sanctity are made available for political theorizing, but we lose something of value when such concepts are stripped of their religious heritage. We also lose something of value when every mention of concepts like tradition, liturgy, and sanctity brings with it unwanted commitments that are specifically theological. Some middle path must be possible: it is precisely the task of this book to identify and traverse that path.

As political theology has gained traction in the humanities, the supersessionist logic undergirding the field has gone unquestioned. Keywords in recent essays and books on political theology include *ontology*, *infinite desire*, *reenchantment*, and *the political*. The project of this book is to offer a new vocabulary. Instead of "ontology," I focus on social practice. Rather than focusing on what there is, I focus on how things are or what people do. Instead of "infinite desire," I focus on specific goal-directed actions, desires that can be sated. Instead of "reenchantment," I focus on sober appropriation of religious language for political analysis and action. Instead of "the political," I focus on specific personal and collective practices of politics.

It might seem as though detaching religious language from religious thought, from comprehensive stories about how the world is and how we ought to act, would lead to a project that is rhetorical rather than substantive. Religious language evokes a special affective response: am I simply attempting to harness the political potential of that affect? No: it is the current discourse of political theology, the discourse that needs to be reconfigured, that is using religious language in a purely rhetorical sense. Subtly in Carl Schmitt's work, and less subtly afterward, the observation that there are historical correlations between religious thought and political thought has led theorists to offer religious redescriptions of our world in order to push political thought in the direction the theorists desire. Schmitt quietly laments the loss of the transcendent relationship to religious-political sovereignty in an age of immanence; latter-day political theologians expose the "enchantment" underlying modernity, or the "infinite desire" expressed in actions, or the possibilities of an alternate "ontology," to motivate political change. These dulcet phrases are evocative because of a theological ground from which they are plucked, but away from that story they quickly wilt. Their force is relative to the theological stories that form their background; they lack independent standing.

In contrast, my interest is primarily in the practices to which religious concepts refer, not in harnessing the affect that religious language produces. My interest is in the social world, richly textured with practices and norms. Religious concepts help describe that texture. While pragmatists blithely gesture at the primacy of social practice, pragmatists' allergy to conceptual analysis and to metaphysics assures that this gesture remains unarticulated. Social practices and norms must be rigorously distinguished and individuated, their workings carefully analyzed. The most interesting recent work from both "pragmatic" (e.g., Robert Brandom) and "Continental" (e.g., Judith Butler) theorists has moved toward this approach. Only once that complex texture of the social world is acknowledged can we understand the usefulness of religious language in naming practices of political significance. Tradition, liturgy, sanctity, revelation, prophecy, faith, and love are all ways of exploiting the difference between practices and norms, and it is with such specific concepts, not with supersessionist logic, that the work of political theology must begin.

IT IS TEMPTING to read *Manderlay*, released in 2005, as a tale that speaks to the contemporary U.S. administration's blind zeal for spreading democracy, or, more generally, as a critique of the efficacy of liberal politics. Grace is confronted with oppression: a community of black people is living in slavery. At the moment she happens upon the community, one of the black people is going to be whipped. While her father argues that it is merely "a local matter" that is "not our responsibility," Grace says that "we" (white people) have created the situation and so have a "moral obligation" to fix it. Grace, with the support of her father's gangsters, informs the former slaves that they have rights. She tells them that each human being has inherent worth and dignity that must be respected. "They can now enjoy the same freedoms as any other citizen of this country," Grace proudly announces. She creates a forum for democratic participation in the governance of the community, complete with a system for voting.

Indeed, Grace not only creates the political institutions that she thinks are necessary for ending the oppression of the former slaves; she also tries personally to reach out to them. She buys an easel and paints for one young man (because his face "possess[es] an artist's sensitivity") and proudly presents the supplies to him with the words "because we believe in you." But her high hopes are soon dashed: Grace discovers that she has confused the artistic young man with his brother. Timothy, a strong-spirited former slave, looking on, notes facetiously how all black men look alike. The attempts that Grace, as representative of liberalism, makes at recognizing differences within the community of Manderlay fall short.

Moreover, the newly constituted liberal democratic polity miserably fails. First, it implodes, with its newly "liberated" members using the democratic processes just established to their own advantage and in "inappropriate" ways (voting on when a jokester can laugh at his own jokes; sentencing to death a woman accused of stealing food). Then, after the initial troubles seem resolved, the community self-destructs. Set off by the theft of the harvest profits, Manderlay goes up in flames. Liberalism has failed. Empowerment did not end oppression; it merely transfigured oppression.

It is also tempting to read *Manderlay* as a Nietzschean critique of values, complementary to the critique of liberalism. Not only does liberal politics not work, but it is based on values with suppressed, dark origins. Before Grace arrives, Manderlay is ruled by the noble and powerful. The whites at Manderlay have guns and whips, in addition to their fair skins and civilized culture. With the help of a priestly class, Grace and her entourage, the weak overthrow the strong in a "slave revolt." The priestly class institutes its own set of rituals to secure its power: democratic community meetings, votes, and celebrations replace inspections and whippings. At first, the former slaves are wary of Grace and her entourage, but eventually they forget the founding moment of their community and seem to live in harmony, not only with Grace but also with the white former slave owners. Grace, as Nietzsche diagnoses the Judeo-Christian consciousness, is plagued by *ressentiment*: "The sins of the past are sins I cannot and do not wish to help you erase." As Grace later puts it, "Manderlay is a moral obligation, because we made you."

But history is not complete. There is still a noble man—strong, physical, cunning—who has not been entirely domesticated by the slave revolt. Timothy appears to have just the sort of character that Nietzsche holds in high regard. When he hears Grace talking about "moral obligations" and "truth," Timothy memorably responds: "Luckily, I'm just a nigger who don't understand such words." He has a haughty attitude, replying cuttingly to Grace's apparent desire for gratitude: "When we were slaves, we were not required to offer thanks for our supper, and for the water we drank, and for the air we breathed."

Timothy is classified by Mam's Law as a "Proudy Nigger," and he is said to come from a line of ancient African kings ("that old-fashioned morality," we are told). However, at the end of the film it is revealed that, in fact, he is actually classified as a "Pleasin' Nigger," a "chameleon," who is "diabolically clever." He could "transform [himself] into exactly the type the beholder wanted to see." Nietzsche writes that the character type he endorses is "necessarily a great actor" whose goals are "achieved by the same 'immoral' means as any other victory: violence, lies, slander, injustice."[1]

Timothy tricks the community in revolt against the "slave" values brought by Grace—values which he never accepted. The community disintegrates and the strong, who have hidden their power until then in the mask of "pleasin'," reveal themselves.

Here we find the standard critique of liberalism advanced in recent political theory. Liberalism, as the continuation of Socratic-Judeo-Christian values under another name (according to Nietzsche), faces an inherent contradiction which is bound to explode in internal rupture—what Sheldon Wolin calls "Nietzsche's prophecy of the disintegration of the liberal-democratic state."[2] The liberal project does not end oppression; it simply replaces one set of values with another while the masses remain subordinated to an aristocratic elite. This new set of values is particularly pernicious because it advances under the label of universalism, providing a "tolerant" umbrella for all points of view. It is agonism, not suppression of conflict, which holds the potential to affect a decisive switch out of an oppressive problematic, many critics of liberalism contend. This agonism is a performance, its achievement always "to come."

However, reading *Manderlay* in this way misses what is most interesting about the film: its critique of political theology. *Manderlay* calls into question both the political theory of liberalism and the political theory of many of its critics. In reading *Manderlay*, we must not overlook what is most obvious. The main character is named Grace. Grace is the name of the protagonist in all three films in von Trier's American-themed trilogy. Two of von Trier's earlier films, *Dancer in the Dark* (2000) and *Breaking the Waves* (1996), while not featuring main characters named Grace, feature female protagonists of a similar type. In each case, the female protagonist feels as if she is sacrificing herself to help others. She imagines herself as pure and selfless, putting the needs of others in front of her own and making of herself a gift to them. In *Dancer in the Dark* and *Breaking the Waves*, this sacrifice results in the death of the protagonists, a death intended to give others a better life (acknowledged at the end of *Breaking the Waves* by the ringing of supernatural church bells). In *Dogville* and *Manderlay*, the sacrifice apparently misfires. It results in the deaths of some of those Grace is trying to benefit as a direct or indirect result of her intervention. But in these cases, Grace is still aligned with Christian grace. When she is first informed of the persistent slavery at Manderlay, her slave informant describes Manderlay as "this godforsaken place." Grace's arrival at Manderlay is an (attempted) gift to the inhabitants of the plantation, intended to improve their condition, to help them form a new community.

Grace is not the only explicitly theological word that plays a central role in *Manderlay*. In addition to Grace, there is Law. Referred to as "Mam's Law" (from Mam, the plantation mistress, its supposed author, played by Lauren Bacall) and regarded as "almost sacred," we first encounter this Law when Mam, moribund along with—likely, because of—the dying way of life she represents, asks to speak privately with Grace and requests one favor from her, "one woman to another" (to which Grace responds that gender offers no privilege). Mam asks Grace to destroy the book of Law kept under Mam's bed. It contains the rules and customs by which the plantation operates, "well-filled with bizarre and vicious regulations," we are told by the narrator. Grace flatly refuses, asserting that any decision should be made in public, by the community as a whole: "It's my view that anything, no matter what, is best served by being brought out into the open." By bringing it out into the open, Grace can demystify the Law, destroying its authority—through her own authority.

As Grace encounters difficulties guiding the liberated plantation, she considers revealing the book of Law to the community. She is convinced by Wilhelm to wait, accepting his advice that the community might not yet be ready. After the community has gone up in flames, as Grace is departing, she delivers the book of Law to the community as a parting "gift" (her gift: to overturn, to turn over, the Law). The film dramatically reveals that Wilhelm, the elderly former slave who had seemed most sympathetic to Grace and her project, had written the Law: "I wrote Mam's Law for the good of everyone."

Wilhelm had tried, long ago, to formalize the best customary practices of the community. Each of the apparently meaningless or simply oppressive regulations had a significance which was, on his view, in the best interest of the community. All slaves had to line up in a particular part of the plantation each day because that was the only part of the plantation that had shade during the hottest part of the day; paper money was prohibited so it would not be gambled away; cutting down trees in the "Old Lady's Garden" was prohibited because they blocked the wind from covering crops with dust; and the slaves were divided into categories (e.g., Group 1, "Proudy Nigger"; Group 2, "Talkin' Nigger"; Group 5, "Clownin' Nigger," each receiving different amounts of food and permitted different liberties) because this allowed for the best organization of the plantation based on the psychologies of its members. These categories kept the plantation "in an iron grip," according to the narrator, who here identifies with Grace. After Wilhelm explains the advantages he perceives of the Law, Grace retorts, "Damn it, Wilhelm, they're not free!"

Simply by looking on the surface, at the relationship between "Grace" and "Law" in *Manderlay*, we can begin to understand what the underlying political theological project of the film might involve. Before Grace comes to Manderlay, the plantation was ruled according to the Law. Grace overthrows the Law. She says that the Law no longer matters. She thinks each former slave, regardless of his or her "group," should receive the same amount of food; she thinks it silly that the former slaves line up on the parade ground each day; and she suggests that the "Old Lady's Garden" be cut down in order to improve the decrepit cabins in which the former slaves live. We cannot help but think of the Christian narrative: Old Testament Law overturned by New Testament Grace.

The results of Grace's attempt to overthrow the Law are calamitous. A dust storm destroys most of the crops that the community had planted because, in violation of the Law, Grace encouraged the community to chop down the trees in the Old Lady's Garden. With the abolition of the "groups" into which the slaves had been categorized, those who, by their "psychology," were prone to take advantage of others did so. Wilma steals food from a dying baby and Timothy steals money from the community as a whole. Both acts result in further violence. One is reminded of the violence that Walter Benjamin suggests lies at the foundation of the law. For Benjamin, law-making violence is hidden by the law, and the law is sustained by law-preserving violence. When the law is suspended, such as in a general strike, law-making violence is exposed. Benjamin seems to relish this violence, aligning himself with an anomic apocolypticism and praying for a messiah to sweep away worldly law with divine violence. In *Manderlay*, it seems as though we witness the moment at which Law is superseded by Grace—and we witness the violence that necessarily ensues.

But this reading, which relies on the same supersessionist logic as the initial reading, misses the dramatic revelation at the end of *Manderlay*: the Law was written by the slaves themselves (at least, by one of the slaves, with the supposed best interest of the slaves as a whole in mind). With this information, von Trier forces us to reevaluate our understanding of the relationship between Law and Grace; he forces us to push beyond any simplistic story relating the two. The Law is not imposed from the outside by some supernatural force. *Manderlay* exhibits the problems that result when Law is misunderstood: it appears that Grace is necessary for salvation because Law is a foreign imposition. The result is that we appear to be faced with a choice between the violence of Law and the salvation—or the redemptive violence—of Grace.

POLITICAL THEOLOGY, as it is currently understood, rests on a supersessionist logic. According to Carl Schmitt, in the seventeenth and eighteenth centuries, God was understood to be transcendent, as was the political sovereign.[3] God was thought to create the world, and to set in motion the laws of nature; so, too, with the political sovereign and the laws of the state. In the nineteenth century, God was understood to be immanent, and so was the sovereign. Ruler and ruled became one and the same in democratic polities, just as the distinction between God and history (and society) collapsed. The political-theological correlation concerns legitimacy, or rather perceptions of legitimacy. Schmitt argues that commitment to a particular theological configuration makes the structure of that configuration plausible in politics. If God is thought to be able to suspend the laws of nature to work miracles, then it is plausible that the sovereign can legitimately suspend the laws of the state in times of emergency. This seminal formulation of political theology rests on the observation that the world is perceived to be fallen, incomplete, and in need of redemption (where these terms are understood in the broadest senses). The world is made right, both religiously and politically, from outside or from within.

Mark Lilla's recent reflection on political theology, like Schmitt's, traces various forms of the relationship between religion and politics in the West, but concludes on an equivocal note.[4] Lilla recognizes the role of Grace in political theorizing: he calls it messianism and the "inverted messianism" of theorists of secularization and modernity. Such stories make sense of our world, and this is something we innately desire, according to Lilla. But it is not inevitable. After the West underwent what Lilla calls the "Great Separation"—the early modern divorce of theology and politics—it became possible to understand politics independent of legitimacy derived from theological structures. For Lilla, there are two responses to this departure from what he calls political theology. One descends from Hobbes and erects the sovereign as an "earthly God." The other is found in Rousseau and his intellectual descendants, retaining a role for gentle religiosity in political life. Lilla claims that the debate between the intellectual descendants of Hobbes and those of Rousseau is "philosophical" rather than "theological"—they all reject "political theology." But Lilla is using the language of political theology in an idiosyncratic manner. The difference between Hobbes and Rousseau maps precisely onto the difference between transcendent and immanent political theologies, in Schmitt's terminology. Lilla understands political theology to involve debates about God that directly affect politics; Schmitt understands political theology as a correlation between religious and political beliefs. The net result is that Lilla's excitement at the end of messianism and inverted messianism conceals his wholehearted endorsement of what, in Schmitt's terms, is a political theology governed by two options: immanent and transcendent. Supersessionist logic remains at work.

Supersessionist logic is not pervasive only in political theology proper; avatars of this logic are found in related explorations of modernity and secularization. To take but two recent examples, Marcel Gauchet and Charles Taylor both build their stories of secularization around the opposition of immanent and transcendent societal self-images.[5] In Gauchet's story, the premodern world is a spatially integrated whole. Gods, spirits, humans, animals, and the rest of nature all occupy the same space. But the source of normativity, the place where the ordering principles of society come from, is in the mythical past—not in historical time, but in a time of heroes or gods absolutely separated from the present. All that is possible is to repeat the events and social structures of this mythical past; it is so separate from our world that no one can claim special privilege as an interpreter. With the advent of the "axial age" (the term is Karl Jaspers's), the gods of the mythical past are condensed into one God, and that God recedes ever farther from our world, both temporally and spatially. God becomes Wholly Other. The less content that can be ascribed to God, the more there is need for human interpreters (Gauchet singles out the Christian paradox of the Incarnation as particularly inviting earthly interpreters). As God recedes, according to Gauchet, religiously sanctioned hierarchy develops; it is now possible for a state to develop independent of society, a state which embodies the earthly presence of the religious Other. Immanence has transformed into transcendence.

Taylor tracks how the transcendence of the axial age transforms into the immanence that characterizes modernity and postmodernity. Through the emergence of conceptions of instrumental reason, an inner will, and universal sympathy, morality—which was once understood to originate outside—was "immanentized." This shift was not just about morality; the cultural changes of modernity, such as the growth of government bureaucracies, economic development, state "disciplinary" practices, and science all led to a change in the conditions of possibility for religious belief. But modernity is unsatisfactory; it produces alienation, malaise. Religions framed in terms of transcendence no longer offer comfort; religions became compatible with immanence, through romanticism, rationalism, or, most recently, a spiritual marketplace. Contemporary science-versus-religion battles play out on the plane of immanence. But these debates presuppose a "closed" form of immanence; Taylor wants to replace it with an "open" form that makes room for human aspirations to higher meaning—indeed, transcendence—on the plane of immanence.

It might be objected that political theologians and secularization theorists are simply describing how individuals in a given culture imagine their worlds. Supersessionist logic, as I have described it, suggests overturning one world and replacing it with another. But ascriptions of transcendence and immanence are more than simple historical descriptions; they are attempts to identify the governing logic, the "essence," of the cultures in question (for instance, of "modernity").[6] To suggest that a culture sees itself primarily in terms of immanence or transcendence, in whatever configuration, is to suggest that individuals in that culture see their lives as needing to be perfected through some mechanism beyond themselves. I think this is a faulty account of the human experience. Individuals spend most of their time and energy navigating their social worlds, doing what is done, making commitments, spending time with friends, bantering about what ought to be done. Concerns about the sorts of "big questions" that might call for answers involving immanence or transcendence, or that touch on the source of normativity, arise only infrequently.

Perhaps, then, it is not on the level of human experience that immanence and transcendence are relevant, but on the level of political concepts and organizations. I am willing to accept the point that, on this superstructural level, there are parallels between ideas about the state and ideas about religion. But the discourse of political theology is never content to stop there. Schmitt's intellectual history (particularly the eponymous chapter 3 of his *Political Theology*) is an aside to the thrust of his project. It is the transcendent conception of politics that he favors—his text is an extended exegesis of its opening sentence: "Sovereign is he who decides on the exception"—and his historical narrative serves only to highlight the conceptual confusion into which sovereignty has fallen, making his conceptual clarification all the more necessary.

Moreover, even if a project of pure historical description were possible, to use immanence and transcendence as the overarching categories for governing such an analysis would be misguided. To do so would be to buy into the theologically freighted (not purely descriptive) notion that all religious concepts point to God, who is beyond the world or within it. A political theology—that is, an analysis of the role of religious concepts in political theory and practice—without Christian presuppositions would not subsume religious concepts under their relationship with God by privileging the relationship of God to the world. This is the reconfiguration of political theology that I am urging, and that I perform in the chapters that follow: an analysis of the rich variety of religious concepts that have political relevance. This same point could be made from the political rather than the theological direction: to privilege questions of sovereignty and legitimacy is already to view political theory from a partisan perspective that ultimately desiccates political analysis. Only by removing that privilege, looking at a rich texture of political concepts and practices, can political theory flourish.

Supersessionist logic appears yet again in another discourse around political theology: it appears in the choice posed between Athens and Jerusalem, Hellenic reason and Hebraic faith. Leo Strauss contrasts "Philosophy and the Bible," where "Each of the two antagonists claims to know or to hold the truth, the decisive truth, the truth regarding the right way of life. But there can be only one truth . . ."[7] Levinas and Derrida position themselves as partisans of Jerusalem, understanding the task of philosophy (and ethics and politics)—the work of justice—to be that of tugging at the threads left loose in the web of reason. Our modern world may be modeled on Athens, but by noting the incompleteness of reason, we can transform it (eventually, in a time "to come") into Jerusalem. In the attempt to transform our world into either Athens or Jerusalem, in the embrace of modernity or its other, we find ourselves yet again entranced by Grace, yet again denigrating Law. To want to make the world either rigid and rational or fluid and faithful is to forget what the world is: textured, messy, viscous, difficult. It is to focus on the world we might wish for, not the one we have—and so to authorize violence against the world.

In the reading of *Manderlay* that I initially proposed, critics of liberalism saw von Trier as an ally. But this reading is undercut by the film itself, by the resilience of Law in the face of Grace, and by the demonstration of the explosive combination of the two. It is not coincidental that critics of liberalism would be entranced by a story of Grace. They, too, are often bewitched by a supersessionist logic. Instead of trying to redeem the fallen world through reason, like the liberals they critique, scholars such as Bonnie Honig and Ernesto Laclau embrace agonism. Politics happens through contest, through articulating political positions and pitting them against each other, not through quieting that contest with a vision of justice that we can all share. This contest, which must take place in very carefully constructed parameters, is what becomes a new avatar of Grace. Wendy Brown, another critic of liberalism, understands herself to be working "in the wake of metaphysics and metanarratives" that legitimize liberalism—modes of thought that have a past but no longer hold sway. She concludes *Politics Out of History* with the wish that her work might offer "modest new possibilities for the practice of freedom."[8] Brown has cast herself as Grace, shrugging off metaphysics and metanarratives and instead offering freedom. For these critics of liberalism, Grace is just as necessary as it is for liberals; it is just a feisty, loud sort of Grace, Grace with an attitude, rather than the quiet, demure, calming Grace of liberals. For critics of liberalism fear that, without the Grace of their favored variety, there will be totalitarianism—either the crude totalitarianism of fascism or the polished totalitarianism of modern rationality and technology, with its dark underside of colonialism and genocide.

Pragmatists, it would seem, ought to be the most suspicious of supersessionist logic. Are not avatars of Grace discarded along with all other metaphysical mystifications? Just the opposite: it is the pragmatist's self-confident dismissal of metaphysical mystifications that casts her in the role of Grace. The pragmatist, like Grace arriving in Manderlay, cheerily announces (already present) freedom: No more metaphysics! Essence is a hoax! Ontology is over! These conceptual clarifications are supposed to allow the pragmatist to focus on what is really important: how people live. For instance, instead of trying to figure out what race "really" is, the pragmatist dismisses any "ontological" conception of race, instead looking at "social context" and imagining how race language could be strategically employed to better the lives of those in need.[9] Grace entered Manderlay to inform the slaves that they were free. Grace brought conceptual clarity to the slaves. A few of their rituals changed: they held democratic meetings and each received an equal share of the food supply. But, for the most part, their lives remained the same—until the changes ushered in by Grace led to various increasingly violent acts. Pragmatists claim to be bringing clarity, to be informing us that race does not "really" exist—indeed, that the whole metaphysical enterprise is superfluous. Certainly, the practice of the social critic must change slightly. She must no longer talk about race in certain ways. The former slaves at Manderlay must no longer refer to each other as "Pleasin' Niggers" or "Proudy Niggers." But the real effects of such changes are questionable—and, as *Manderlay* demonstrates, possibly quite dangerous.

The pragmatist claims to be interested in "social context," in "the messiness of life." So is Grace. But by dismissing Law, Grace is bereft of resources to engage with social context. The pragmatist is similarly bereft of resources, for the pragmatist dismisses the necessary intellectual resources—posited distinctions, claims about representation, classificatory schemas—as "metaphysics." Grace, the character, refuses to use Mam's Law to classify the different "groups" of former slaves, with the eventual consequence that the community goes haywire and self-destructs. Further, recall how Grace at one point purports to have an interest in the textured life of the former slave community. She tries to give little Jim an easel and paints—but she accidentally gives them to his brother, Jack. From the perspective of Grace, all black people look alike, for Grace has overturned Law and all of the distinctions which Law entails.

Avatars of supersessionist logic bring with them melancholia. Fixation on a lost object makes the existing world appear in shades of gray. The fixation never loosens. In fact, it tightens when it is coupled with hope: fixation on a lost object in the past is maintained by projection of a desired object into the future. Schmitt's discontent with the immanent political-theological model and his longing for a return to the transcendent—a longing that skews his political judgment about his contemporary world—shows this melancholia. So do secularization theorists who meditate on modernity in a meandering manner—the culminating instance of this being Taylor's melancholic desire for an open-ended form of immanence. So do theorists meditating on the distinction between Athens and Jerusalem, with their fixation on mythical cities at the expense of the cities in which they actually live. So do critics of liberalism, even those who acknowledge the danger of melancholia yet in their very acknowledgment of this danger fall into its orbit. Such critics fixate on the melancholia itself, offering only a vague gesture toward a "mixture of heaviness and hope" as an alternative.[10] And so, finally, do pragmatists, who acknowledge the "tragic" dimension of life yet respond to it with rhetoric rather than analysis—who offer as an antidote the language and "spirit" of hope. A recent book on pragmatism and politics, for example, bears the title *In a Shade of Blue*, unintentionally foregrounding its thoroughgoing melancholia.

LET US RETURN to *Manderlay*, examining what it does, not what it says. And let us look at how it persuades. It inflates Law and Grace until they burst. What remains? Practices and norms are left, the practices and norms that compose filmic conventions, on display for all to see. The enchantment which makes up cinema, which gives it authority, which allows it to dazzle, is undercut when the individual ingredients that compose a film are paraded before the viewer as these conventions are manipulated or toyed with.

Manderlay is visually striking. It is set on a simple white stage with only blackness beyond the stage's edges. All of the characters remain on the stage all of the time—it is Manderlay, their home. There are only the most minimal props on the stage: Mam's bed; the pillars representing the plantation house which, significantly, support a beam engraved with the slogan "LITTLE LITTLE CAN I GIVE;" a few pieces of wood representing the leaky slave cabins; and one or two other props. Many locations are designated by labels written on the floor in white lettering. There are not doors: when a character needs to represent going in or out of a doorway, he or she knocks and then turns the air like a doorknob.

The result is a visual minimalism, sometimes disorienting, sometimes claustrophobic. Indeed, the style is nearly the opposite of von Trier's earlier ("dogma-style") films such as *Breaking the Waves* and *Dancer in the Dark*. These earlier films were made almost entirely on location in quasi-documentary style (they were, in turn, a response to von Trier's technically sophisticated earliest films). Moreover, in both the on-location films and the entirely set-bound (indeed: theater-style) *Dogville* and *Manderlay*, von Trier uses a hand-held camera which he himself operates much of the time. This has an effect both on the actors and on the viewers. The relationship between actor and director is dramatically altered when the director is constantly only a few feet in front of him or her. The viewer is taken into the scene; the detachment allowed by an "objective" view through the lens of the camera is taken away. There is no framing: the viewer is not allowed the relaxation of symmetry or ordering in what she sees. Another effect of the handheld, director-operated camera is that the film is often momentarily but noticeably out of focus.

Dominating the feel of Manderlay is the voice of a narrator (John Hurt). This voice—strong, masculine, mid-Atlantic, authoritative—booms across the plantation set. Despite his authoritative sound, the narrator is not, in fact, an authority. He misleads us, and his allegiances are unclear. When Grace first liberates blacks at Manderlay and begins to facilitate their transition to "freedom," the narrator reassuringly tells us, "Her actions would comprise an unconditional enrichment of these people's lives, there was no doubt about that." Notice also the excessively—facetiously—pretentious language and stance. It provides a clue that something is amiss, that the authority of the narrator should not be taken for granted. Yet the narrator himself brings his authority into question. After making the statement just quoted, we are shown the skeptical faces of the former slaves. The narrator adds: "or was there?" In another case, the narrator tells us that the slave community is "Living proof of the devastating power of oppression"—a statement that, as the finale of the film shows, is at the very least misleading.

The voice of the narrator is complemented by "chapter" titles displayed in black lettering on a white screen—for example, "Chapter ONE: In which we happen upon Manderlay and meet the people there" and "Chapter EIGHT: In which Grace settles with Manderlay and the film ends." The combination of narrator and titles serves to replicate, in excess, the Hollywood conventions which guide the viewer through an ordinary plot. The narrator's voice is too strong, too masculine . . . too authoritative. Similarly, the chapter titles tell us too much. It is not that their content gives away what is about to happen in the film, but rather that, like the restrictive set, they frame the narrative excessively.

Finally, when we turn back to the narrative itself, we find even more examples of convention-bound unconventionality. The narrator's voice banally opens the film, "It was in the year of 1933 . . ." There is a main character who encounters difficulties while trying to do the right thing. A woman lusts after a forbidden man, the "wildest" of the former slaves, Timothy. The winds of fortune blow this way and that: Grace's difficulties are sometimes resolved, sometimes compounded. There are Hollywood stars: Bryce Dallas Howard plays Grace (Nicole Kidman was set to reclaim the role, which she played in *Dogville*, but she had a scheduling conflict); other actors include Danny Glover and Lauren Bacall.

At the same time, these Hollywood conventions are altered: the main character is female, not male; the difficulties she faces are largely her own fault; her moralism is explicit and ubiquitous; and, dramatically, there is no happy ending—or even any resolution. It is not clear what will happen to Grace at the end of the film. She simply runs away, escapes. And it is not clear what will happen to the remaining former slaves, who seem to have internalized some democratic values (e.g., the right to vote), but who remain tied to the old customs of Manderlay.

In each of these ways, *Manderlay* toys with rules. Indeed, rules—Law—have long been a fascination, perhaps an obsession, of von Trier. He famously distributed little red pamphlets containing the new "rules" for filmmaking in 1995, the organizing document of what came to be known as Dogma

95. Billed as a response to Hollywood excess, the Dogma rules prohibited filmmakers from using music, required filmmakers to use digital cameras, and prohibited lighting and special effects. In 2003, von Trier challenged fellow Danish filmmaker Jørgen Leth to remake the latter's 1967 film *The Perfect Human* with five obstructions. These obstructions were each rules constraining what Leth could do. One obstruction was to have no shot with more than twelve frames, another was to use only animation.

Unlike von Trier's project with Leth, the way that *Manderlay* toys with rules is not purely constrictive. *Manderlay* takes familiar conventions and follows them in such a way that they are brought into question. It follows norms alternately excessively and deficiently, denaturalizing them. At once, the film is restricted to a stage and is filmed through a handheld camera. At once, we see familiar Hollywood faces and we see those faces in the roles of ill-fated characters. And, at once, we are reminded of the formality of the plot by a narrator's voice and the standard rules which characterize a "good" plot are violated.

Von Trier practices what might be called anti-Aristotelian virtue. Instead of striving to meet the community norm, he tries to exceed that norm or to fall below it. Aristotle would call such practice vice. But it is not that von Trier is uneducated, and it is not that he was insufficiently acculturated into the norms of the filmmaking community. Rather, the excesses and deficiencies of his filmmaking practice are always conscious and intentional, with full knowledge of the rules that are not being perfectly followed. *Manderlay* rejects the opposition of Law and Grace. In its style, *Manderlay* investigates the interstices of Law, highlighting and toying with specific norms. *Manderlay* invites political theorists to investigate the ways in which Law—that is, customs, norms—are manipulated. And *Manderlay* invites political activists to stop arguing about, or waiting for, avatars of Grace and to instead proceed with the difficult work of highlighting and challenging specific problematic norms and conventions. The film does this by using aesthetics to persuade. In fact, might it be possible to read *Manderlay* as arguing for the *necessity* of political theology, of the rhetorical force of political theology? Perhaps the problem it identifies is that political theorists and political activists have repressed political theology; what they need to do is reconfigure it.

IN THE PAGES that follow, I seek to constitute an antisupersessionist canon of political thought. The writers involved—Franz Kafka, Simone Weil, and James Baldwin—are in some sense "too Jewish to be Christian and too Christian to be Jewish" (a phrase Gillian Rose used to describe herself).[11] Anodyne labels like "spiritual but not religious" or "religious without religion" miss the significance of these writers' work for political theology. I argue that they use the rhetoric of political theology to make supersessionist logic self-destruct, and to open up space for thinking and acting in a way that accepts, rather than rejects, the richly textured world of social norms and practices. They return to the ordinary, and the ordinary, understood rightly, is political.

There are resources for exploring this world of norms and practices to be found in recent writers. I have found particularly helpful the work of Robert Brandom, Judith Butler, Jeffrey Stout—and, almost as a muse, the late Gillian Rose.[12] Brandom, Butler, and Stout do not see their work as part of a concerted effort to overturn supersessionist logic; Gillian Rose does. She offers both theoretical resources and literary work deserving a place in the antisupersessionist canon. Rose's wide-ranging work addressed issues of sociology (the field of her academic appointment), philosophy, religious thought (both Jewish and Christian), and political theory. Rose urged a switch from melancholia to mourning, from unending fixation on a lost object (reason or faith, a time in the irrecoverable past or the always-distant future) to a sadness that propels the mourner back into engagement with the world.

Rose was a committed Hegelian. She understood herself to be faithful to Hegel against his many betrayers, ranging from Marx to poststructuralists. According to Rose, Hegel has been betrayed because of the allure of an insidious neo-Kantian problematic. The defining feature of neo-Kantianism is its "diremption," or splitting, between the empirical world and some set of transcendental presuppositions not accountable to the empirical world. To take two disparate examples, Rose argues that Durkheim took "society" to exist in the transcendental register and then applied the category of "society" to his investigation of the empirical world without allowing the empirical world to feed back into his understanding of society. Similarly, she argues that Foucault took "power" to exist—unaccountably—in the transcendental register as he applied the category of power to his investigations of the empirical world. This latent neo-Kantianism is the root of supersessionist logic (though the latter is my term, not Rose's).

In opposition to this neo-Kantian apostasy, Rose locates herself as a (perhaps the) orthodox Hegelian. She does this by understanding philosophy and social theory as the study of social norms.[13] True to her Hegelian commitments, Rose emphasizes the unavoidability of "metaphysics." She argues that metaphysics and politics are always already intertwined. Philosophy and social theory go wrong when they attempt to disentangle the two, when they repeat the neo-Kantian diremption between, shall we say, Law and Grace. To think that metaphysics and politics, Law and Grace, are inextricably entangled is a "disturbing possibility." Rose suggests that this view is, and will be, strongly resisted: "In both the world of politics and the intellectual world, there seems to be a low tolerance of equivocation. The result of this intolerance and unease is the reproduction of dualistic ways of thinking."[14]

Rose only gestures toward an alternative to the diremptive tradition with which she disagrees. In her constructive vision, the theorist (or subject) acknowledges that action, power, law, and violence are always intertwined. Her slogan "mourning becomes the law" means that the frustration effected by the violence inherent in the social world must remind us of our commitment to justice, and it must return us to the political realm "renewed and reinvigorated for participation, ready to take on the difficulties and injustices of the existing city."[15] We are not to slip into melancholic fixation on a fantasized but ever distant "New Jerusalem," a fantasized land of Grace. Instead, we are to be committed to "political action" tied to "structural analysis"—which is to say, we must commit ourselves to a thorough investigation of the social world of practices and norms, and we must commit ourselves to act based on the results of that investigation.

Rose's intellectual voice has not as yet found a wide audience. This is in part because of her liminal academic position—too much a sociologist to be a philosopher, and too much a philosopher to be a sociologist—but also because of the rapid Christian appropriation of her thought.[16] The Anglo-Catholic theologian John Milbank has skyrocketed to academic fame in large part by Christianizing Rose's insights. Like Rose, Milbank argues that there are appeals to transcendence latent in, and undergirding, the work of nearly all ostensibly secular social theorists. Unlike Rose, Milbank embraces this structure—but replaces latent neo-Kantianism with blatant Christian triumphalism. He does this via a return to immanence, an immanence through which transcendence percolates.[17] Our shared world, when we live rightly, is sanctified. There can be unity through difference, Milbank argues, when that difference is viewed aesthetically, as with musical notes functioning together harmoniously. But Milbank's theological project is supersessionist—both in the broad sense I am using here and in the narrow, theological sense.[18] In our everyday lives, we must dance to the beat of Christian music. If we don't, according to Milbank, discipline must be applied. Milbank's appropriation misses what is most interesting about Rose's thought: her examination of the difficulty involved in navigating the social world, and her accounts of the virtues of faith and love as crucial tools for that arduous task.

THE FOLLOWING CHAPTERS offer resources for a postsectarian, postsecular political theology that is "too Jewish to be Christian and too Christian to be Jewish." Each chapter focuses on one religious practice. Through conceptual analysis and engagement with theoretical and literary texts, I show how the practice in question can be understood in terms of its relationship to social norms and practices, thereby detaching it from an overarching theological narrative and exploring its political potential. The first three chapters consider the theological virtues: love, faith, and hope. While political theorists such as Richard Rorty, seemingly unaware of or uninterested in these virtues' religious heritage, commend the "fuzzy blend" of the three, I carefully analyze each separately. The invocation of this triptych draws on a specifically Christian heritage which needs to be reformulated for political theorizing. In fact, hope is not a virtue at all: it is a rhetoric that can be exploited for good or ill. What seems like the virtue of hope is actually an incongruous blend of the virtue of faith and a rhetoric of hope.

These initial three chapters also develop the account of social norms and practices on which the rest of the book builds. In the discussion of love in Chapter 1, I read Rose's memoir, *Love's Work*, a book about love that, curiously, says virtually nothing about desire. The entanglement of love and desire relies on opposing immanent and transcendent notions of love, and Rose's memoir demonstrates the inadequacy of both. In its place comes a virtue of love. For Rose, love is exercise for life. Navigating the practices of lover and beloved as they conflict with and complement each other, an always difficult process, is intense preparation for navigating the social world writ large, and for navigating political practices and institutions specifically.

It is only possible to work through love—through the inevitable conflicts between lover and beloved—with faith. I understand faith not as a belief in particular propositions but, like love, as a virtue, a disposition to remain committed to a project even when it seems as though all is going wrong. Faith is necessary for love, and, I contend, it is necessary for life in the political world. In this second chapter I tap the resources of Robert Brandom's account of social norms and practices, but move beyond it by noting the need for a supplement. Judith Butler offers desire as such a supplement. However, putting desire in this role, instead of faith, is an (in this case explicit) endorsement of supersessionist logic. I show how Gillian Rose's writings offer resources for developing a nonsupersessionist account of the virtue of faith.

The Christian theologian Charles Mathewes has recently argued that cultivating the theological virtues in individuals makes them better citizens, because in political processes (for example, at a neighborhood association meeting or school board meetings) love, faith, and hope are necessary to get results.[19] Mathewes also argues that the more time Christians spend engaging in politics, the better Christians they become because participation in politics cultivates the theological virtues. I endorse and develop Mathewes's sentiment, but I see no reason that it needs to be understood as specifically Christian. Faithful and loving individuals make better citizens, and the duties of citizenship make individuals who are more faithful and more loving. But hope must not be included in this triptych of virtues. In Chapter 3, I demonstrate how political theorists who have praised hope, including Richard Rorty and Christopher Lasch, have really been talking about faith, about the commitment to persevere and continue negotiating the difficult world. The rhetoric of hope is potent, but it also quickly hypostatizes, causing slippage into a supersessionist logic.

The five chapters that compose Part II follow an arc that tracks the relationship of social norms and practices. These chapters progress from tradition, which I analyze as the strategic explication of social norms hollowed of practices; to liturgy, sanctity, and revelation, which I take to be means of stepping aside from (and gaining critical perspective on) social norms; and then to prophecy, which I take to be the integration of critique and tradition. While liturgy, sanctity, and revelation all involve a split between social norms and practices that has critical potential, they do not involve a space "outside" of social norms. To say that they involve stepping outside, living outside, and allowing the outside to come in (for liturgy, sanctity, and revelation, respectively) would be to invoke exactly the supersessionist logic to which I am offering an alternative.

How can we make sense of stepping aside from social norms without stepping outside of them? To begin, practices and norms never perfectly match up. Pace some pragmatists, norms cannot simply be "read off" practices. This has been poignantly shown in Judith Butler's work: norms for "woman" involve an alignment of female anatomy, feminine behavior, and desire for men.[20] Yet there have been, are, and will be many individuals who inevitably fail to live according to these norms, individuals who meet only one or two of these components. To live outside the norm, as lesbians and transgendered individuals do, is not to live in a realm of absolute freedom. Quite the opposite, it is to continually feel the violence of the norm—that is, the reprimands with which the norm is enforced (and by which it is constituted).

We act as if there are norms: we praise and reprimand those who follow or do not follow norms. In other words, norms are not "really there"; rather, they are fictions that we live by, and that thus have real effects. They are social fictions: closing one's eyes to them does not make them go away. We normally act as if there are norms; we can also act as if there are no norms. Acting as if there are no norms does not make us free, for we are still acting in relation to norms. We are constituted by norms; they are what makes us humans and individuals. But we can act as if the bonds of the normative universe are loosened, as if it is somehow hollow, simulacral. To do so is not straightforward opposition to norms, for such opposition is coded as pathology, and the normal and the pathological are equally norm-governed. Butler's work identifies parody as a means by which the pull of the normative can be loosed, that its ultimately fictional nature can be revealed. A woman wearing men's clothes reminds us of the disconnect between practices and norms, and so frees us to understand gender norms less strictly, to imagine new possibilities for gendered life. I argue that liturgy, sanctity, and revelation, understood in the ways that I present in Chapters 5 through 7, are practices that have a similar effect. In the moment of liturgy, the lifetime of sanctity, and the event of revelation, our relationship to norms is complicated in a way that opens new, politically potent possibilities.

In Chapter 4, I analyze tradition as a way of politically mobilizing norms. I develop this concept of tradition by reading the novels of the conflicted Jewish writer Franz Kafka in implicit opposition to recent partisans of tradition. There is an underlying contrast of Kafka's *Amerika* and the account of the American democratic tradition provided by some of its recent partisans, such as Jeffrey Stout. Kafka's work suggests a theopolitical account of tradition as norms untethered from practice. This effect is achieved through rhetoric which does more than explicate already existing practices of a community.

Liturgy, the topic of Chapter 5, is a space and time in which it is as if social norms are suspended, allowing for politically potent critical reflection on the social world. I develop this understanding of liturgy by contrasting recent enthusiasm for liturgy from Christian theologians such as Catherine Pickstock and William Cavanaugh with the accounts of liturgy developed just a couple decades earlier, in the wake of the Second Vatican Council. I argue that, while recent enthusiasts claim a radical potential for liturgy, in fact it is earlier theologians of liturgy whose work escapes the logic of supersessionism and has theopolitical potential. Simone Weil's account of attention, I suggest, resonates with the work of these earlier liturgical theologians.

In liturgy it is as if norms are suspended momentarily but repeatedly; in sanctity it is as if norms are suspended for a larger time and space. Sanctity involves acting as if the social world is irrelevant to one's actions. I develop this analysis of sanctity in Chapter 6 through a reading of the Jewish writer-philosopher-mystic Simone Weil's so-called spiritual writings. Weil performs a maneuver typical of sanctity to avoid entanglement in social norms: she decides that she will say yes to whatever she is asked (with sharply delimited exceptions). Instead of navigating the complexly textured social world, Weil carves out a space apart by imposing on herself a rule of acceptance—acceptance that refuses political impotence.

In Chapter 7, I analyze revelation as an event when a space seemingly outside of social norms comes in contact with norms, forcing revision of those norms. My discussion is informed by a comparison between the work of the Claude Romano and Alain Badiou, both of whom build philosophical projects around "the event." Against this background, I turn to the short stories and essays of James Baldwin. In his work, I am particularly interested in the connection between paternity, theology, and law, and the role of the stepson as the locus of nonsupersessionist revelation.

Prophecy, the topic of the final chapter, need not be understood as predicting the future or calling on the spirits of the past. I understand prophecy as calling out the gaps between social norms and practices that account for the tragic nature of social life, and marshaling the strategies of tradition, liturgy, sanctity, and revelation as means of coping with this tragic condition. Here, again, I turn to the work of James Baldwin, this time with emphasis on the figure of the father. I argue that putting the father under erasure is a precondition for prophecy. This is uniquely possible when the father does not serve as a proxy for the social world, but represents a conflicting authority.

The Conclusion examines the aspiration to represent ordinary life, which I understand to consist of navigating social practices and norms. This aspiration often goes wrong. In the films of Robert Bresson, the everyday is portrayed as obvious with the result that transcendence percolates through immanence—and a supersessionist logic is entrenched. In a sense, von Trier's films offer a parody of Bresson's style that highlights and undercuts Bresson's serious religiosity. Another attempt to represent the ordinary, the recent subgenre of American microbudget films labeled "mumblecore," turns the everyday into effective silence (into mumbles). I argue that these filmic attempts to represent the ordinary illustrate pitfalls which political theorists interested in the ordinary often meet. It is by paying heed to rhetoric that these pitfalls can be avoided.

Throughout the book I introduce certain concepts without explaining what I mean by them, for example the concepts of enchantment, the hegemony of the visible, and the ordinary. I would like to think that the Appendix functions as the obverse of a glossary. It is meant as a counterpoint to the text, glossing certain concepts that might otherwise seem to be used for purely rhetorical purposes by putting these terms together in a different, though perhaps equally difficult, way.

THE FOCUS of this work is on supersessionism as a political problem. My earlier book *Law and Transcendence* considered supersessionism as a philosophical problem. As I completed this project, a brilliant account of the cultural-theological implications of supersessionism appeared: J. Kameron Carter's *Race: A Theological Account*. With broad and deep learning, Carter shows how Christians in late antiquity racialized Jewishness and then constructed a theology that shut down that race. He demonstrates how blacks have replaced Jews as the victims of supersessionist theology, and he gestures toward a reconfiguration of black liberation theology that would focus on the lived experiences of the oppressed rather than the existential condition of blackness. This reconfiguration, he argues, undermines supersessionism, and thus offers the opportunity for true emancipation—in Christ.

Like Carter, I am a black American. I suspect the concern with supersessionism that Carter and I share has a common provenance. We both find in supersessionism—in his case, theological; in my case, philosophical and political—a logic that authorizes insidious forms of oppression. Unlike Carter, I have not written as a black American, or as a Christian. I have written about how we humans navigate our life together. There is no shelter from the treacherous waters of this common life. Taking race or Christian commitment as organizing principles supposes such shelter. For me, overturning supersessionism does not offer relief; it exposes the messiness of the world from which there is no escape. Identity must be worked philosophically, employed rhetorically. Rhetoric brings with it the illusion of Grace. And rhetoric offers the only possibility of redemption.

PART I

THEOPOLITICAL VIRTUES

CHAPTER I

LOVE

LOVE OPPOSED TO LAW: THAT IS THE QUINTESSENTIAL IMAGE OF supersessionism. Where we were once shackled by senseless rules, we are now embraced by that sensuous blend of the affective and the ethical which goes by the name of Love. In the regime of Law, we must be made to do good; in the regime of Love, we do good because we want to do good. Citizens of the City of Man live in a regime of Law; citizens of the City of God live in a regime of Love.

This is the image that grips and enchants us. Yet as soon as it is thought, rather than regurgitated, it becomes almost impossibly perplexing. It is, after all, a metaphor, and a strained one at that. What if all our life was really like love? What if all we did was like that one human practice which seems to have so much appeal, which seems to bring with it affective, ethical, and religious dimensions, to intermingle these dimensions into a fuzzy, spiritual experience? There seems to be no better tool to combat the rational, material, secular character of the modern world than a certain image of love— love as we imagine it in the modern world.

To live in a regime of love: this is a perplexing metaphor because love seems supremely personal, unique to one individual and directed at another for highly contingent, possibly mysterious reasons. To reconcile the specificity of the modern experience of love with the universalities to which the metaphor is applied—the social, the political, the religious: must this require some third, supernatural term that reconciles the universal and the particular, some third, peculiarly Christian term? Or is there a way for the universal to supersede its particular counterparts through its own power? The supersessionist imagination cannot just oppose law and love; it must derive love from law, derive the universal from the particular. Love does not offer an alternative to law, love completes law.

Perhaps it is not in this image of love, this enchanting love, but in the phenomenology of love, in the lived experience of lover and beloved, in the tension and teasing, in the fulfillment and frustration, perhaps in the sorrow and in the confrontation with another being, distinct yet demanding—perhaps this is where the political potential of love resides. This is where Gillian Rose turns in *Love's Work*, her philosophical memoir, at once a work of autobiography and an ethical-political polemic. The culmination of two decades of investigation of Hegel, Marx, the Frankfurt School, poststructuralism, Christian theology, and the Jewish tradition, as well as four decades of living life as sensually suffused as it was intellectually robust, *Love's Work* offers a (Hegelian, not Husserlian) phenomenology of love. It not only lays the groundwork for understanding love as a virtue but also exposes the supersessionist deviations that enchant love, deviations that lead to frightening political conclusions.

The question of the relationship between love and politics is posed allegorically through Rose's narration of the story of Camelot.[1] The question is posed but not resolved. The resolution, or rather the work of resolution, is the project of *Love's Work* as a whole. The story Rose retells is this: In a time of endless feuding and bloodshed, King Arthur had a vision. He wanted to create a kingdom based on justice and equality. There would not be favoritism, the rule of law would be respected, and knights would sit at a Round Table to participate in the governance of the regime, each with an equal voice in the kingdom's affairs. A regime founded on justice and equality, King Arthur believed, would be an island of peace and prosperity in a sea of chaos and violence.

King Arthur recruited knights to Camelot who shared his aspirations. The French knight Launcelot, passionate and idealistic, befriended King Arthur and joined the Round Table. King Arthur, too, was idealistic. His ideal was to create a transparent law that would best suit those who lived in Camelot, would best match their customs. Launcelot's ideal, in contrast, was not to take the people as they were, but to transform them, to perfect Camelot. He was idealistic and passionate: when he slew a knight while jousting, he publicly wept.

Launcelot's passion was without restraint, and it brought about his downfall. He fell in love with King Arthur's wife, Guinevere. According to the laws of Camelot, Launcelot had to be banished and Guinevere had to die. But King Arthur deeply loved both his wife and his friend. The king faced a choice. If he followed Camelot's laws, he would stay true to his ideal of governing a kingdom based on the rule of law; however, he would lose those individuals who are dearest to him, Launcelot and Guinevere. If King Arthur made an exception to Camelot's laws, he would be able to save his wife and friend but Camelot would be tainted. The people would know that the laws are not always applied fairly, that exceptions are made for those whom the king favors.

The choice that King Arthur had to make was a choice between his two loves, between his love for the ideal of Camelot and his love for his wife and friend. It was a conflict of ideals, a conflict of loves for ideals, that gave rise to this choice. King Arthur's ideal of transparent and equitable law arising from the customs of the community was incompatible with Launcelot's ideal, the passionate drive for perfection. It is the tension between these pairs of loves which opens a phenomenology of love. Framed by passionate conflict, this is the experience of love: the working of love's apparent conflicts. What proclaims itself most loudly as love gives way to a practice of love. King Arthur and Launcelot began enchanted by the rhetoric of love; through the experience of conflict, King Arthur learned the practice of love. He became skilled in the virtue of love.

King Arthur decided to follow the law, but Launcelot managed to rescue Guinevere before she was executed. The banished Launcelot and King Arthur fight a war which King Arthur won. But Camelot was no longer a peaceful kingdom, and King Arthur had lost his wife and his friend. Rose concludes that, regardless of what choice King Arthur would have made, "the King must now be sad." This is the heart of the allegory: "sadness is the condition of the King" (123). When law is understood as an ideal, whether imposed by a King or a sovereign people, "humanity is forgotten, and so will be the law" (124). The focus on a distant ideal allows lawmakers, be they monarchs or democratic citizens, to forget their personal vulnerability and power, with inevitably grim results. But grim results would have just as surely followed had King Arthur forgotten his ideal and favored his family and friends.

When philosophy is done right, Rose asserts, it is about the sadness of the king. When philosophy is done wrong, it is about finding an easy way out, accepting one of the king's options as obvious, ignoring (but actually repressing) this sadness. The result is melancholy: interminable fixation on suppressed sadness (Rose names neo-Kantianism, poststructuralism, and neopragmatism as victims of this melancholy). Philosophy done the right way acknowledges that, regardless of the choices made, there inevitably will be regret. Philosophy done the right way does not dwell on this regret but is propelled by it back into the fray to try again at getting things right, and to try again at justice. Metaphysics, according to Rose, is "the perception of the difficulty of the law," while ethics is "the development of it . . . being at a loss yet exploring various routes, different ways towards the good enough justices, which recognizes the intrinsic and contingent limitations in its exercise" (124).

The work of philosophy is the work of telling stories like the story of Camelot. It begins with discernment, looking carefully into muddy waters. Out of these waters a governing opposition is posited. Then, the philosopher tracks the conflicts to which the governing opposition gives rise. This final stage is animated by what Hegel calls the speculative identity of the governing opposition. The two posited concepts are at once identical and nonidentical. Rules of logic are moot because this is a work of rhetoric, of persuasion. A speculative identity is "a result to be achieved" through adding social and historical detail. This detail makes both claims of identity and nonidentity plausible.

Rose follows Hegel in telling such a story about jurisprudence.[2] Having surveyed the history of jurisprudential thought, she posits natural law, the belief that law has some transcendent foundation, and positive law, the belief that law is a product of human societies, as organizing moments. It is examining the tension between these two moments which becomes the work of the philosopher of law, telling the story of that tension. That one of these moments is taken to point to the transcendent and the other is taken to refuse the transcendent is not coincidental.

For this is the work of philosophy generalized: setting transcendent and immanent apart and witnessing the instability that results. But does this not sound uncomfortably similar, in form if not in content, to supersessionist logic? The problem with supersessionist logic, in its most generic form, is opposing immanent and transcendent, thereby ignoring the ordinary. Rose's phenomenological method certainly opposes immanent and transcendent. That is where it begins. But Rose understands Hegelian phenomenology to be a narrative, a compelling story, not a "first philosophy."[3] In other words, Rose's phenomenology is a rhetorical strategy, a tool to persuade. Yet it would still seem a questionable rhetorical strategy: it attempts to shift the focus away from a supersessionist logic through a discussion organized around the pillars of a supersessionist logic. Regardless of intent, is it not likely that the pillars, transcendence and immanence, will be reinforced rather than displaced?

What is important is "the middle." This is what Rose took to be her innovation, a restoration of what is most powerful from Hegel—and a return to what Hegel really says. The middle is between the posited poles, between the immanent and the transcendent. It involves the difficult work of the ordinary, of negotiating practices and norms. To some readers, the middle appears too difficult, inscrutable—and too much like deconstruction.[4] Why is focusing on the middle not just another way of reveling in the indeterminacy of meaning? But the objection seems less plausible if we take the story of King Arthur as paradigmatic of an opening onto the middle. The point of the parable is not that the concepts of ideal law and ideal love slip into each other, as it would be for a deconstructive reading.[5] The point is that they are both wrong, that we should shake free of their domination and turn our attention elsewhere—to the middle.

Perhaps we can say: Rose's phenomenology is a rhetoric of two which she opposes to a rhetoric of one. A rhetoric of one is organized around inflating or deflating a privileged concept. Various resources are marshaled to advance that one cause, to deliver one packet of information. If the King Arthur story were a rhetoric of one, it would aim to persuade the reader that the concepts of law and love are x and y (or, in the deconstructive case, that x is y). A rhetoric of two is a rhetoric that self-destructs. Its aim is to persuade the reader that the way she currently see things obscures. It persuades by inflating, into caricature, the way things are currently seen. Thus, it is not any two concepts that can be chosen in a rhetoric of two (as would be the case in a deconstructive argument, which would show that any two concepts slip into each other). The two concepts are not taken as given, they are constructed, and they are constructed in such a way as to capture the aspiration of a domain to supersede itself.

A rhetoric of one does not recognize itself as rhetoric so it puts on the pretence of naturalness. Deconstructive rhetoric is parasitic on a text; constructive rhetoric is parasitic on the world. A rhetoric of two is parasitic on its listeners, choosing its poles so as to maximize its appeal to them. A rhetoric of one is necessarily supersessionist. It is animated by an object, whether present or absent, named or unnamed, that effectively exerts a gravitational (that is, libidinal) pull. But it is that very object which is being transformed by its discourse: the one is both cause and effect, origin and end. If it succeeds as rhetoric—that is, if it persuades—it does so because its core is aligned with regnant enchantment, with ideology.[6] It thickens enchantment, offering new, more clever, more eloquent, more sophisticated ways to say what is obvious. It is only by means of a rhetoric of two that we can get to the middle, because a rhetoric of two takes aim squarely at enchantment. How the two pillars, inflated into caricature, contaminate and animate becomes evident as the story of their coevolution unfolds. The dual pillars tell a tragic tale, which is to say they speak of the ordinary. In each moment when they conflict, when the two pillars pull against each other (not just slip into each other), enchantment fails. With each conflict, the desire that animates the poles loses its potency and the grip of enchantment fades. As we will see, love is the rhetoric of two made flesh.

Rose does not explicitly follow this procedure in her discussion of love. She only gestures toward it with the allegory of Camelot. Yet her entire memoir, *Love's Work*, is doing this philosophical (self-consciously rhetorical) work autobiographically. Before directly approaching Rose's text, let us follow the method I am ascribing to her. Let us turn to ancient Greece in order to sketch what immanent and transcendent, worldly and otherworldly, conceptions of love might look like. As was the case in the Camelot story, such a historical sketch is an allegory; it is history put to use by rhetoric.

In Homeric Greek, forms of the verb *philein* were used in a broad variety of contexts, ranging from friendship to spousal love.[7] They were also used in contexts which seem quite strange to the modern ear: *philos* was used reflexively to indicate a special bond with something, rather like the English adjective *dear*. A soul, heart, life, or breath could be *philos*, as could a body part, such as a knee. In addition to the reflexive *dear* usage, *philos* was used to describe bonds of friendship. When there was some sort of reciprocal agreement between two parties, an agreement creating what might be called a friendship, the individuals became *philoi*. Gods could have *philoi* among humans, those whom they favored and whom did them favors. The word also applied to less formal arrangements, such as between comrades in war. The verb *philein* took on the meaning "to kiss," as a kiss was an action which signified a reciprocal agreement between friends.

To make sense of these varying uses, Émile Benveniste suggests that *philein* began meaning a formal, reciprocal agreement but later evolved to mean a relationship with "emotional color" involving a "sentimental attitude" beyond the formal institution of friendship. *Philos* described things that were, broadly, mine: things relating to my household and my family, as well as my physical body and spirit. *Philos* described "'a scale of affection' involving 'a fixed gradation of friends and relations,'" where a wife was situated near the top of the scale.[8] Affection for one's wife was not qualitatively different from affection for servants or colleagues or even one's own soul. Rather, affection for a wife was different only in quantity, in the special degree to which she was close to oneself. A wife was most dear. In sum, love in the Homeric, pre-Platonic sense was a special quantity of affect, where affect attached to objects and people because of their closeness to oneself. Closeness here does not refer to physical proximity but rather to the amount of comfort and attachment that one has to the object or person in question. The more comfort and attachment, the closer it is. What one loves, on the Homeric view, is that with which one is most comfortable, that to which one is most attached. Love is entirely this-worldly, immanent. It simply describes a fact about human existence. Everyone loves just as everyone eats, just as everyone has parents.

In the Socratic dialogues we occasionally see the implications of this immanent conception of love. In the *Gorgias* and the *Republic*, for example, concern with helping friends (*philoi*) and hurting enemies is presented as a naïve understanding of justice. On this view, what one ought to do to be just is to benefit those who are closest to oneself, those whom one loves. For this immanent conception of love, there is no need to change one's self because of one's love. On the contrary, one becomes more entrenched in one's self (one's body, the people one likes, the things one has) as one acts to advance the interests of those one loves. This, of course, is exactly what Plato's Socrates argues against. He argue that one might—indeed, will— have to change one's behavior, to alter one's self, based on love for something which is otherworldly, transcendent. To be just is not synonymous with benefiting one's friends. What it means to be just might be unfamiliar, and it might be counterintuitive. It might take some strenuous physical or intellectual effort. It might make one uncomfortable. Through his persistent questioning, Socrates pushes his interlocutors to abandon their comforting beliefs and practices. He forces them to part with those things which they love in the Homeric sense.

On Plato's view, the world is full of deception, of mere images. But Plato is concerned with reality, and he thinks reality is what everyone ought to be concerned with. For Plato, love (*eros* now, not *philia*) has to do with desire. But desire can be deceptive. We desire to go to the doctor for the sake of our health, but we desire health for the sake of being able to do activities we enjoy and we desire activities we enjoy because . . . into an infinite regress, or so it seems. But, Plato argues, these worldly things we desire are mere images, the equivalent of shadows in the *Republic's* allegory of the cave. The question which interests Plato is: what is the "first object of love, for whose sake we say all other objects are loved?"[9]

This question is addressed, among other ways, in terms of the ascent from worldly love to otherworldly love described in Plato's *Symposium*. Although readings of this passage, and its relationship to the dialogue as a whole, are contentious, for the presentation here we can simply note the ascent from the material world to the transcendent. Diotima instructs Socrates on the ways of love. First, the young man should love just one physical body. Then, he advances to loving all beautiful bodies, finding his earlier fixation on just one body petty. Next, he advances to love for mental beauty. He can now love someone without attractive physical attributes but with an attractive mind. He penultimately advances to love for what makes minds attractive: knowledge. Finally, he ascends to love for something eternal and purely attractive, the form of beauty in which all other instances of beauty participate. The young lover has advanced from the state of a "small-minded slave," focusing on individual, material instances of beauty, to one who gazes on "the vast sea of beauty" (*Lysis* 210d). This transcendent conception of love functions as an escalator out of the material world to something higher.

If we were to track further the immanent and transcendent conceptions of love, we might note how the Homeric conception of love is refined in Aristotle's discussion of friendship and virtue, and we might note more distant echoes in Aquinas and recent communitarians. Nietzsche vividly described the avatars of the Platonic conception of love in Christianity, Kant, and beyond. Further, we would trouble these conceptions, noting their longings for sufficiency frustrated by their interdependence.

Instead of pursuing that historical phenomenology, we will turn to Rose's memoir, an autobiographical phenomenology. But first, let us refine the immanent and transcendent moments of love by thinking through how they are tied to value. If what one values is what one will organize one's life around or, less abstractly, what one will change one's behavior in response to, then both immanent and transcendent conceptions of love are deeply concerned with value. On the immanent view, one values what is close to one's self. One works to advance the interests of those one loves (helping friends, hurting enemies). On the transcendent conception of love, it may seem less clear how one can organize one's life around "the beautiful" or "the good." But perhaps it is possible: one's daily practices and beliefs are changed on the basis of the transcendent object of one's love if one is a committed Platonist—and, of course, if one is a committed Christian.

Rose's "first love," as she describes it, was of a distant object. As a child, she was infatuated with Roy Rogers. She writes, "It caused me acute physical pain just to think of him, and the high point of every week was watching his programme on television" (61). The young Rose wore cowboy clothing, played with plastic pistols, and taught herself to urinate standing up. In short, she had an "unshakable desire *to be* him" (61). Rose's love for Roy Rogers appears at first to be of the transcendent variety. Roy Rogers was not a real person, not a material entity with whom Rose had become comfortable, used to, attached to. Certainly one could describe Roy Rogers. His name did attach to some definite characteristics, though most of Roy Rogers was mystique. And Rose's behavior certainly did change because of Rogers. She started to imitate his behavior, to change her life to more closely resemble his.

Rose very quickly reminds us of the ubiquitous but often hidden link between the transcendent and immanent conceptions of love. Every week, Roy Rogers was on television at the exact time that she was supposed to leave her mother's house to visit her father (her parents had been involved in an especially acrimonious divorce). Despite the appearance of distance, of abstraction from her material surroundings, Rose's love for Roy Rogers was very much rooted in those things and people around her which she cared about, to which she was attached. Like the view of justice that Socrates so forcefully denounced, Rose's love for Roy Rogers was a means for her to help her friends and hurt her enemies, for her to attach herself to her mother's house, the house she felt most attached to. Her love was a means through which she could express resentment at her distant father's intrusion.

The sort of love that Rose had for Roy Rogers, like the sort of love that King Arthur began with, was the enchanted sort of love. It involved elements of both immanent and transcendent conceptions of love. But it did not synthesize them; it did not put them in dynamic tension. It allowed for a seemingly easy choice—a choice for one (Roy Rogers) which was really the other (Rose's mother): just the sort of easy choice that blinds one to the middle. In her description of writing, an activity Rose describes as a less intense form of loving, her account of love in the middle begins to unfold. Writing is a "mix of discipline and miracle, which leaves you in control, even when what appears on the page has emerged from regions beyond your control" (59). Here we find, first, the opposition between immanent and transcendent, between Law (discipline) and Grace (miracle). Instead of standing in confrontation, "discipline and miracle" mix, they are somehow (through speculative identity) both present in writing. Indeed, writing is the product of the fecundity of their tension. Discipline, the worldly, immanent ingredient of writing, "leaves you in control." You feel as if you are determining the outcome. You have created the regimen, you have set pen to paper for this hour, you have created this outline, you are addressing these topics. So what you write is yours. Yet, somehow, what you write—that is, what appears on the page to yourself and to your readers—is always alien. What is written "emerged from regions beyond your control," it includes an element of miracle. To take another example, the concert pianist who rehearses hours each day for a performance has a highly disciplined regimen, yet the product that the concert goers, and the pianist, hear at the performance is somehow not reducible to that regimen—nor is it possible without that regimen.

In the space between presenting one's self in words on a page and that self being represented as those written words are read, there is an unbridgeable gap, the entry point of miracle. As the author is confronted with the words that she wrote, she is forced to change herself to accommodate the different person she now sees that she is. In the case of writing, the words written remain static, engraved in ink, as it were. But in loving, when the relationship is between two individuals, there is dynamic feedback. Each presentation and representation is constantly forcing alterations in the two parties. The lover and the beloved, as they interact with each other, are constantly forced outside of themselves by the miracle of love, by the miracle enacted in the space between them. Neither party remains who she or he was before the interaction; each, through the interaction, is forced to become a new person. Loving involves greater intensity than writing; it is punctuated by "joy" and "agony" to a degree which writing is not.

Rose describes the experience of love as being one in which there is "someone who loves *and* desires you, and he glories in his love and desire, and you glory in his ever-strange being, which comes up against you, and disappears, again and again, surprising you with difficulties and with bounty" (60). When Rose writes of one who "loves *and* desires," we can quickly think of *philos* and *eros*, the immanent and transcendent conceptions of love in Homeric Greece and in Plato. The conjunction is crucial because it reaffirms the distinctness of the two conceptions of love while also linking them in the new formulation Rose offers. The "ever-strange being" is equally crucial, for it reminds us of the mechanism by which Rose seeks to synthesize and surpass the immanent and transcendent conceptions of love. In the immanent conception of love, those who are loved are never strange. Indeed, they are the opposite of strange: they are as familiar as possible, for that is precisely the reason that they are loved. Yet it is them, those very specific "beings," who are loved. They are not loved because they are representatives of something else; they are not loved because of the bit of beauty or good (or God) in them.

The precise mechanism of love, as Rose describes it, is a pushing and pulling, an ever-present tension which performs what love is. The lover "comes up against you, and disappears, again and again" (60).[10] The lover challenges you, surprises you, makes you uncomfortable. In reacting to the advances of the lover, one changes oneself, grows in response, and through response, pushes back at the lover, forcing the lover to respond—"again and again." This process is not an easy one, but it is a rewarding one. It is characterized by "difficulties" and "bounty." It is painful to be pushed, to be ill at ease, to be forced to respond in ever novel ways. But this is where the grace of love in its most powerful sense, neither immanent nor transcendent but the speculative identity of the two, resides.

The intensity of love, greater than that of other relationships in life, is due in part to the absolute vulnerability that love entails. Colleagues have roles to play. They interact with each other as colleagues, following the scripts assigned to their positions. Their interactions are mutually beneficial, but they are like trains on a track: they may be able to travel far and in varied directions, but their interactions are always closely guided by prelaid rails. In contrast, lovers interact with each other not as people putting on a performance, not as people playing a role. You do not see your lover as a postman, a brunette, or a golfer; you see your lover as a human being stripped of all social roles.

Because of this nudity, because of this lack of rails, anything is possible. Our beloved is under no obligation to act toward us in a predictable way. As Rose writes, lovers "have absolute power over each other." Because there is no "contract," no agreed-upon rails to guide the interaction, "one party may initiate a unilateral and fundamental change in the terms of relating without renegotiating them." In short, "There is no democracy in any love relation: only mercy" (60). Although the push and pull that characterizes love also characterizes life in the world more generally—as a version of the struggle for recognition, perhaps—in love this struggle is magnified because it starts ex nihilo; it cannot rely on social norms as a starting point. The miracle of love, in other words, is that lovers walk together over a cliff, on thin air. Occasionally, they may experience vertigo, but they continue walking, the only thing that they can do, together.

"Happy love is happy after its own fashion," writes Rose, while "all unhappy loves are alike" (62). This conclusion straightforwardly follows from Rose's phenomenology of love. Happy love is no more than the performance of the give and take between lovers. This is a dynamic performance, ever changing, involving different pulls, different pushes, as the personalities, and the persons, of the lovers differ and develop. Unhappy love, in contrast, always follows the same structure. Unhappy love has an effectively empty content: it is either solipsistic (on the immanent conception) or refers to an effectively empty signifier (on the transcendent conception), both of which collapse into one and the same thing—as Rose showed with her example of Roy Rogers. In unhappy love, one elevates an opaque object to the position of most loved, one structures one's life around that object—an object which, it turns out, is really just a reflection of one's own self, of one's own desires.

But the story is more complex still. "The unhappiest love is a happy love that has now become unhappy" (62). In such cases, there was once the dynamism of happy love, performed in the space of the "middle," between the two lovers and between immanence and transcendence. But, for whatever reason, the love has been lost; its dynamism has been stilled. It has become a memory, incorporated into the being of each lover, part of them in love's immanent form and projected as a broken hope in love's transcendent form. The pain of happy love turned unhappy is especially acute because of the loss involved, because of the personal knowledge that it was once animated. If I may suggest a slightly disturbing image: it is a taxidermied pet rather than a taxidermied animal in a museum diorama.

Rose's first love, her love of Roy Rogers, was a story of failed love, of loving the wrong way. Her relationship with Father Dr. Patrick Gorman (Rose's pseudonym for the priest-scholar) illustrates love in the middle. Their relationship begins with exchanged notes and mystery: Gorman claims to have seen Rose; Rose searches her memory to recall on what occasion this might have been. At a faculty meeting, Rose senses "an intense aura emanating from someone whom I had never seen before, an intense, sexual aura, aimed precisely and accurately at my vacant being" (65). She is later introduced to Gorman and realizes that he is the same man she earlier sensed at the meeting. She is invited to dine with Gorman and, as she entered, she says, "He gripped my hand and, looking straight in the eye, did not release the tension between our clasped hands and locked eyes" (66). It is in this tension, this exchange of advances in which each party's desire manifests itself in varying modalities as the love progresses, as the future lovers become closer, that love is performed.

"We knew we wanted each other in the way those who become lovers do—with simultaneously a supernatural conviction of unexpressed mutual desire and a mortal unsuresness concerning declaration and consummation" (68). Here again, in yet another form, the transcendent and the immanent meet. The practical realities of growing closer, of physical proximity, the material manifestations of love as deep bodily, sexual attachment, these are set in tension with desire, *eros*, the "supernatural," the transcendent conception of love in which the object is purely desired but only vaguely defined. As Rose points out, in her particular circumstances this tension was magnified: there was a material obstacle (the priestly vocation of Gorman) as well as a supernatural supplement (again, the priestly vocation of Gorman).

Rose and Gorman finally consummate their love. In her graphic yet delicate description of their physical intimacy, Rose again explores the phenomenology of love. "The sexual exchange will be as complicated as the relationship in general—even more so. Kiss, caress and penetration are the relation of the relation, body and soul in touch" (69). Each touch, in love, is a push, at once eliciting a response, at once transforming the lovers and propelling the performance of love forward. In bed together, the nudity of the lovers is literalized: their vulnerability and their power magnified. The immanent (body) and the transcendent (soul) are put in dynamic tension, "in touch." The lover "succumbs so readily and with more joy than I could claim" (69), with an excess which is reducible neither to the immanence of the material bodies of the lovers nor to the transcendence of their desire for their ideal images of each other.

Rose characterizes a night spent together as a "shared journey," "unsure yet close" (70). The immanent conception of love is "close," that is its defining feature. Yet it is also sure of itself, it is characterized by certainty, predictability, lack of surprise. In the immanent conception of love, one loves what one is most used to, what is closest to one's self and so is most well understood, not what one is "unsure" of. Yet the "unsure" character of the love, and its nature as a "journey," does not unequivocally point to the transcendent conception of love. Although the transcendent conception of love involves a movement forward, an alteration of one's own conduct and life based on an underdetermined object, the transcendent conception of love takes love to be an individual phenomenon. Rose most definitely considers love "shared" and "close." In her phenomenology of love, love is definitively between two material beings, yet the two beings move beyond themselves through their interactions with each other.

In an opinionated aside, Rose articulates her opposition to "sex manuals" and "feminist tracts which imply the infinite plasticity of position and pleasure" (69). Her opposition arises from the same roots as her opposition to the stark choices which King Arthur sees. To imagine countless varieties of pleasure is to settle for an ideal, to imagine—and to seek to create—a Camelot. Such a project is inevitably doomed. But, more important, even the consideration of such a project is problematic. It is an easy solution, a way out of the difficult work of negotiating the push and pull of life and love. Sex manuals are "dangerously destructive of imagination, of erotic and of spiritual ingenuity" (69). It is against the stasis implied by both immanence and transcendence and in favor of the dynamism of negotiating their synthesis that Rose's phenomenology is positioned.

Lovers walking together without rails, walking together over a cliff—this is how Rose links love and faith. In the morning, after a night spent with a lover, Rose writes, "there can be no preparation or protection for this moment of rootless exposure" (70). The lovers have opened themselves to each other; love has been performed. They have walked over the cliff and they now, in the morning light, realize where each stands, together, walking on thin air—this "holy terror," this "rootless exposure." At this moment, Rose writes, love is replaced by faith. It is only faith which keeps the lovers together, keeps them walking on thin air, prevents them from falling—against all odds.

One of the most profound elements of Rose's account of love—and morality, and politics—is her explicit acknowledgment of the pervasiveness of tragedy in a way that few others dare. "There are always auguries, not only of future difficulties but also of impossibility" (71). During the love affair, as the love is performed through the tension of push and pull between lovers, the tragic nature of love is forgotten, elided. In Rose's own case, her relationship with Gorman, this was particularly acute and explicit. He was, of course, a priest. In the performance of their love, the impossibilities inherent in the situation are easily overlooked. But Rose suggests that her relationship with Gorman is just a particularly acute instance of a much more general phenomenon. Love that is happy becomes unhappy. Lovers change irreconcilably. Lovers die.

Yet the inevitably tragic nature of love should not discourage us from participation—in love, as in life. As the epigraph of *Love's Work* extols, "Keep your mind in hell, and despair not." Rose offers the vivid image of the paradoxical circularity involved in learning to swim. Before one enters the water, one must know how to swim, yet one cannot know how to swim by being told how on dry land. One must enter the water. To think one knows how to swim before entering the water is to believe in Camelot, to believe in the immanent-transcendent ideal. In our short lives, in our few loves, we will never learn to swim well, Rose suggests. We will only flounder about, thrashing our arms and legs, pushing and pulling ourselves against the water as we try to learn to swim. Once in awhile, we succeed, beginning to find a rhythm, but more often we thrash about, gasping for breath. Yet there is something indisputably more desirable about the novice swimmer thrashing about in the water than the person who has never been in the water but believes she can swim because she read how to in a book.

Again, Rose's view of love functions as a microcosm of her view of life. *Love's Work* is decorated with examples of decline and death, ranging from a friend dying of AIDS to an octogenarian cancer survivor to vivid descriptions of Rose's own terminal illness. In all of these cases, Rose admires and advocates persistence in the face of apparently insurmountable difficulties. King Arthur cannot remain silent. He must choose, and then he must move on to choose again. His weakness is that he imagines that he can avoid difficult choices, avoid the work of love, the work of ethics, the work of life. Rose concludes, on the final page of *Love's Work*, that she aspires "to be exactly as I am, decrepit nature yet supernature in one. . . . I will stay in the fray, in the revel of ideas and risk; learning, failing, wooing, grieving, trust-ing, working, reposing—in this sin of language and lips" (144).

What can Rose's phenomenology of love tell us about the relationship between love, ethics, and politics? Perhaps we can address this question by trying to make sense of two statements. Rose writes: "To spend the whole night with someone is . . . ethical. For you must move with him and with yourself" (70). She also describes love as offering the possibility that lovers can "achieve the mundane" (71). So it seems as though Rose is suggesting that, somehow, the experience of love alters one's experience of the world. Somehow, love offers a conduit of the holy (in an unconventional sense) into the ordinary—and this is ethical. On the immanent conception of love, love reinforces the way one already lives. On the transcendent conception of love, love forces one to change one's way of life in accordance with an underdetermined abstract object. In contrast, Rose's development of a spec-ulative identity between the two conceptions turns love into an exemplary instance of how one should live. Rose suggests that a life lived well is a life continually pushing and being pushed, by and against individuals, groups, and institutions. When we are in a love relationship, we are taken into a cor-ner of the world where life is lived more intensely and from which we can return to life all the more dedicated to participate in the difficult work of living, all the more committed to rejecting the easy options of falling into the stasis of pure immanence or the fantasy of pure transcendence.

Rose's phenomenology of love uncovers the theopolitical potential of love. What her phenomenology does is make explicit misconceptions, crip-pling the enchantment which gives the immanent and transcendent con-ceptions of love their force. They are crippled by filling in the details of experience. With these misconceptions out of the way, we can begin to see that the political potential in love lies in considering love a virtue. This possibility is foreclosed by both immanent and transcendent approaches. On those views, love is an affect. The two views present two stories about how that affect comes about, or rather two versions of the same story. In both cases, love is opposed to law. On the immanent view, what one loves is proximate, and proximity trumps social norms. Love spreads naturally outward from what is closest to me, regardless of the socially authorized pathways. On the transcendent view, what one loves is an object outside of oneself, or rather the signifier of that object. The effect of this object is to motivate change in oneself. Here again, the effect is to disregard social norms in favor of an object imagined to be immune from them, above them (sometimes quite literally).

Love, in the immanent and transcendent senses, does not produce anything new. It refines, polishes, and thickens. Because it has no traction, because it refuses the texture of norms, love secures those norms. The tension between norms, the difficulties involved in the relationship between norms and practices, these are made invisible. They are reified and relegated to the domain of law opposed to the domain of love. On the transcendent view, any compromise will be made because the lover is in love; on the immanent view, no compromise will be made because none is necessary. Compromise is at issue, never negotiation. When lover and beloved come near each other, their norms and practices conflict. But this conflict cannot be acknowledged on the immanent or transcendent views of love. So the conflict is either suppressed (I will change for you) or ignored (I am who I am and you are who you are); the two, of course, are the same. Suppressing and ignoring only work for so long. Love fades.

As we have seen, in the experience of love, there may appear an alternative to the immanent and transcendent conceptions. It may appear; this is not certain. When the immanent and transcendent conceptions exclude all other representations of love, when they come to exclusively determine the ways in which love is spoken about, they also come to determine how love is practiced. Only the remnants of an alternative may remain. The phenomenology of love recovers those fragments. This alternative involves love as a practice of intense negotiation in which one's self, in all its complexity, is at stake. Life in the world involves—in fact, just is—negotiating between practices and social norms, what one does and what one ought to do. Love is an intensification of life: it is negotiating between practices of lover and beloved. Each is multiform. The negotiation is complicated, and never-ending. It is necessary because lover and beloved put themselves at stake. They set aside their social roles, bracketing the norms which would give them guidance, would provide a neutral third to which practices could be brought to match. Love does not occur between two individuals following social norms; it occurs when it is as if those norms are absent. Of course, they are not absent, but the ability to act as if they are when one person is in the proximity of another makes love possible. To have this ability is to have the virtue of love.

Once immanent and transcendent conceptions have been set aside, once it is the experience of love that is at issue, what is uncovered are the contours of love as a virtue. A virtue is a disposition, a tendency to act certain ways in certain circumstances. To have a virtue is not to be competent at following a norm. It is not the ability to do what one ought to do when one ought to do it. Rather, it is to have a capacity to deal with all norms in a certain way. In the case of love, it is the capacity to suspend norms and negotiate practices in proximity to another, to put one's self, in all its complexity, at stake. It is a virtue because it is a capacity that is unequivocally beneficial for life as such, even as love itself relishes in equivocation. It is unequivocally beneficial because it provides a training ground for life in the world. The better one is at negotiating between practices of two, the better one is at negotiating between practices and social norms. Love is a virtue and not a strategy: the point is not that, faced with a particular challenge, the best course of action is to love. Cultivating love is beneficial for facing all challenges. Love is a political virtue because having it makes life with other people easier. It equips the loving person with abilities that will help her in political life. Love is a theopolitical virtue because it refuses the hegemony of the visible. The experience of love is constituted by this refusal, setting aside social roles and then negotiating, between two, in such a way that new practices, unexpected, will necessarily arise.

It is easy for this theopolitical dimension of love to vanish, even when love is understood as a virtue. For example, Iris Murdoch, drawing on the suggestive work of Simone Weil, writes of love as "the liberation of the soul from fantasy" through shaking away the "false unity" of the world created by the self and, instead, seeing things as they are.[11] To love is to see rightly. Love, like art, allows for "merciful objectivity."[12] The thought here seems to be that the world is enchanted, clouding our view. Love disenchants. Yet there is a sense in which Murdoch's account of love, as a virtue, takes away its theopolitical potential, for the "merciful objectivity" of love would always result in right action. In other words, the virtue of love leads to a collapse between practice and social norms. If a whole society were gifted with the virtue of love, everyone would act as they are supposed to act, all of the time. The hegemony of the visible, suppressing the tragic and the comic, failure and surprise, stifles.

Perhaps the appeal of this misconception of love, as seeing rightly, comes from its affinity with parenting. From the perspective of the child, her parents' love may manifest itself through strict rules which are to be followed for the good of the child, or it may manifest itself through an acceptance of whatever the child happens to do, acting as if the child is never wrong. More often than not, the child perceives that one parent loves one way while the other parent loves the other way. This is how it seems, love as Law or love as Grace—until the child grows up (of course, not all children grow up). Then, the child realizes that the parents' love was aimed at raising a child who would act rightly. The child realizes that the parent perceived as a disciplinarian suffered when she punished, that the parent perceived as all-accepting suffered when the child acted badly—though neither of these parents let that (redemptive?) suffering show. The child who has, in growing up, completed a phenomenology of parental love, sees in the parent's actions "merciful objectivity," where before these actions appeared egocentric. Of course, it is only in the movies that this is realized in a moment. The realization is present in the experience itself, though often it is ignored. Both suffer, the parent quietly and the child loudly (loudly not only at the hands of the disciplinarian but also at the hands of the all-accepting parent: *Why don't you care?*). Sometimes it appears that the parent loves too much, wrongly; sometimes it appears as though the child does not love at all.

In the experience of parental love, in the virtue of the parent and in the virtue of the child, there is training for life in the world. Suffering is necessary in this love, as it is necessary in life. Yet this is a different sort of training than the training provided by the theopolitical virtue of love. Practices conflict, parent and child shout, but the parent is always a proxy for the social. The whole of the child is at stake, but the whole of the parent is never at stake, regardless of how she might feel. Child and parent come to love better, and they come to see more clearly. But what they see is what everyone sees when they see clearly—the hegemony of the visible. Is this not also the case in the desire, perhaps love, between teacher and student, where it is not social norms as a whole but a specific domain into which the student is raised through love? And perhaps it is also the case with reading, as opposed to writing. A text is given, it can be worked, and in this work the reader puts her self at stake. After reading, the world is seen more clearly. But something much more radical happens, or can happen, in writing. The writer interacts with a doppelgänger of herself on the page, each pushing and pulling at the other. Might this also be the sort of love that is in play in patriotism, love of nation. Like a parent, the nation may seem disciplinary or merciful, and the citizen with such a love must put herself at stake, yet the outcome, again, is predetermined.

The difference between this virtue of love which brings clarity and the immanent and transcendent conceptions of love may seem great. The former introduces objectivity, the latter entrenches subjectivity. Yet the subjectivity entrenched is enchanted, and the enchanted subject is always already interpellated, embedded in a world of social norms. To be well-enchanted is to be well-acculturated—which is to see things rightly.

Love, understood as a theopolitical virtue, has to do with two. It disposes the lover to act in certain ways when in proximity to the beloved. It is more than the increased intensity that privileges the dyad. It is not just that this intensity is diffused in groups of three, four, ten, one hundred. The pair is privileged for the same reason that a rhetoric of two is uniquely efficacious. The two decenters while refusing mediation. Its significance does not derive from an asymmetry, as Emmanuel Levinas would have it, or from pure contradiction, as Alain Badiou would have it. Its significance comes from its efficacy at opening the middle through effacing itself. The two is fecund because it self-destructs: the purported unities of lover and beloved are inflated until they pop, leaving practices performed by each, practices in conflict, and, out of that conflict, from the invisible, come new practices performed together.

CHAPTER 2

FAITH

LOVE IS AN EXERCISE FOR NAVIGATING THE SOCIAL WORLD. THE challenges and frustrations of social and political life are condensed in dyadic love relations. But love is exhausting. It is tempting to quit love, to walk away. The rewards of loving may be many, but they do not clearly exceed love's trials. Utilitarian calculations do not make love. Faith makes love. In the high-pressure environment of a dyadic love relation, there are always reasons, good reasons, to walk away. Walking away means contentment with stasis. It means ending the work of love, even if the relationship continues. Faith is commitment even when there are good reasons to walk away. My interest is not in faith as holding a specific belief, it is in faith as a virtue. The virtue of faith is the twin of love. If the virtue of love is an exercise for life in the world, the virtue of faith is the spaghetti dinner that provides the calories.

This, of course, is an unusual understanding of faith. The everyday language of faith is quite different. When believers *really believe*—that is, when there is an excess of belief—then there is faith.[1] Faith is about improper beliefs, beliefs that go beyond what ought to be believed. People object. Faith causes arguments. How could you believe *that?* To the unfaithful, faith seems peculiar, sometimes frightening, sometimes just odd. Its object is not of this world: an alien or a god, a monster or a miracle cure. The faithful are committed to their excessive belief in the face of worldly condemnation. It runs counter to prevailing social norms. The object of faith has an authority which can trump the authority of norms. Faith calls for reprimand, if only in skeptical glances when the object of faith is brought up in casual conversation. More dramatically, it may call for persecution; less dramatically, it may call for tolerance.

The everyday language of faith is especially peculiar because it makes faith out to be both exotic and commonplace. It is otherworldly, but it is also so worldly as to be banal. We have faith in what is most familiar. We have faith in our town and its football team. We have faith in our family and friends. We have faith in our community. When hard times hit, we are sure that those we have faith in will pull through. They will pull through because they are *our* family, *our* friends, *our* community. It takes a lot to lose faith in the familiar. It takes betrayal. Things have not just gone wrong; they have intentionally gone deeply wrong. It is an affront to us, to the faithful. A man of faith is upstanding, doing what is required of him and more, treating others as they are to be treated; he is respectable, righteous. In short, a man of faith is a man who has mastered social norms, although his faith is independent of those norms. The everyday language of faith and love are entangled: we have faith in the familiar because we love it; we would not love it if we did not have faith in it.

The case of faith in one's nation brings these two senses of faith together. As Herbert Croly wrote in 1909, in *The Promise of American Life,* "The faith of Americans in their own country is religious, if not in its intensity, at any rate in its almost absolute and universal authority. . . . We may distrust and dislike much that is done in the name of our country by our fellow-country-men; but our country itself, its democratic system, and its prosperous future are above suspicion."[2] Here is American democratic faith. Democracy creates uncertainty: there is no monarch or deity to provide stability, to assure that things will be right again when they go wrong. So faith is necessary, faith both in one's nation as a whole and in one's fellow citizens. For it is the citizens who compose the nation, and if the citizens are fundamentally flawed, the nation will fail. Faith in the familiar must be extended to the unfamiliar, must be extended to an object composed of components that are worldly but not of this world. As these two views of faith—faith in the familiar and in the unfamiliar, faith in fellow citizens and in our country itself—are brought together, it appears at first as though the object of faith simply is social norms, the way we do things here. "Here" equivocates between those around us and our imagined community, those around us projected outward into the nation. The projection is a shared fantasy, a way in which many local familiars can be unified into one. And vice versa: the familiar is seen in light of the projected object, the faith in our family, friends, and neighbors now resulting from their status as democratic citizens. The richly textured world of social norms has no place in these conceptions of faith. In them, immanent and transcendent are bound together, their tension refused.

Let us ponder an alternative, one that might put that richly textured social world at its core. This is a world that is composed of norms and practices; life in this world involves navigating between the two. A social norm differs from a practice in a way vaguely analogous to how a concept differs from an intuition in the Kantian tradition. Norms without practices are empty, practices without norms are blind. The one is reality presented; the other, reality represented.[3] A norm makes an approximation. It says, in *those* circumstances, *these* are the proper things to do. If *these* actions do not follow from *those* circumstances, the actor will be reprimanded by members of his or her community. Like a judge discerning the law from past practice and community values, an individual discerns social norms by taking into consideration the practices of a community and its history. Social norms are in this way accountable to social practice. If a norm is posited, it can always be invalidated by noting that people do not do what the norm says they ought to do (or people do what the norm says they ought not to do, and there is no reprimand).

Norms are violent. They never perfectly match social practice, and they conflict with each other. Representations never lay on top of the world without remainder (this image, of course, is imprecise). To call norms violent is not only to speak metaphorically. Norms exist where there will be a community reprimand in store for those who do not do what one is to do (that is how they are identified, by the possibility of reprimand).[4] The reprimand can vary from disdainful glances to severe penalties enforced by the institutions that codify social norms, for example, police, courts, and government agencies. When posited norms do not match practice, there will be unwarranted penalties. As norms always mismatch practice, there are always unwarranted penalties. To suppose that norms receive their force from some unquestionable authority, whether other-worldly or this-worldly, is to put them beyond question. It is to sanction violence.[5] Is this not, precisely, faith: commitment to an authority for norms that is other-worldly or that is this-worldly, where ultimately the two options are one and the same? The challenge, then, is to reverse our understanding of faith, to offer an account of faith that takes what seems to be the most faithful to be the most faithless, and the most violent. For faith in the ordinary senses of the word suppresses the violence of norms by sanctioning that violence through enchantment, through a compelling story. The brutality of the police officer is excused because she is enforcing the laws to which we all, in some original position, agreed.

To see how we might think of faith as growing out of navigating the world of practices and norms, let us first turn to two proposals that also take navigating the social world as their starting points. From this shared starting point, these two alternative accounts move in quite different directions. While both authors of these proposals attribute their views to Hegel, Robert Brandom takes freedom to be uniquely privileged while Judith Butler gives this privileged position to desire. Where Brandom and Butler move, in a sense, from Kant to Hegel, I will argue that another step is necessary, one which Gillian Rose's work illustrates: from Hegel to Kierkegaard.

Brandom begins his discussion of freedom by offering an account of action according to norms.[6] He agrees that norms involve praise and blame—praise for acting correctly according to a norm (an action which is right), blame for acting in a way which is not in accordance with a norm (an action which is wrong). On his account, norms are based on convention. Which actions are praised and which actions are blamed could be entirely different. To understand what a particular norm is, on Brandom's view, we have to look at actual social practice. Which actions do real people in a community praise and which do they blame?

But Brandom's Wittgensteinian instincts prevent him from endorsing any view that would present a realm of norms as a metalanguage, set above the practices of a community. In the case of linguistic norms, the norms of what is correct or incorrect to say, Brandom suggests that it is impossible

norms are implicit in practice of

comm for Brandom

to construct a list or algorithm that would encompass or produce every correct linguistic expression. If it was supposed that such a sufficient list or algorithm could be constructed, we would be in the untenable situation of having rules, and rules for the application of rules, and rules for the application of rules for the application of rules . . . ad infinitum. Brandom argues that this conclusion can be applied to social norms in general. However, this lack of a metalanguage of norms need not trouble us because norms are "implicit in the practice of the community," according to Brandom. Instead of constructing a metalanguage which would describe which acts are in accordance with norms and which are not, we can just *look*: if the action results in a reprimand, it is not in accordance with norms. As observers of a community, even if that community is our own, we divide behavior into social norms based on what we see of how community members act. The way that we divide up the behaviors we witness need not correspond with how members of the community themselves ordinarily understand their activities. For members of the community, norms often remain implicit; it is the observer who makes them explicit.

social practices must be understood holistically

An implication of Brandom's proposal is that social practices must be understood holistically, not in isolation from each other. One social practice is correct if it is responded to without reprimand, if members of a community take it as correct. Even so, the responses of the community are themselves social practices that can be correct or incorrect, as determined by further practices of reprimand, and so on, all the way down. To avoid being stuck in this infinite regress, all social practices must be considered together at once. This holism means that social practices cannot be individuated: to convey the norms of a community we wish to describe, we need to perform a "translation," not simply identify and describe one practice in which we are interested.

implicit norms must be made explicit

Brandom thinks that it is possible for norms to accurately reflect social practice: norms are *implicit* in practice and they just need to be made *explicit*. To do this accurately, holistic translation is necessary. In contrast, in the account I have sketched, norms and practices are associated, but every attempt to articulate a norm will fail. There will be reprimands that cannot be accounted for by the articulated norm. This is not just a matter of imperfect translation, there is an unbridgeable, inexplicable gap. However, that

Norms as Tool / Fiction

does not mean we should not attempt to articulate norms; doing so is how
we go about the necessary task of explaining and critiquing, and living in,
the world. We say that an action is right or wrong because it is authorized
or unauthorized by a specific norm. Brandom's gestures toward holism and
translation are an attempt to still the violence of the mismatch between
social practices and norms. Norms are not implicit in practice, waiting to
be revealed. Although Brandom understands himself as a pragmatist, perhaps
there is an even more pragmatic approach here: norms as a tool, a fiction for
describing social practice. People act *as if* there are norms.

Ordinarily, we think of freedom as a lack of constraint. We are free when
there are not rules telling us what we can and cannot do; freedom is freedom from social norms. Brandom's account of freedom concludes just the
opposite. From his "Hegelian" perspective, freedom consists in "the self-
expression made possible by acquiescence in the norms generated by an
evolving community" (187). This understanding of freedom makes it possible to speak of "the artist and the genius" as free (not just, as a "Kantian"
conception would have it, freedom being the condition of "the peasant and
the worthy Pietist"). This is because freedom is "enabled by but not reducible to constraint by communal norms" (193).

Freedom as Communing with Communal Norms

New Performances Enabled by Mastery of Norms

This Hegelian understanding of freedom matches aspects of our everyday use of freedom. To master a language is not simply to be able to speak
without making mistakes, without being reprimanded. To master a language
is to be able to say things which have not been said before, to combine
words in new ways which, despite their novelty, will not result in reprimand
by one's community. Only then can it be said that an individual is a competent language user. Freedom consists in the possibility for new performances enabled by the mastery of a "framework of norms." In this case, that
"framework of norms" is "inherent in the social practices which make up
the language"; in general, that framework of norms is inherent in the social
practices of the community as a whole (194). In sum, for Brandom freedom
is a feature of social practice, made possible by social norms; it is not the
ability of an individual to transcend social norms.

On Brandom's account of freedom, there is no need for faith. Social
practices form a seamless web: practices, practices for correcting practices,
practices for interpreting practices, and so on. If a community member is

No need for faith

well acculturated, she can be sure no situation will arise which is not part of a familiar social practice—except for the innovations of the "artist or genius" which beget new social practices. Yet even in these cases of innovation, there is no sense of the tragic, no sense of necessary conflict. Such conflict is suppressed, for there would presumably be practices for interpreting apparent conflicts, and practices for righting practices gone wrong, and so on. This social world is smooth, it has no texture. Social norms, which could provide texture, are understood to be of secondary importance, guides for practice which are sometimes explicit—or, even when they are implicit, they can always be made explicit.

Is it possible to account for what Brandom calls freedom if one takes seriously the gap between norms and practices? Gillian Rose's work suggests that it is. Reminiscent of Brandom, she writes of "our infinite capacity for self-creation."[7] Rose's account of law (by which she means something akin to social norms) refuses stasis; law is always in flux. Out of the tension between social practices and norms emerge new practices and new norms which are surprising, which were unknown previously. What Rose has to say about flux is made clearer by her descriptions of reading and writing. Rose describes reading as "the repository of my inner self-relation: the discovery, simultaneous with the suddenly sculpted and composed words, of distance from and deviousness toward myself as well as others."[8] By reading, Rose was able to call herself into question by leveraging the tension between practice and norms, presentation and representation. In other words, she was able to step back from the norms through which she understood herself, the norms she unquestioningly accepted because of their apparently seamless connection with who she was. In fact, these norms had just been borrowed from those around her and applied to herself. Her encounter with the explication of community norms through the written word, in the texts she read, distanced her from those norms, revealing the tension between social norms and practice, between her concept of herself and who she really was (that is, how she really acted). It allowed her to become "devious," to open new possibilities for herself, new ways of acting that were previously unimaginable.

The same process, but with an escalated intensity, occurs in writing. For Brandom, writing would seem to be a paradigmatic instance of "making it explicit," of articulating norms implicit in social practice. Jeffrey Stout uses Brandom's work to suggest that this is how we should understand great American writers such as Whitman, Ellison, and Baldwin.[9] They have made explicit the norms that are implicit in the American democratic tradition. For Rose, writing shows the fecundity of the tension between social practice and norms, rather than showing how norms are implicit in practice. Recall how Rose describes writing as a "mix of discipline and miracle, which leaves you in control, even when what appears on the page has emerged from regions beyond your control."[10] Writing involves grappling with received norms ("discipline"), and attempting to creatively follow those norms to produce an acceptable, desirable product ("control"). On the other hand, something else is at work, something utterly unexpected based on existing norms. This is exactly what a "miracle" is: a phenomenon not explicable in terms of existing laws, in terms of existing norms. Writing involves miracle because, in the process of confronting existing norms—norms which are necessarily incomplete, which necessarily do "violence"—something new appears in ink on the page. This something that appears reflects neither the existing norms nor the "personality" of the writer, but a Hegelian (on Rose's nontotalizing reading of Hegel) synthesis of the two. Rose characterizes these possibilities as an unexpected "paradise" that is "unlocked as a result of coercion, reluctance, cajolery and humiliation."[11] The new possibilities open up through a confrontation with the law, through being forced to grapple with the rigors of reading and writing.

Freedom — through the impossibility of mastering norms

For Brandom, freedom is possible through the mastery of norms; on this alternative account, endorsed by Rose, freedom is possible through the impossibility of mastering norms. It is made possible by the fecundity of their failures. Even a competent practitioner is wrong some of the time simply because of the necessary mismatch between norms and practice. It is out of such mismatches, especially when harnessed in practices such as reading and writing, that new norms and practices emerge. Put another way, Brandom's account succumbs to the hegemony of the visible. Novelty arises on top of the visible, as embellishments to the already existing fabric of social practices. The alternative account, endorsed by Rose, refuses this hegemony. The image of an unbroken fabric of the social world is an illusion. When

Brandom succumbs to the "hegemony of the visible"

it is refused, it becomes clear that the social world is already broken, that social life is always tragic. By acknowledging this picture, radically novel possibilities open up, but to acknowledge this picture, to acknowledge the fundamentally broken nature of the world, faith is necessary.

Once one acknowledges the perennial conflict between practices and norms, does it not beg the question to say that faith is the answer? If, paradoxically, faithlessness is simply succumbing to enchantment and faith is refusing enchantment, is the concept of faith doing any work besides pointing to this paradox? Before considering Rose's account of faith and exploring how it might address this situation, let us consider an alternative. What if it is desire, not faith, that animates life in the ordinary, that allows for the navigation of a difficult world of practices and norms? This suggestion can be found in the work of Judith Butler, from her early writings on Hegel through her writings on gender. The juxtaposition of Butler and Rose is provocative. They both began their careers studying Hegel and immersed themselves in the tradition of critical theory. Later their paths diverged as Rose's work increasingly concerned itself with questions of religion while Butler's work became increasing concerned with culture, particularly issues of gender, sexuality, and race. Yet even in their later work, Rose's and Butler's shared concerns with the violence inherent in norms persists; what is different in their approaches is how this violence can be addressed, a difference that has its roots in the way each understands Hegel.

Butler and Rose both refuse the image of a "totalizing" Hegel against which much twentieth-century French thought reacted.[12] They both refused the image of Hegel as having offering an all–encompassing, closed system, dominated by an Absolute, a system which purported to unify all history and knowledge. It was not the case that all truths were contained in or directly derivable from the books of the Master. Butler argues that this image of Hegel runs counter to both the content and method of the *Phenomenology of Spirit*. The *Phenomenology* should be read as a narrative. It follows a movement, but it also has a movement, taking the reader along its journey. It is a bildungsroman with "comic, even burlesque" elements.[13] There is growth, struggle, failure, tragedy, and resumption of the journey. Just when we think we have arrived at where we are going, when we have figured out what the world is like—then, again, we realize that it is a deception.

It is realizing that what we are doing is different from what we intend that
reveals this deception. It becomes necessary to move beyond the deceptive
state of affairs, to supersede it, a process fueled by desire. Thus, Butler translates the key Hegelian term *aufgehoben* as "superseded," and concludes that
"desire is nothing other than the action of supersession itself" (43).

On this reading, desire becomes the animating force of the *Phenomenology*.
It is desire that drives the narrative (even though desire only appears midway
through the text, Butler argues that it is implicitly present throughout). At
any moment along the path of the *Phenomenology*, it seems as though desire
would be satisfied, but it is not. To say that the Hegelian subject is a desiring
subject is an understatement. The Hegelian subject "is not a self-identical
subject who travels smugly from one ontological place to another; it is its
travels," and these travels are fueled by desire (8). For a subject desire is a
"necessarily ambiguous movement toward the world, consumption and ex-
ternalization, appropriation and dispersal" (42). The subject is always getting
the world wrong. It is as if the world is playing tricks on the subject. But the
subject is able to continue her movement toward the world despite these
dispiriting fits and starts because the subject desires.

Butler positions her work against what she sees as the efforts of main-
stream philosophers to ignore or control desire, who present desire in opposition to reason, the proper domain of philosophy. If ignoring and controlling prove ineffective, then desire is integrated with reason. The alternative
that Hegel presents is more radical: desire is unavoidable, it disrupts, but it
also engages. To do philosophy with a focus on desire is to do philosophy
critically, to acknowledge and work through difficulties instead of submerg-
ing them in enchantment. This turn to critical philosophy is what makes
possible Butler's famed work on gender and sexuality. Risk is crucial to ethics, she suggests. Rather than retreating into enchantment, into set ways of
thinking and acting which take our "I" as a "self-possession," Butler urges
that we recognize ourselves to be constantly navigating a world of norms
through improvisation fueled by desires. If we recognize that we are impro-
vising, we can improvise strategically. Norms have their hold on us through
desire, and our performances in relation to a norm are animated by desire.
It is thus by taking ownership of our desire that we are able to access a
"transformative potential" that could result in new norms that no longer

foreclose the existence of some individuals. Queers, transgendered people, and the disabled are always in error, are never able to lead livable lives.[14]

But what is this category of desire which animates, and why does it deserve autonomy? The epigraph to Butler's introduction comes from a Wallace Stevens poem:

> The greatest poverty is not to live
> In a physical world, to feel that one's desire
> Is too difficult to tell from despair.

These lines wonderfully, though paradoxically, illustrate Butler's conclusion that "desire is nothing other than the action of supersession." Desire is in the world, the physical, sensuous world, but desire is also what makes life in that world possible. When desire and despair mingle, desire is impotent. It cannot pull one out of and into the world at once. What is left is the grubby mix of desire and despair, love and loss, mourning and joy—the world unpurified by desire. This is the picture that Butler paints. Against this understanding of the centrality of desire, with its accompanying supersessionism, it will be, strangely enough, faith that does not denote the action of supersession. It is precisely the otherworldly status of faith which allows it to signify what desire attempts to signify without bringing along an association with supersession. If what is at issue is simply a structure, as it were, the mismatch between practices and norms which does not lead to abandon, it is an empty name that can most safely denote such a structure.

Like Butler, Gillian Rose provides an alternative to the "totalizing" image of Hegel. A response to this totalizing image in twentieth-century French philosophy had been to reject Hegel's "conservative system" but to endorse his "radical method." Rose takes aim at just such an image of Hegel. But by focusing on Hegel's "radical method" alone, the Absolute disappears—and to understand Hegel, one must think the Absolute. In a sense, this is precisely what Butler does. With her reading of the *Phenomenology* as a narrative, Hegel appears to have a "radical method," a way of implicating the reader in a shared, tragicomic journey. Butler's account of the Absolute suggests that it is "something like the dramatic integrity of a comedy of errors" (23). In other words, the Absolute just names Hegel's "radical method." While Rose concurs with the focus on narrative, she argues that

For Rose, Hegel
Present Announce an end to
History but the beginning
of Faith

the content of that narrative must not be ignored, or be separated from the narrative method. Central to that content, at the heart of Hegel's system, is religion. To think about God is a precursor to thinking the Absolute philosophically. Philosophy picks up where religion left off, but both are engaged in the same task. Critical philosophy has "faith." According to Rose, Hegel does not announce an end of history or an end to religion. He announces the beginning of genuine faith, philosophical faith, in work which is, in Rose's words, "not a success" but "a gamble."[15] To acknowledge inherent, irreparable conflict and to continue to gamble—that is faith. Hegel's work tracks the history of this gamble, which is a religious history.

Rose reintroduces faith in her later work, when Kierkegaard has come to deeply inflect the Hegelian currents of her thought. Rose had grappled in *The Broken Middle* with Kierkegaard's account of faith, trying to find a way to assimilate faith into her thought through critical encounters with writers ranging from Lacan to Kafka to Arendt to Milbank. Faith had become a living intellectual topic for Rose; it would soon become a living personal issue as well. Rose writes that her interest in Judaism, her "return" to the faith of her ancestors, was spurred by a dinner party conversation. A friend explained to her, "An orthodox Jew doesn't have to worry about whether he believes in God or not. As long as he observes the law."[16] This struck a chord with Rose, offering the possibility that the Jewish tradition might be mined as a resource for her jurisprudentially oriented philosophy. She studied ancient and modern Hebrew and the works of Jewish writers; she also served on a commission charged with memorializing Auschwitz.

Rose's interest in issues of faith underwent a change from intellectual to personal, from Kierkegaardian to Jewish. Her faith later underwent a second change which coincided with her fatal illness. Rose's interest shifted from Judaism to Christianity, culminating in her deathbed conversion. In her last writings, especially *Paradiso*, she explores the intellectual and spiritual resources of the Christian tradition, ranging from the significance of monasticism and seclusion to Augustine on the virtues of faith, hope, and love. Nonetheless, in each of these three phases of Rose's relationship to faith, the way that she understood faith philosophically remained consistent. Faith for Rose always remained a feature of life in the social world. From Kierkegaard she took an interest in moments which reveal faith, from

Rose's account
of Faith draws
from Kierkegaard,
Judaism &
Christianity

Judaism she took an interest in the centrality of law for faith, and from Christianity she took an interest in the role of love in faith.

In contrast to almost every other topic she discusses, Rose presents a straightforward statement of her understanding of faith. The difficulty comes in trying to make sense of how this statement, offered in her final, posthumously published work, illuminates the variety of statements that Rose made about faith at other points during her life. Rose asserts that faith has a twofold meaning. On the one hand, Rose follows Keats in describing it as "the capacity of being in uncertainties, mysteries, doubts, without any irritable reaching after facts and reasons"; on the other hand, Rose asserts that it is "the enlarging of inhibited reason in the domain of praxis, of practical reason, Aristotle's *phronesis*, the educating of wisdom that knows when to pass unnoticed and when to act."[17] Faith is a practice: it is the practice of continuing to grapple with the world, realizing that the world is, and always will be, uncertain. Commitment to this task leads to excellence in navigating the world, excellence at the job of being a lawyer whose specialty is social norms.

The example that provides the centerpiece for Rose's account of faith is Abraham's preparation to sacrifice Isaac. Constructing her argument in dialogue with Kierkegaard's renowned reading of the biblical story, Rose begins by rejecting any reading of the story that would take the sacrifice to be "a pre-ethical condition of a founding murder."[18] What is at work is a *suspension* of the ethical—which immediately entails that the ethical already existed before its suspension. The sacrifice is not the moment when norms arrive on the earth from the starry skies above; social practice and norms have always existed.

Instead of focusing on the "leap" of faith so often read into Kierkegaard, Rose is at least equally interested in what happens *after* the moment when faith is tested. Indeed, what happens during the moment itself can remain in brackets—its only salient feature is its existence, that such a moment does happen. After the moment, the individual who has experienced it returns to his ordinary existence. Kierkegaard's heroes return to the ordinary world. However, their lives afterward are subtly altered. It is this new style of living, inflected by the moment when faith was tested, that Rose identifies with faith.

The "suspension of the ethical" (Kierkegaard's phrase, appropriated by Rose) only occurs for an "imperceptible" moment, "for the movement of faith does not take place in time, or, it takes place in every moment of time."[19] This perplexing observation is a reminder that faith, like freedom, is a mode of living, a stance toward social norms. It is not a feeling or a belief or a decision that happens in a "moment." The moment simply allegorizes the lifestyle of faith, condensing it to a point. The story of Abraham and Isaac is a fiction; it forces us to think about what it would be like if social norms were suspended, even though they really are not and cannot be suspended. To suppose that social norms actually are suspended, and that such a suspension is the foundation of ethics, would be to separate ethics and law—it would be exactly the supersessionist move Rose so vehemently opposes. *Rose* *however* "*moments* *of* *suspension*"

Abraham's willingness to sacrifice Isaac is just one of many examples of *forever* suspensions of the ethical to which Rose points. Moments of suspension *to* *radically* *alter* occur in much less supernatural circumstances. Rose cites illness, bereavement, separation from a loved one, and natural disasters as moments which *norms* fulfill this function—"to loose and to bind, to bind and to loose."[20] All of these circumstances function to radically alter the norms by which one lives; each results in a re-formation, in the emergence of new, previously unforeseen norms. "*life* *of* *faith*"

What does a faithful life look like, a life informed by stories of faith such as those told about Abraham? Rose describes the life of faith as one in which an individual is continually "willing to stake oneself again."[21] By this she means that a person with faith will wholeheartedly engage in the activity of positing concepts (norms) and testing them against reality (practice), and will always be willing to revise the concepts he or she posits. A faithful person will not exempt herself from this process; she will remain sensitive to the evidence of experience, never dogmatically holding to concepts that are not supported by evidence, to norms not supported by practice. It is thus only faith "that prevents one from becoming an arbitrary perpetrator or an arbitrary victim; that prevents one, actively or passively, from acting with arbitrary violence."[22]

To hold dogmatically to a view of the world is to act with arbitrary violence because it is to offer reprimands that are not supported by the evidence of experience and are only based on personal whims or social conventions held as dogmatic truths. A faithful person does not imagine that she can act without violence; rather, she realizes that all actions are continually implicated in violence. Yet she perseveres in acting, in positing concepts and testing them against realities. In this struggle, "'violence' is inseparable from staking oneself, from experience as such—the initial yet yielding recalcitrance of action and passion."[23]

This is why Rose opposes much contemporary religious thought, both Jewish and Christian. She takes the project of religious thinkers from Buber to Fackenheim to Metz to Milbank to be one of "mending the world" which has the effect of "betraying" the hard work of living.[24] In short, they lack faith. They lack the commitment to persist in the "revel of ideas and risk" that is social life and instead opt for an easy out, for the fantasy of an ethics purified of law.[25] The "New Jerusalems" that they posit foreclose the possibility of critical analysis of social norms, of the worldly power and worldly institutions from which they recoil. "Against the tradition from St. Paul to Kant which opposes law to grace and knowledge to faith . . . the modern congregation of the disciplines—from philosophy to architecture—*loses faith* when it renounces concept, learning, and law."[26] Supersessionism was once religious, now it is secular; once it was theological, now it is academic.

If Kierkegaard identifies and describes the problem of anxiety, the solution he offers, on Rose's reading, is a lifestyle of faith. Anxiety is experienced any time one genuinely grapples with the law. To live life without anxiety would be to shut oneself off from a central feature of the world; it would be to live in delusion (in enchantment). Living life without anxiety is like living life without freedom; possible, perhaps, but only when one understands social norms to be absolutely rigid and static.

Rose charts Kierkegaard's two-stage move, which demonstrates the relationship between law, anxiety, and faith. First, there is a movement "from law to anxiety." A person who is living an ordinary life experiences anxiety for some reason, perhaps because of a moment of crisis when social norms are suspended. Then, faith allows the individual to return from the moment of anxiety to the law, to the world of social norms. Instead of despairing indefinitely because of anxiety, faith allows the individual to go back to ordinary life. However, the ordinary life of the individual before the experi-

Freedom is thus linked to anxiety [handwritten annotation]

ence of anxiety is subtly different from that ordinary life afterward. What was before simply a life lived with "ambivalence" becomes a life lived with full-blown existential angst, with deep "equivocation."

Rose explicitly links freedom to anxiety—and hence to faith. "The art of power is 'freedom': how to be always all-ready for anxiety."[27] In this rather bewildering sentence, we find a tangled knot of Rose's key concepts. To begin untangling: the absent center of Rose's sentence is law, which we have been associating with social norms. Law is infused with power, according to Rose. To navigate the law, to find one's way around the world of social norms, to use *phronesis*, is what Rose here calls "freedom." Let us think of anxiety as what happens when law is suspended—for instance in Abraham's case, or in the case of disease or disaster. The *phronimos*, the person with practical wisdom, the person who has the ability to navigate the law with excellence, will be able to continue to act when it seems as though the law is suspended. This person has freedom, and also faith. In fact, it is not only in moments when the law is suspended that this ability to have faith is needed. Faith is needed all of the time because social norms always involve anxiety. In a sense, they are always suspended, for they are just fictions trying, and failing, to match social practice. This being the case, to be free is to have faith, because freedom is the ability to navigate social norms, and faith (not desire) is the energy that fuels that task. *Faith is to continue to struggle w* [handwritten annotation]

Faith is also a central topic of Rose's philosophical memoir. Disease and *the world* [handwritten annotation] hardship without despair pervade *Love's Work*. We encounter character after character who has gone through great ordeals, ordeals which only reinvigorate his or her zeal for life. "Keep your mind in hell, and despair not," the epigraph reads. This is the core of faith for Rose, to continue to struggle in the world instead of opting for easy escapes. One's mind—and body—may suffer unspeakable travails, yet one who has faith will persevere in the engagement, in the struggle. In the first pages of Rose's memoir, we meet the nonagenarian Edna, a woman who "exudes well-being" despite a battle with childhood cancer and various other ailments. Edna is a model of the understanding of faith endorsed by Rose; Edna "lived sceptically."[28] Despite her age, she continued reading, thinking, and engaging with the world of ideas and people. Edna is not perfect and is not even extraordinary. She makes mistakes, frequently. Yet Edna believed in "the quiet and undramatic transmutation that can come out of plainness, ordinary hurt, mundane mal-adies and disappointments" (6).

In contrast, Rose describes her own mother as faithless.[29] The Holocaust claimed the lives of fifty of her mother's relatives, yet her mother lives in de-nial. Her mother claims that the loss caused no suffering, yet this only masks the depth of the suffering which remains unresolved. Her mother's refusal to "live in hell" results in melancholia, in an entrenched despair which will not budge because it is denied. Her mother appears content, she wears a smile, yet she has an "all-jovial unhappiness." The trauma is not *worked*, in Rose's idiom, because it remains unthought. Rose's understanding of her mother's denial, and faithlessness, is parallel to Rose's critique of postmod-ernism and neopragmatism. Rose argues that these movements evade the difficulty, violence, and suffering of the world. They claim to sweep away metaphysics and law, they claim to offer a possibility for ethics without law. However, in doing so, they merely exemplify a form of incomplete mourn-ing—mourning for reason itself, lost because of its now all too evident entanglement in violence.

Faith is a virtue. It is the virtue that Rose accuses her mother of lack-ing. As a virtue, it is an aspect of character; it is the disposition to persevere in the face of conflict. Better, it is to acknowledge conflict, for the way that the faithless retreat from conflict is by refusing to acknowledge it. To smooth over the world so that difficulty never comes into view, this is the work of enchantment. Enchantment is always imperfect; there are always hints of conflict. The virtue of faith, then, is the disposition to take seriously these hints, to stare at them, to be willing to set aside enchantment if this is called for by the investigation of the moment of conflict. To be faithless, thus, is vicious. It is to suppress difficulty, to perpetuate the illusion that enchantment is impeccable. As a virtue, faith can be cultivated. Love is an education in faith (and love is impossible without faith).

This conception of the virtue of faith differs from the conventional wis-dom that faith involves belief with insufficient evidence, belief that is not "beyond a reasonable doubt."[30] And it differs from the conventional wis-dom that faith involves conviction in the face of detractors. On the con-ventional view, one will occasionally encounter evidence against beliefs in which one has faith. Because one has faith, that evidence will be dismissed.

Dramatically, in a society suffused with evil, an individual will constantly encounter reasons to doubt beliefs about being good. While to the average Joe in contemporary America it might seem reasonable that honesty is the best policy, no doubt about it, unless Joe has *faith* in the goodness of honesty, his belief in the goodness of honesty will quickly evaporate when he finds himself in a totalitarian state. Dishonesty will seem more expedient, more beneficial for him—unless he clings to his belief in the goodness of honesty. Morality in general is a good example of this sort of faith. Even if reasons are presented for belief in morality, these reasons can never be totally conclusive. A student who has taken for granted a belief in morality may take an ethics class or an anthropology class (or an economics class) and begin to doubt that her belief is correct. The student might read about people in far away lands who act in dramatically different ways than the way she acts. To be moral requires having beliefs about good and evil, but the student now doubts her own beliefs about good and evil. Consequently, to be moral, she needs faith—or so the conventional view has it.

Yet these examples seem to be compelling accounts of faith because of the moments they describe when belief is challenged. A belief that is simply held despite the possibility, but not the reality, of a "reasonable doubt" would not qualify as faith. The virtue of faith involves the willingness to grapple with a possibility of reasonable doubt. To address those doubts as reasonable instead of dismissing them out of hand, that is what takes the virtue of faith. More generally, faith is the willingness to countenance moments when beliefs normally taken for granted are put into question. When we read in a Marxist newspaper that morality is the tool of the oppressing class, we are shaken from our default belief in morality. If the concerns raised by the newspaper are taken as genuine rather than dismissed as excessive rhetoric or dismissed as "ideology"—even if we persist in our original belief—the virtue of faith is exercised. Of course, if we genuinely take seriously the doubts raised by the Marxist newspaper, it will be impossible for us to return precisely to the position from which we started.

What are we to make of the example of the average Joe who finds himself in an oppressive regime but clings to his forbidden belief in the goodness of honesty? Does he have the virtue of faith? The question is not whether it is appropriate to say that he has faith—that is a question of everyday language—but whether he acts as one who has faith. It is tempting to obscure the issue, to be distracted by language, by enchantment. If the virtue of faith is understood as this sort of commitment in the face of overwhelming odds, it is not a theopolitical virtue. It is caught in the hegemony of the visible: the beliefs of the embattled Joe and his surroundings are not put in play. Indeed, this embattled Joe likely does not imagine that doubts about his beliefs are at all reasonable. Even though it appears that he is constantly forced to question himself, the situation may have the opposite effect. It may quite closely resemble the situation in which Joe is at a barbeque, surrounded by those who share his values. In neither the case where Joe is embattled nor the case where Joe is surrounded by those who share his views is his conviction at stake. This is not to say that Joe has the vice of faithlessness, though it is a vice that is likely to develop in either case.

Is this virtue of faith at work in the faith that seems to be necessary to live in a democratic community? Recall how this democratic faith, at least as it appears in everyday language, is a synthesis of immanent and transcendent conceptions of faith, of faith in a proximate community and faith in a distant object, an ideal of the democratic state. If all citizens had the vice of faithlessness, a democratic community would quickly descend into totalitarianism. Democracy takes discernment and judgment that cuts deeper than enchantment. Totalitarianism relies on smooth edges and veneer. Friction is the last thing totalitarianism wants, and friction is what faith creates. Those who advocate democratic faith often associate specific beliefs with it—for example, a belief in the underlying equality of human beings, which, they admit, cannot be proved beyond a reasonable doubt. However, it seems compelling that a culture of faith, a culture that is religious without religion, is closely tied to democracy.[31]

But crudely combining immanent and transcendent conceptions never moves beyond the hegemony of the visible. To combine faith in what is familiar to us, those particular practices and institutions of our community, with faith in an ideal: this results in the opposite of faith. It is the quintessential enchantment, sanctifying the worldly with the authority of the otherworldly. This is the dangerous potential of democratic faith. Moreover, there is a tempting but confused misconception about the virtue of faith. This misconception relies on the notion that where virtues are concerned

the more the better. But that is not how virtues work. Virtues are disposi-
tions to act in certain ways in certain circumstances, not to act those ways
all of the time. To have the virtue of faith does not mean that one must
be constantly faithful. There may be whole domains where faith may not
be exercised, just as there are times and places where one should not love.
Political institutions do not necessarily call for the virtue of faith. Love,
the virtue of love, always involves faith, but politics does not always. In the
domain of politics, as in any domain, there may be times when accepting
enchantment is called for. But this does not mean that faith is abandoned.
In the practice of love it is sustained. Faith remains political whether or not
it is employed in particular practices of politics, because faith, with love,
makes the invisible visible.

CHAPTER 3

HOPE

HOPE IS NOT A VIRTUE. THIS IS HARD TO SWALLOW. FAITH, HOPE, and love seem to form a natural triptych. They are what make people good, and they are what make people happy. It is hard to think of a hopeful person who is unhappy, or a hopeful person who is bad. A hopeful person whistles while she works. She skips down the street for no reason. She lights up a room. She is ebullient. There is something about her character, something that disposes her to, as Bing Crosby would say, accentuate the positive and eliminate the negative. How could this not be the virtue of hope?

The extent to which we cling to hope, to the idea of hope, illustrates the difficulty of disentangling everyday language from rigorous thought, and the grip that enchantment has on us. How could it be worth living in a world without hope? There must be hope! It is tempting to say something easy: hope is many things to many people. It is a cluster of concepts. Hope is multivalent. It is a conjunction of affect and object. Everyday language, on these approaches, is the starting point. It is to be organized and theorized. Instead, we should be concerned with what hope does. If hope is a virtue, then there are certain circumstances in which, because an individual has the virtue of hope, she will act in certain ways. That seems simple

Hope isn't a virtue but a Rhetorical technique

enough: someone with the virtue of hope will, when things are not going *Rhetoric it* well, imagine that things will, eventually, go better. But what are the effects, what does this hopeful person *do*? In the face of adversity, she perseveres. That sounds very familiar—because it is the virtue of faith.

Hope is not a virtue, it is a rhetorical technique. It is part of everyday language, not ordinary life. It is used to persuade. Whatever remainder of hope there is beyond its rhetorical nature is the virtue of faith, but often there is no remainder. Put the other way around, sometimes the virtue of faith is expressed in the rhetoric of hope. There is a triptych of Christian virtues, the "theological" virtues of faith, hope, and love, and these have been secularized with barely a change (not even their names).[1] But when rhetoric is left to one side, there is but a diptych of theopolitical virtues: faith and love. To say that hope is a rhetorical technique is not to dismiss it. Rather, it is to acknowledge its ambivalence. Hope can be used for good or for ill. There are no guarantees. Faith and love, understood theopolitically, are always virtues; they are always beneficial.

Gillian Rose, whose work suggests how love and faith can be understood as virtues, has very little to say about hope. Perhaps this is because hope is unequivocal, and Rose's work is, if anything, an embrace of equivocation. Augustine's seminal account of the theological virtues may help illuminate Rose's reticence about hope. Augustine asserts that one of the differences between faith and hope is that the objects of hope can only be good while the objects of faith must be both good and bad.[2] One hopes for eternal life but one has faith in the possibility of eternal damnation. One does not hope that millions of individuals will go to hell, but one believes it to be so as an object of faith. The closest Rose comes to a discussion of hope is her discussion of those who would posit a "New Jerusalem," an antinomian future which would be purely good, which would be free from violence. Although she does not use the word supersessionism to describe advocates of a "New Jerusalem," this is the problem she finds with their work.[3] The land of milk and honey that they posit explicitly has its origins in the ordinary world, yet it moves beyond the ordinary world to what is effectively an antinomian simulacrum of the ordinary. The object of hope, Rose seems to suggest, is to be free from laws, free from social norms—and so hope must be resisted. Faith, in contrast, is commended by Rose because it grapples

For Rose, Hope must be resisted

with both good and evil; it grapples with the realities of the world without solace in any fantasy of escape.

Perhaps this helps to explain Rose's puzzling response to an interviewer's question: "Do you believe in eternity?" She replied, "Definitely. It's the only thing I believe in." Her next remarks are even more confounding, "If there is eternity, then it's now. . . . Time is devastation. You can't believe in time. Time is going to destroy you. So you have to believe in eternity."[4] The interviewer's question solicits a statement of hope, not of faith. He is asking Rose for her thoughts on a future which will be unequivocally good, a future outside of time, outside of Law. Rose manipulates the question, toying with the concept of eternity by rejecting its projection into the future. Eternity offers an alternative to time, where time is understood (counterintuitively) as stasis. For Rose, eternity is present in the freedom made possible by faith. Eternity is the transcendence made visible by the unexpected, by the surprising fecundity of norms. In a sentence which could apply to both her writing and to her own life, Rose writes, "The rhetoric of virtue, virtue alive to the negative, is discernible in the pathos of syntax, where eternity shines through violence."[5] This eternity is neither in the future nor the past, and it is not outside of the world. It points to the theopolitical, that which is not captured by the hegemony of the visible.

To believe in eternity means to refuse both hope and melancholia. Both involve fixation on an object. In hope, that object is projected into the future, in melancholia, it is projected into the past. In both cases, the world is clouded by the fixation. Critique is impossible, enchantment is all-embracing. Recall Freud's distinction between mourning and melancholia.[6] In both, an object is lost. To the individual for whom the object was significant, there is something missing from the external world, and this loss provokes a conscious sadness. Melancholia is mourning without end, mourning that "cannot work." In melancholia, loss disturbs the unconscious, and the bereaved individual feels the loss not in the external world but in herself. In the face of this sort of loss, the outside world no longer matters. The bereaved person spirals inward as she no longer feels capable of attachment. Yet this inward spiral does not regress to a firm core of the self, but to an empty, reviled self. The world is distorted by the lost object,

MELANCHOLIA & HOPE SHARE — BOTH ENCOMPASS THE SAME STRUCTURE (THE) PLURAL DEFICIENCIES (OF THE WORLD)

and it seems as though there is no sense in navigating the world any longer. There is no need to work the world, or the loss.

Melancholia and hope, when the latter is taken as more than rhetorical, share the same structure. What differs between them is how they are expressed. The plural deficiencies of the world, the many moments that do not make sense, moments of tragedy, of failure, of inexplicable disturbance, these *HOPE* are condensed into one. When one object is pushed so far forward that it is *REFUSES* no longer part of our time, it is just hope. The specificities no longer mat- *MOURNING* ter. That is what produces both hope and melancholia. Mourning must be refused in order to sustain hope, and hope sustains the refusal of mourning. Engagement with the world is thoroughly and constantly refused.

Put another way: norms and practices are in tragic conflict. When one tries to do what one ought to do, one falls short. Norms are misperceived. It seems like they are one thing, but actually they are something else. Norms conflict. It seems as though two different norms speak to the same practice, that there are two quite different things that one ought to do in a given situation. As soon as one acts according to one norm the action will be wrong according to the norm not followed. This is why life is saturated with mourning. Every action is tragic, every moment produces a new loss. It would be easy to be overwhelmed. The simplest solution would be simply to ignore the constant mismatch. Or, more precisely, the simplest solution would be to buy into a story, an enchantment, which would make it seem as if there is no mismatch. The harder solution would be to have faith: *TO* to acknowledge an instance of the tragic and to work through it, refusing *MOURN* enchantment. To have faith is to mourn; to buy into enchantment is mel- ancholic. To mourn is to acknowledge loss, to work it, and to thrust oneself back into the fray, back into life in the world, to find again the mismatch between norms and practices, But the world of practices and norms is now inflected by that experience of mourning, it is different than it was before. This is what is meant by the title of Rose's book *Mourning Becomes the Law*.

When melancholia is the response to tragic conflict, the conflict does not inflect the world. The conflict is ignored; it is as if it did not exist. Of course, the conflict remains—at what we might call an unconscious level. It is not worked, it wells up. It must express itself somehow, and it does: in an affective remainder affixed to a projected object. The object cannot be of this world; if it were, the tragic would be acknowledged, would be visible. The object must be otherworldly: this is the object of hope. What better object of otherworldly attention than the generic future, "a time to come"? The affect associated with hopefulness, the cheery disposition for which no cause can be found, is in fact the affect produced by a most profound melancholia. Why does it appear so strange, so unmelancholic? Because the affect produced by the repressed tragic is harnessed by enchantment. The object of hope only seems empty. In fact, it has content, and that content is shared. It is a collective fantasy. It binds a community by offering an explanation for the tragic so that the tragic need not be acknowledged. With the tragic now ignored, it is again repressed, generating more affect, projected again into an object of hope, the content of which binds—and on and on. This is the libidinal logic of enchantment, the logic which clothes melancholia in the guise of hope.

There are, necessarily, cases in which enchantment fails and melancholia is left exposed, cases in which the unconscious wounds of the tragic are never salved. There are those who are unrepresentable, whose very representation would mark a failure of enchantment. Their identities are failures: to acknowledge their identities would be to acknowledge the tragic. Women are to desire men, are to wear feminine attire, and are to have female anatomy—this is part of our enchantment. Lesbian identity is a perpetual failure.[7] There is no way to recognize the lesbian without being constantly reminded of the tragic, precisely what enchantment prevents. The figure of the homosexual haunts enchantment, or rather certain enchantments. Each enchantment has a specter, whether it be the disabled, or the transgendered, or the biracial. From the perspective of the specter herself: she feels a "wounded attachment" to her identity.[8] The identity the lesbian is attached to necessarily causes her pain because it is unauthorized, it runs counter to norms, always bringing reprimand with it. Yet that is who she is: any other identification would cause even greater unconscious repression. For such spectral figures, there is no hope, no future.[9] The identity to which she is attached is constituted by her exclusion. The necessary injury is part and parcel of who she is. If she were to be incorporated into enchantment, given an object of hope, she would have to disavow who she is. Recognition would be transformation—and loss. Is this double loss not the origin

RESSENTIMENT IS A SIMULACRUM OF
HOPE AT ITS PUREST

of the politics of *ressentiment*? Might *ressentiment* be a simulacrum of hope
at its purest, hope so infected with melancholia that it can no longer be
projected into the future?

HOPE ISN'T A DESIRE

If hope is not a virtue, then might it be a desire?[10] It would seem to be
so: the desired object of hope marking the missing cause of melancholia.
But let us look at the effects of hope. The language of hope mobilizes the
commitments of an audience by representing them, explicitly or implicitly, as an object of hope. In the object of hope, the commitments of an
audience are displayed as if in a carnival mirror, one especially tailored to,
yes, accentuate the positive and eliminate the negative. This may be done
directly, through description, or indirectly, through paralipsis, hinting at but
passing over the content of the object itself—though of course the audience has no difficulty filling it in.

RHETORIC OF HOPE
CONVINCES AUDIENCES TO

The rhetoric of hope need not, and does not, confine itself to the propositional; it is equally concerned with the affective. It mobilizes the emotions of its audience, emotions generated by the elision of the tragic. The *OVERLOOK*
language of hope calls forth these emotions and attaches them to its object *THE TRAGIC*
in order to convince. What does the rhetoric of hope convince an audience of? It convinces listeners to overlook the tragic. It smoothes over the
rough edges of social norms, disappearing apparent conflicts and filling in
apparent gaps. The result, of course, is more affective remainder, more of
the tragic repressed—making an audience all the more susceptible to the
rhetoric of hope.

It may be tempting to suggest that the rhetoric of hope cultivates the
virtue of faith. After all, the rhetoric of hope urges its audience to persevere
in the face of the tragic. But this would be to misunderstand. The virtue of
faith requires acknowledging the tragic. The rhetoric of hope persuades by
eliding the tragic. The virtue of faith involves mourning, but the rhetoric
of hope conjures an object which can never be lost. This is not to say that
the virtue of faith might not, on occasion, call for the rhetoric of hope.
Sometimes, in order to persevere in the face of acknowledged difficulty, the
most effective technique is to elide that difficulty and harness the affective
remainder produced by that elision. The most effective technique may be
to employ the rhetoric of hope. But the virtue of faith and the rhetoric of
hope exist in different registers, the former concerned with what one does,

the latter with what one says; the former with the ordinary, the latter with enchantment of the ordinary.

As soon as theories of hope are pushed, they often collapse into theories of the virtue of faith coated in the rhetoric of hope. Take the work of Richard Rorty, who fashions himself a great enthusiast of hope.[11] Of course, Rorty does not purport to be engaging in more than rhetoric; he relishes his vocation as a rhetorician. On his account, in the olden days, religion (or religion sublimated in metaphysics) held communities together. Now, in our age of atheism, social hope can serve the same function. It can build solidarity. Solidarity founded on hope is more palatable to Rorty than solidarity founded on religious or metaphysical belief. Hope is open-ended and undogmatic. That is why it appeals to "us"—postmodern bourgeois liberals—and appeal to its audience is precisely what good rhetoric is supposed to do. While Rorty is clear about his status as a rhetorician, it is often overlooked because his rhetorical flourishes seem to beg a nonrhetorical reading.

Rorty writes of faith as well, but he does not distinguish, and is emphatic about not distinguishing, between hope and faith. He also adds love into the mix. He writes of "a faith in the future possibilities of moral humans, a faith which is hard to distinguish from love for, and hope for, the human community," and continues, "I shall call this fuzzy overlap of faith, hope, and love 'romance'" (160–61). Romance can gather around anything with future possibilities in which individuals have, in some sense, a stake. To the conventional religious examples of a congregation or a god, Rorty adds a trade union, a novel, and a child. If we take a moment to reflect on the faith involved in this "fuzzy overlap" of the three traditional theological virtues which Rorty is reappropriating, if we step back from how nice it sounds to us, what Rorty is saying about faith hardly sounds like faith at all. It sounds like hope, like the rhetoric of hope. It is entirely directed at the future, while the rhetoric of faith concerns the present and past as much as the future (the virtue of faith is concerned exclusively with the present). Also, the faith in question is faith in a particular depiction of the future, a rosy future. Again, this is typical of the rhetoric of hope, not of the virtue of faith. The powerful commitment that the virtue of faith makes possible is entirely absent from the notion of "romance" that Rorty advocates. Rorty's romance

For Rorty
FAITH ≠
BELIEF

is appealing because it paints a rosy picture; faith is efficacious because it is a commitment to a project through thick and thin.

Rorty does write specifically about faith, arguing that faith and belief should be strictly distinguished. He associates belief with specific creeds, with specific propositions held to be true or false (e.g., Jesus rose from the dead). Aligning himself with Paul Tillich, Rorty argues that faith, like love for a spouse, child, or god, can seem inexplicable because the goodness found in spouse, child, or god is not visible to one who lacks faith in or lacks love for that object. Moreover, one who has faith and love does not "predict and control" the behavior of the object of his or her faith and love (158). The faith that Rorty is writing about here does sound closer to the virtue of faith than to the "fuzzy" overlap of faith, hope, and love he elsewhere describes. Yet the virtue of faith involves attention to detail. It involves beliefs about specifics. It does attempt to predict, or even to control. To have faith in a particular trade union, you must believe, without sufficient reason, that this specific trade union is organized rightly, is engaged in endeavors which are at least well intentioned, and so on. Very rational people may, and will, disagree about whether these beliefs about the trade union actually are true, yet the faithful trade unionist will remain committed to her or his beliefs even after hearing and acknowledging rational objections. Again, we are left to conclude that it is not the virtue of faith on which Rorty leans.

The payoff for Rorty in assembling this rhetorical arsenal, for secularizing the language of the theological virtues, is to arm contemporary leftists with a patriotic language which will not make them queasy. Early twentieth-century leftists exhibited a patriotism that is now lacking. The defining characteristic of that patriotism was its endorsement of a romance of the nation, of faith, hope, and love directed at the United States. It boiled down to "emotional involvement with one's country," "feelings of intense shame or of glowing pride aroused by various parts of its history, and by various present-day national policies."[12] Here is another dimension of the importance of romance as rhetoric. If what rhetoric does is persuade, and if one of the most effective techniques of persuasion is to draw on the emotions of one's listeners, what Rorty is commending in the early twentieth-century leftists is a rhetorical tradition that has been lost. What he seems to be saying is that leftists these days just are not very persuasive. Their

Rorty secularizes
theological
for leftist-patriotism

rhetorical repertoire could be expanded by studying historical precedent. The language of "emotional involvement," then, is misleading; it conjures amorphous sentimentality instead of specific affects in one's listeners for specific purposes.

According to Rorty, recent American leftists have misused romance—a critique that is clarified when romance is understood as the rhetoric of hope. For the rhetoric of hope to work, it must take an object with which we are associated and project an image of that object into the future, an image with the positives accentuated and the negatives eliminated. Recent American leftists, on Rorty's rather idiosyncratic view, have been hoping that America as we know it will be eliminated and "replaced, as soon as possible, with something utterly different."[13] This is an infelicitous rhetorical technique because there is no continuity between the present and the future objects with which we are associated. Listeners are not persuaded to act by a vision of the future that does not include them, or at least the objects and projects presently dear to them. The critical voice so important to recent American leftists need not be lost when the rhetoric of hope is employed; it can complement the rhetoric of hope. Rorty points to Sinclair, Dreiser, and Steinbeck as writers who hoped for a better America and simultaneously brought their critical force to bear on the actual existing America. There is critical potential built into the rhetoric of hope. When the rhetoric of hope juxtaposes, explicitly or implicitly, images of the object of hope with its present reality, the shortcomings of the present become all the more evident and the object of hope is no longer free-floating. This, of course, is how the rhetoric of hope effects change: it solicits approval for a future, perfected vision, and then demands action in the present to bring about that future vision.

In his lament for the lost rhetoric of hope, Rorty also seems to be grasping after, but never quite articulating, a lament for the virtue of faith. Both early and late twentieth-century leftists met with resistance from their fellow Americans. In response to this resistance, early twentieth-century leftists persisted in working the idea of America; late twentieth-century leftists abandoned ship in favor of a cosmopolitan, post-Marxist, or otherworldly utopian vision—or at least that is how Rorty sees it. The contrast recurs when Rorty discusses Elijah Muhammad and James Baldwin: "Neither forgave, but one turned away from the project of achieving the country and the other did not."[14] Baldwin and Muhammad certainly had reasonable doubts about whether America was a project to which they should remain committed. Baldwin acknowledged those doubts but maintained his commitment while Muhammad abandoned the project of America. Rorty notes that there is no "neutral" or "objective" way of deciding in which cases one should persevere and in which cases one should jump ship. Although Rorty, the rhetorician, does not say it, this is precisely where the virtue of faith comes in. It is necessary to countenance doubts and make a commitment when there are not "neutral" or "objective" criteria. Faith is not only commitment to persistence, but commitment to acknowledging and interrogating doubts—and being willing to act on the results of those interrogations.

The late American political theorist and social critic Christopher Lasch unabashedly asserts that hope is a central democratic virtue.[15] However, Lasch makes what he takes to be a crucial distinction between hope and optimism. He argues that optimism is about progress; hope is about a better but insuperably distant future. According to Lasch, hope has often been confused with optimism, but it is hope, not optimism, which is a genuine democratic virtue. For optimists, limits are threatening: they hint that progress may not be unbounded. For the hopeful, limits are expected because hope is directed over the gap that divides the present from the future. There is no way to anticipate or imagine what lies over that gap. Yet if we carefully examine Lasch's thoughts on hope, it will again become clear that he is equivocating between a rhetoric of hope and a virtue of faith.

Millennialism is a form of hope, not optimism, according to Lasch. Millennialism is about the end of the world, outside of time, while the optimist understands a better future to be inevitable within time, in the foreseeable future. Lasch suggests that the religious language that has been so much a part of the American democratic tradition is about optimism, not hope. The American conception of progress is the Christian commitment to providence, secularized. But instead of putting millennialism in tension with providentialism, Lasch at least partially reconciles the two by suggesting that the split between hope and optimism is relatively recent. Once upon a time, presumably while a Christian outlook was accepted without question,

(handwritten top margin) IN THIS ERA, OPTIMISM + HOPE WERE LINKED → PROGRESS → MILLENIUM, → CHRIST'S RETURN

progress was understood to culminate in the millennium, in Christ's return to earth (or, in its secularized version, the creation by humans of utopia on earth). Once the idea of the millennium, whether caused by God or by man, was discredited, what remained was an idea of progress without telos. What Lasch advises is that we reverse the results of the split between hope and optimism, retaining the telos without the idea of progress.

(handwritten left margin) LASCH WOULD CLASSIFY RORTY AS OPTIMISTIC

This is strikingly different from Rorty's rhetoric of hope. Rorty's view— that the hoped-for future be recognizable as deriving from the present— would be dismissed by Lasch as optimism. This is because Lasch understands himself to be concerned not with the rhetoric of hope but with the virtue of hope, though clearly the history of hope's rhetorical uses plays

(handwritten left margin) LASCH ABT THE VIRTUE NOT RHETORIC of HOPE

an important part in his analysis. Although he proclaims his interest in the virtue of hope, as soon as he describes the workings of hope it sounds strikingly like the virtue of faith. Lasch frames his inquiry into hope with the question, "How does it happen that people continue to believe in progress, in the face of massive evidence that might have been expected to refute the idea of progress once and for all?" (13). In this question we find that the virtue of faith and the rhetoric of hope are knotted. Lasch queries the possibility of persistence in the face of acknowledged reasonable doubt; at the same time he asks why this persistence would be expressed in the idea of progress, that is, the rhetoric of optimism.

To make sense of this knot, Lasch turns to the flipside of the rhetoric of hope: the rhetoric of nostalgia. The connection between future and past suggested by Lasch is twofold, corresponding to his distinction between

(handwritten left margin) OPTIMISM ALWAYS ACCOMPD BY NOSTALGIA

hope and optimism. He argues that optimism, which is committed to a belief in an ever-increasing improvement in the human condition, is always complemented by nostalgia. Nostalgia is a way of looking back on an idealized past, not of remembering things as they actually were in the past. As Lasch puts it, nostalgia is "an abdication of memory" (14). Both optimism and nostalgia disparage the present. They offer a picture of future and past which is more appealing than the present. In doing so, they refuse ambivalence. They lean on idealized futures and pasts, the rough edges smoothed over, the lovely memories and possibilities brought to the fore. They do the work of the rhetoric of hope: accentuating the positive and eliminating the

(handwritten left margin) ONE SHD ACKNOWLDGE AMBIVALENCE

negative.

In contrast, Lasch views the virtue of hope as enabling us to acknowledge the ups and downs that will inevitably confront us in the foreseeable future, yet he also suggests that the virtue of hope will allow us to see promise in the unforeseeable future. Hope, on this view, does not denigrate the present. It sees present and foreseeable future, as well as the past, as ambivalent. When optimism and nostalgia are set aside, replaced with the virtue of hope, the good and the bad can be thought together. This permits us to remember the past as it actually was, and thus to harness the past as a resource for confronting the challenges which we will encounter in our present world.

Michael Walzer's contrast between messianic politics and exodus politics grippingly, and hyperbolically, captures the distinction which Lasch seems to be making.[16] Messianic politics is concerned with collective action for ultimate purposes. It is ready to "force the End," because this is what God wants. Messianic politics refuses to see itself within history, for its political cause surpasses history. Limits are refused. Consequently, messianic politics refuses to see itself within a world of ups and downs, of ambivalence. Things are about to get better, dramatically better, and any means necessary are justified in accelerating this change. It is not the time for deliberation, for argument, or for compromise. Might we be able to read messianic politics as progress sanctified—or, the politics of progress as always already sanctified?

The Exodus narrative poses an alternative both to messianic politics and to the status quo. It offers a possibility to productively channel transformative energies which does not blind the transformers to the ambivalences of their worlds—and thus avoids harnessing those energies in a way that would be counterproductive. Exodus politics offers hope, as Lasch would describe it. The Israelites are in captivity, and they are animated by the promise of a better life. But this better life is always at a distance, always across an unbridgeable divide. The Israelites, collectively, are committed to this hope. It does not flatten the ambiguity of their world. Their world is still difficult. Sometimes the Israelites resist action called for by God's promise (this obstinacy, Walzer suggests, also prevents the Israelites from forgetting God's promise). As they wander through the wilderness, the Israelites are transformed, but their ultimate hope is not realized. It is not realized because the Israelites always fall short: "Since the laws are never fully observed, the land is never completely possessed. Canaan becomes Israel, and still remains a *promised* land."[17] The promise, the hope, is always across a divide, yet it animates action on this side of the divide. In Lasch's terminology: messianic politics seems hopeful but actually relies on optimism; exodus politics, rather, genuinely relies on hope.

But, again, is this really a distinct virtue of hope, or is it simply the virtue of faith with added oomph—with the rhetoric of hope on top to spice it up? Lasch opposes the distortions created by the optimism-nostalgia pair to the clarity brought about by hope paired with attendant careful memory. Walzer opposes messianic politics, with its refusal of worldly ambivalence in favor of a quickly approaching End, to exodus politics, which is animated by hope but which remains clear-sighted and evenhanded (Walzer also considers a third option: the status quo, which he associates with the ritual requirements administered by priests). These theorists' rhetoric creates a false dilemma, making it seem as if some version of hope is necessary and we just have to choose which we prefer. But can we not agree that messianic politics and the politics of optimism distort without our necessarily being forced into the alternatives that we are presented?

Lasch writes about the role of hope in dealing with misfortune in a way that sounds suspiciously like a discussion of the virtue of faith: "The worst is always what the hopeful are prepared for. Their trust in life would not be worth much if it had not survived disappointments in the past, while the knowledge that the future holds further disappointments demonstrates the continuing need for hope" (81). In other words, if the disappointments of the past are whitewashed, any disappointment of the present seems novel. The optimist's spirits are thus fragile; her optimism is crushed at the first sign of things going wrong. Those with the virtue of hope "trust in life," they remain committed in the face of disappointments. But Lasch's presentation seems to obfuscate the causation here. Why is it hope that leads to an acknowledgment of disappointment which leads to a trust in life? Does it not make more sense for trust in life—the virtue of faith—to lead to acknowledgment of disappointment? If the language of hope is found, could it not be understood as a way of describing this virtue of faith, a rhetoric that persuades others to persevere in the face of disappointments (but does not make sense of disappointments: that would be optimism)?

Faith does explicitly enter into Lasch's discussion when he criticizes liberals for "their faith in administrative expertise [which] offended those who put their faith in common sense" (38). Those commonsense citizens, the petite bourgeois with whom Lasch aligns himself, are distrustful of the bureaucratic machinery that is supposed to make possible the progress so lauded by liberals. The sort of faith in common sense discussed here by Lasch is a commitment, but it is limited to the concrete world, and on his view politics is not part of the realm of the concrete. Lasch does not see commonsense faith as a directly political virtue, but rather as an earthy character trait which inhibits the growth of bad politics. However, perhaps it is possible to read Lasch's remarks on commonsense faith together with his faithlike discussion of hope. The practical, this-worldly orientation—and commitment—of those with commonsense faith, as well as their realistic view of history, is buttressed by their talk of a telos. What does this telos do but offer a rhetorical boost? It is, after all, entirely inaccessible. Lasch is attempting to recover part of the American democratic tradition, complete with its millennial and providential heritage, while jettisoning its commitment to progress. In doing so, what he finds most important is faith, not hope, even though he retains the branding of hope.

Let us turn to one final theorist of hope. Drawing on Lasch's work, Patrick Deneen reformulates questions of faith, hope, and democracy by bringing explicitly religious faith into the conversation. Like Lasch, Deneen endorses democratic hope. But Deneen makes two further claims: he rejects democratic faith and he suggests that religious faith should be viewed as a positive additive to democracy. The central goal of Deneen's effort is to untangle a paradox, to answer the question of "how a political system designed to minimize claims of faith itself rests on faith."[18]

Deneen argues that almost all contemporary political theory rests on an implicit faith in democracy. Reasons always prove insufficient to justify democracy, even when political theorists claim to be relying exclusively on sound reasons. In both liberal theorizing and radical democratic theorizing, there are "ground rules" at the core of the theories that must be accepted but that cannot be justified. Although radical democrats such as Chantal Mouffe, Bonnie Honig, and William Connolly claim to be "antifoundational," in fact their understanding of democratic citizenship requires faith that the citizen's own perspective is limited, that the citizen does not have all the right answers. Radical democrats implicitly argue that citizens must have faith that beliefs about important topics are essentially contestable. In short, for these theorists, before there can be politics, there must be an agreement to disagree. This is a proposition about which—regardless of radical democrats' wishes—there can be reasonable doubt. Viewed in this way, the position of radical democrats comes closer than they would like to that of liberals. For liberals too have faith, but their faith is "in the possibility of near-universal 'reasonableness'" and amelioration through progress (29). Both liberals and radical democrats have a commitment to democracy itself: regardless of conflicts, regardless of the severity and depth of those conflicts, the project of democracy must not be abandoned.

In place of democratic faith, Deneen holds up skepticism. When faith in democracy is allowed free reign, it leads to "unwarranted optimism, utopianism, and fanaticism" (xvii). While a central tenet of democratic faith involves human perfectibility, Deneen suggests that democracy should be premised on the imperfection of human beings. This starting point, he claims, is not a result of faith but of skepticism. Deneen charges that, in the face of human imperfection, democratic faith should be abandoned and democratic hope should be cultivated. Democracy should not try to make humans divine—the desire Deneen associates with democratic faith—but should instead simply try to improve the lot of us sinful creatures. Thus, Deneen, unlike Rorty, sees it as crucial to distinguish faith from hope. Drawing on Aquinas and Augustine, Deneen suggests that hope is rightly held in a communal context, shared with others. Hope strengthens our resolve while reminding us of our personal insufficiency. In short, "humility moderates" but "hope motivates" (244).

Although Deneen is very interested in separating faith from hope, in his account of hope it seems as though the two have become confused once again. Deneen argues that hope is important because it strengthens our commitment to a democratic project (it "motivates," like good rhetoric). But does this not sound more like faith cum oomph? Deneen would demur because his understanding of democratic faith focuses on a "belief in human malleability." But when he writes of this belief, he describes it as a belief, not in malleability in general, but in perfectibility, a belief that human beings can and will improve the human condition through the democratic enterprise. But this sounds like hope, or at least like that variety of hope that Lasch labels optimism. Deneen writes of faith and hope with the concepts reversed. His motivation for this is to recover a place for religious faith in democratic politics. *For DENEEN, RELIGION is THE FIRST LINK*

In opposition to what he takes to be the dominant trend in democratic *or* theory, dismissing or at least distrusting religious beliefs, Deneen suggests that *DEFENSE* religious beliefs are helpful to a democratic culture because they emphasize *AGAINST* "human fallibility, insufficiency, and humility." Religious belief is thus "the *THREAT IS* first line of defense against the threat to democracy that 'democratic faith' *TO* can engender" (11). Faith in God is "more modest" than faith in democ- *DEMOCRACY* racy: while faith in democracy is very specific and concrete, faith in God recognizes the mysterious nature of its object. By recognizing that there is something so great that it is beyond human comprehension, faith in God promotes humility in politics.

This argument does not seem especially plausible. It is easy to think of religious beliefs which are much more specific (e.g., dietary rules, features of the afterlife, etc.) than "democratic" beliefs (e.g., the vague belief that democracy will bring peace to the Middle East). Moreover, if we understand faith as a virtue rather than a specific set of beliefs, the dogmatism that Deneen associates with "democratic faith" vanishes. Faith as a virtue has nothing to do either with human perfectibility or with divinities. It has to do with a commitment to intersubjective reality. This commitment is certainly a virtue in democratic politics. It is a virtue that supports critical interrogation of political institutions and political rhetoric while not holding dogmatically to any precommitments. Indeed, it is the believer in an all-powerful God who is a problematic participant in politics, for the faith of such individuals will preclude them from full participation, from truly risking themselves by exempting no norms from investigation and possible reformulation.

Even once the rhetoric of hope and the virtue of faith have been disambiguated, there remains a common misconception about hope. The rhetoric of hope is a tactic, not a strategy. It is a specific means of achieving a goal that works in some circumstances and not in others. To speak of hope is not necessarily to be persuasive. In some circumstances, where the whole history of American politics is perhaps a striking example, it is extremely

FURTHER, DENEEN HAS A COMMON MISCONCEPTION ABOUT HOPE

persuasive. If tactics and strategy are distinguished in terms of practice—that is, in more than a rhetorical sense—strategies are means of achieving goals that are always effective regardless of the content of specific norms and practices. Strategies are means of leveraging the distinction between norms and practices in order to achieve goals. Strategies are theopolitical. They refuse to be limited by the options on the proverbial table. They bring about new options, unpredictably. By acting, for example, as if there are no norms, or by talking about norms as if practices do not matter, new norms and practices come into being. Politics is no longer limited to judgment between existing options.

The ambivalences of the rhetoric of hope are illustrated by the American jeremiad, "A mode of public exhortation that originated in the European pulpit, was transformed in both form and content by the New England Puritans, persisted through the eighteenth century, and helped sustain a national dream through two hundred years of turbulence and change."[19] Throughout the course of American history, orators have conjured and renewed John Winthrop's imagery of a covenant with God, America as a community favored by God, and a sanctified city upon a hill. This rhetoric of hope, pointing to the positive future in store, certainly could buttress the virtue of faith (sometimes the connection is explicit: Winthrop did not shy away from mentioning the challenges in store, nor did his successors, through Martin Luther King). Yet this does not mean that the rhetoric of hope is *necessary* for democratic faith. As Sacvan Bercovitch convincingly shows, the American jeremiad is a peculiar innovation, and one which carries with it no small number of problems. The tradition of American chosenness fuels a self-confidence in the perceived mission of the chosen, however that mission may be envisioned at a particular moment—whether it be in connection with the civil rights struggle or in connection with the displacement of Native Americans.

The American jeremiad, as a specific rhetoric of hope, illustrates how hope is a tactic, not a strategy, and how it may function at the service of the hegemony of the visible. The American jeremiad forecloses revolutionary possibilities. Any discontent with the status quo becomes a way in which the present falls short of the ideal, a mismatch between the purified object of hope and its present incarnation. There can be no hole so large that the

ship must be abandoned. The rhetoric of hope is constituted by the
closure of the invisible. Yes, new possibilities will arise, which we cannot
predict from our present vantage point, but the path from here to there is
necessarily smooth. At any given point the next point is not surprising.

The American jeremiad pushes the limits of this foreclosure to its extreme. The uniqueness of this case, perhaps, is that the object of hope is hope
itself, pure promise. There are no specificities that connect present and future, no necessary attributes of America, except one: America is the promise
of America. What defines the present object is a commitment to a pure future object and no more (this is in stark contrast to European nations, where
the object of hope has content, it is a people, a land, a history). The American jeremiad offers a simulacrum of the theopolitical. Anything is possible,
every attribute of the present nation may be abandoned in the future. All
that we need to do now is to remain committed, not give up on this project
of pure promise even when faced with difficulties. If hope usually separates
into a rhetoric of hope and the virtue of faith, might the American jeremiad
be an example in which the two collapse, in which the rhetoric of hope
simply is an expression of the virtue of faith? It seems as though, with all
specificities removed from the object of the rhetoric of hope, what remains
is a rhetoric which urges commitment in the face of adversity—not commitment for any particular reason but commitment for its own sake.

In the case of the American jeremiad, the curve of history remains continuous. The particularities of the present are disguised in the supposed
emptiness of the jeremiad's content. The object of hope purifies the status
quo, but in the case of the American jeremiad, that status quo is suppressed.
The nation is everyone and no one, everywhere and nowhere, existing at
all times and never. In fact, it is here, it is now, it is us. It is we who fill in
the content of the object of hope, and it is our false consciousness which
leads us to believe that this object has no content (is this not the quintes-
sence of supersessionism?). But to call this false consciousness is to say too
much; there is no need to be pejorative. The American jeremiad is simply a
souped-up tactic, a more efficacious means of persuasion. It uses the façade
of the theopolitical in order to achieve worldly ends. Yet this makes it all
too easy to dismiss the theopolitical outright, to allow the difference between simulacrum and original to slip away.

American
Jeremiad isn't
False consciousness,
but a super-tactic

Might there be rhetorical power in hopelessness as well? Without an object onto which an audience's desires can be projected, how would such a rhetoric persuade? Perhaps by mobilizing affect. Joy is an affect particularly susceptible to mobilization by hopelessness. The image of melancholia suggests an abyss, a falling without end, even if that falling is into oneself. It suggests retreat prompted by unwanted exposure, a feeling of vulnerability. But in an autobiographical fragment Gillian Rose suggests that it is in joy, not in sorrow, that vulnerability is most acute. In sorrow, there is an object to grab hold of, conscious or unconscious. Melancholia involves a "busy tumult," activity, or busy inactivity, compensating for the lost object. Only in joy, "my soul is naked: it has lost its scaffolding of regret and remorse or even repentance. . . . This does not make me ecstatic, unreal, unworldly: it returns me to the vocation of the everyday."[20] In other words, joy does not elide difficulty, it is exposure to difficulty. In its effervescence, it is unpredictable. It puts the self at stake. Yet this exposure is not frightening. Appeal to joy does not scare the rhetorician's audience away. Nor does joy purify the world. It begins in the ordinary and stays in the ordinary; it does not have pretensions to enchant the ordinary. Such enchantment would be impossible because of the effervescence of joy, its unpredictability.

But is this rhetoric of hopelessness, this language of joy, a tactic? Does its affinity with the virtues of faith and love not accord it some privileged status? Its privilege comes not in the rhetorical register but in the philosophical. Joy is a philosophical rhetoric, appropriate in a place where other rhetorics must be set aside. It is a rhetoric which self-destructs, for its function is, in fact, to persuade that rhetoric should be set aside. What is left when rhetoric is set aside, when the armor of enchantment is removed, is vulnerability. This is the "vocation of the everyday." It is not how the everyday is represented but how it is presented, how it is lived. Faith and love are prerequisites for this vocation. The exercise of these virtues is hard work. But it is a joyful labor: that is how it is sustained.

PART II

THEOPOLITICAL STRATEGIES

CHAPTER 4

TRADITION

[handwritten: TRADITION AS CONDITION OR POSSIBILITY]

THE TRADITIONAL IS TO THE MODERN as the conservative is to the liberal, as preservation is to creation. Tradition is an anchor, a base, a home. It is where we left and where we must return to. We desire to escape it, but it is ever present. It is a burden, a necessary burden, for it is a burden that makes possible—it is the condition of possibility. Noble, elegant, staid, tradition is comfortingly aristocratic; it is also a populist adhesive and a bourgeois aspiration. Tradition binds its adherents and tradition binds its opponents; tradition binds and tradition severs; tradition encompasses and tradition disintegrates. *[handwritten: "ELOQUENCE TRADITION"]*

This is the eloquence tradition, an eloquent hodgepodge. Its power to persuade is perhaps unmatched. It grasps and it holds. The mechanism by which it operates is not complex: it associates us with a mighty past and, perhaps, a mightier future. An invisible shuttle is guided by the speaker, a shuttle of the old fashioned variety. Lifting the warp and interlacing the weft, familiar threads are combined in unfamiliar patterns. As I listen it is woven, in my presence, from my own threads. The cloth is cherished, its aesthetic inevitably delightful—the artisan triumphant. As with any craft, to distinguish affective and rational components is to introduce confusion; persuasive force comes from refusing the distinction. The skilled artisan can

[handwritten: "WEAVING SHUTTLE"]

[handwritten: THIS RHETORIC IS "EXPANSIVE" = ?]

weave the right cloth for the right occasion, the right pattern for the right customer. It is not only the cloth that is sold, but the image of its maker, the quaint artisan laboring at her loom.

That is one rhetoric of tradition; the other rhetoric of tradition is a rhetoric of contrast. Dynamism is opposed to stasis, and the choice to be made is obvious. This is not a rhetoric that crafts but a rhetoric that structures. It uses language with precision to mark, delineate, specify, and otherwise characterize the traditional. That site of bondage repels, and this repulsion is manipulated by the second rhetoric of tradition. What remains unspecified is what is free, and this includes where we stand. The menacing other that is tradition ironically specifies the very means by which it is specified: that which narrows and picks out, confusing the particular and the universal. The danger of tradition is in one place and in every place, a danger that does not respect the line between affect and reason—and so a danger that can be used to persuade.

The two rhetorics of tradition are not symmetrical. The first is expansive, the second is directed. The first motivates through comfort, the second motivates through discomfort. Each rhetoric consumes the other. Artisans innovate and manufacturers replicate. The expansive rhetoric is comforting because it encompasses discomfort; the directed rhetoric evokes the threat of discomfort in order to assure comfort. In both, persuasion is achieved through the knot of affect and reason, achieved through recognition of the familiar (including the familiarly unfamiliar). We have returned to love, to the faux virtue of love. Transcendent love and immanent love are one and the same, and the rhetoric of tradition is nothing but the manipulation of these loves.

There are those new partisans of tradition who attempt to cut through the rhetoric of tradition by refusing to see both of its faces.[1] For them, tradition is not confined to insular communities whose lives are exotically different than ours (the Amish, Native Americans, medieval Europeans). Nor is tradition a story which embraces us and all of our worlds, a story in which we are actors and in which we desire to offer superb performances. For the sacred text to consume the world, and so to thrust us into the tradition where we always already reside, is to weave an elegantly patterned cloth and then to pretend that the pattern was there all along, even when the threads were sitting, virginal, on spools. The new partisans of tradition dismiss these uses of tradition polemically as polemic, as contrary to the values professed by those who wield them. Those who dismiss tradition as insular hold firm to the values that set themselves apart; those who see themselves already embracing tradition ignore the care implicit in that embrace, a care that extends to those who see differently.

With the rhetoric of tradition dismissed, these new partisans of tradition return to tradition purified of polemic. Tradition now refers to the values that are held dear in a community, through its history. These values may be—indeed, always are—opaque and contested. But they are always there, implicit in the practices of any community. The supreme tradition, for these new partisans of tradition, is the tradition in which the central value is the contest of value: the American democratic tradition. This is the only tradition in which the rhetoric of tradition transcends itself, losing its identity as rhetoric because it serves a higher purpose—indeed, the highest purpose, the highest value. Of course, there are other values of the American democratic tradition, and other traditions have other values and other orderings of values, all of which are discerned by community members, sometimes misrecognized, always subject to contest. Community leaders articulate those values. Politicians, novelists, orators, even social critics make explicit those values—and enable their contest. The greatness of Melville, Thoreau, Lincoln, Emerson, and King, in the American democratic tradition, is their ability to discern and articulate such values. They congeal tradition not with the rhetoric of tradition but with the practice that makes tradition, that makes tradition recognizable. If comfort or discomfort for their listeners or readers is a result, it is a result of recognizing the way the audience's own actions conflict with the values to which they are committed, and of which they are reminded. In other words, community leaders do not move the community away from where the community is; leaders remind the community of where they already are. Also, the work of the leader is part of the work of the tradition, not above or outside it.

From the perspective of the new partisans of tradition, the rhetorician of tradition makes tradition too easy. While the rhetorician of tradition also purports to remind the community where it is, and utilizes as raw material what is already accepted by a community, she fails to acknowledge that values may be implicit in the practice of a community. The rhetorician fails to recognize the *difficulty* of her work: values are obscure. Clarifying them is not a task that involves harmonizing differences in practice, or condensing those differences to a point. It involves judgment: locating affinities and contradictions in richly textured community practice and deciding which practices are at the heart of the tradition and which are anomalous. For the new partisans of tradition, it is the *phronimos,* the wise man—perhaps the wise Latina woman—to whom one must turn to find tradition. The *phronimos* sees rightly, and judges rightly, within his community. He may or may not speak loudly; he need not be a rhetorician.

The risk that such a view may slip into its other, into the rhetoric of tradition, is great. Are not the words of a celebrity the articulation of the values of a community? Does not the television presenter articulate the values of a community? But they aren't "deep," which is to say that their practice of judgment, and likely their ability to judge, is limited. More often than the community leader, but less often than the crude rhetorician (the demagogue), these public figures settle for harmony or easy difference rather than working through the contradictions of the textured social world, contradictions that force revision of popular conceptions of value. Is this, which the "soft" public figure avoids, not how a good judge is distinguished from a bad judge? The bad judge relies on the most obvious and most proximate precedent, or on an easy anchor from the past. The good judge works through contradictory precedent, adding nuance to her understanding of law before applying it to the present case.

The new partisan of tradition purports to dismiss rhetoric but actually is committed to it. The language she speaks is more compelling, it persuades more effectively, but it is still subject to the hegemony of the visible. A judge relies on precedent recorded in volumes of case law. The discerning community leader applies her capacity of judgment to seemingly contradictory practices in order to articulate the values implicit in them. But what alternative is there to this exulted *phronimos?* What is tradition if it is separated from a community and its history? Unhitched, tradition requires faith. Judgment does not take faith; it takes skill, a skill not unlike that of the rhetorician (perhaps it also takes desire). For tradition understood as a strategy, judgment is necessary, and rhetoric is necessary, and faith is also necessary. Faith becomes necessary when the difference between practices and norms is acknowledged. The new partisan of tradition fails to acknowledge

[handwritten margin note: For practising norms are implicit in practice]

this difference. For her, norms are implicit in practice. The task of the community leader is to make norms explicit through judgment. Community practices, contemporary and historical, are evaluated in order to find the normative commitments which they indicate. Norms supervene on practice: if it can be shown that the practice is or was different than it seems, the accepted characterization of the norm must be revised. A norm has no hold on a community if a leader cannot convince the community that its members are committed to it, and the community can be convinced by pointing to their own practices.

For the rhetorician of tradition, practices and norms are absolutely identical: each practice exemplifies the norm advocated. The skill of the rhetorician is to present practices in such a way as to make this a plausible claim. For the new partisan of tradition, norms supervene on practices. But for one who employs tradition as a strategy, there is an irreducible, ever-present mismatch between norms and practices. It is this mismatch that requires faith, and it is this mismatch which makes the strategic use of tradition possible. Tradition used strategically exploits the plane of norms, hovering above the plane of practices, by giving free rein to its internal development. Consequently, practices are pulled beyond themselves, in a direction inexplicable by analysis of practices alone. *[handwritten: For partisans, community leaders words express]*

Let us approach this through a contrast. The new partisan of tradition argues that the words of community leaders express norms implicit in the practices of a community, but does this not ignore the rhetorical dimension of the speech of such leaders? Surely their words are doing more than echoing norms that any philosophically oriented historian or sociologist could deduce from empirical study. The community leader is not simply using fancy words in stylized constructions to express the same norms that are stated in dry prose by the historian or sociologist. What the community leader is doing, whether she is a novelist or a politician or a social critic, is exploring the configuration and logic of norms. She is doing more than exploring; she is toying with them, reconfiguring them, altering their logic. As she does this, she brackets practices: it is the norms themselves with which she is concerned, not what lies on the other side of the gap between norms and practices. It would be a mistake to view the speech or writing that constitutes her fiddling as referential; it has set aside the attempt to align the planes of norms

[handwritten margin note at bottom: Yet for Lloyd, this is also a rhetorical aspect]

[handwritten margin notes: "TRADITION AS POLITICAL STRATEGY" at top; "GIVES AUTONOMY TO 'PLANE OF NORMS'" on left]

and practices. This is something the sociologist or historian, always accountable to the empirical data, can never do. It is only the novelist, politician, or
social critic who has the liberty to provide an imaginative account of norms.
In a sense, this is all too obvious: sociologists and historians reflect a community and its history while politicians and poets change it. Politicians and poets
change history when they allow social norms to sprout wings and fly.

This is tradition understood as a political strategy rather than a tactic.
The strategy grants temporary autonomy to the plane of norms. Rhetoric
and judgment are both elements of this strategy. It takes judgment to discern norms, a task which involves looking closely and carefully at richly
textured social practice. It takes rhetoric to set them free, to weave them
together, to set some apart, all without concern for whether the patterns
produced match practice. When tradition is employed as a strategy, the tools
of rhetoric are used without an audience to persuade. Their raw material is
not commonly accepted beliefs but social norms. The goal of the strategist
employing tradition is not to persuade listeners to change their beliefs; the
goal is to tell a story about norms as if it were the true story. It will not be
clear *ex ante* whether or not it will become true.

Tradition thus requires faith. To set aside the security that practice (to
which norms are accountable) provides is not easy to stomach. It is a risk.
Sometimes it works, often it fails. The visionary politician persuades, the
visionary writer changes her audience; other aspiring visionaries are laughed
off the platform, other writers remain unpublished or ignored. Excellence
(at judgment, at rhetoric) is no guarantee of success. This is what always happens when the hegemony of the visible is refused: there are no guarantees.

Tradition is not something to be named; it is something to be used. This
goes unrecognized by the new partisans of tradition, who themselves propose an alternative account of tradition. In doing so, and in their polemics
against the rhetoric of tradition, they are themselves engaged in rhetoric. It
remains mysterious as to why this is not entirely obvious, especially when
the conclusion some of these partisans reach is a triumphalism about American democracy, understood as a tradition. Such conclusions simply attest
to a lack of faith, a risk aversion in the guise of risk taking. It seems risky to
understand the values of a community as contestable, but the terms of this
contest are fixed ahead of time. Arguments must be rooted in the practices

of a community and its history, even if it acknowledged that the community and history remain opaque. A much greater sort of risk taking occurs when tradition is taken to be ungrounded, to float free of the plane of practices. To subject oneself to this sort of tradition is to cede control, for it is to acknowledge the normative force of tradition, the force to reprimand and to praise, while setting aside the aspiration to understand, and so control, this force. Law is not opposed to Grace; there is only Law hollowed of its implicit pretensions to Grace, hollowed instead of hallowed.

Is there any depiction of tradition's opposite more vivid and troubling than what is found in the prose of Franz Kafka? The Kafkaesque is nothing but this, the raw absurdity of the modern world, of system, bureaucracy, depersonalized authority. Tradition has been crushed, the warmth of community, security of history, transmission of values through family have been replaced by icy rules empty of actual people. But if Kafka is read as part of the antisupersessionist canon, if the caricature suggested by the Kafkaesque is abandoned, perhaps it is precisely that opposition between what is most modern and most traditional which suggests a thicker depiction of tradition, and offers resources for the strategic use of tradition.

Indeed, Walter Benjamin presents such a view. Benjamin writes, "Kafka's work is an ellipse with foci that are far apart and are determined, on the one hand, by mystical experience (in particular, the experience of tradition) and, on the other, by the experience of the modern big-city dweller."[2] Benjamin's words leave underdetermined the relationship between the mystical and the modern. Are they each a focus, codetermining Kafka's narrative, or is it after their intermingling that they become two? It would be easy, too easy, to read the force of Kafka's narratives as the result of his bilingual acculturation, the modern European and the Jew, the tension between cultures producing a hybrid irreducible to either.

But this is neither Benjamin's meaning nor an apt characterization of Kafka's work. Kafka's worlds are "prehistoric," as Benjamin puts it. They exist before the Law. Normativity covers the earth, as it always does: there are things that one ought to do and things that one ought not to do. But these are inaccessible. Law makes them accessible, contestable. Law is absent in both its modern and its premodern forms: "Even the world of myth . . . is incomparably younger than Kafka's world."[3] This is also how Marcel Gauchet

Traditional
↓
mystical ≠ mythical

characterizes the world before the Axial Age: all that is possible is repetition, for the source of normativity is located spatially and temporally within the world.[4] It was gods or ancestors who were *here*, long, long ago, who determined what is to be done. It is only when gods are located outside the world that the norms they impose must be interpreted; only then can myth expand unbounded, and only then will the possibilities of human action seem limitless. Mystical experience is not mythic experience. The experience of tradition is mystical, not mythic: the sheer force of norms is exposed but not salved, exposed by its ubiquity which remains unexplained. Norms have nothing to do with practice. The pretense that they do, the pretense of rational or mythical justification, is absent. If Kafka's characters found this disturbing, the significance would be spoiled, for that would make them time travelers. It is we who are disturbed, and this discomfort exposes the dramatic difference between the rhetoric of tradition and the strategy of tradition. To see a world of free-floating norms without flinching seems superhuman. To refuse the superhuman label, to recognize the humanity of K., takes faith.

Tradition
mystical
≠
reason

Kafka's worlds exist before the Law; they also exist after it. The second focus of the ellipse, "the experience of the modern big-city dweller," does not pull in an opposite direction to the prehistorical but doubles it and, in so doing, adds depth. Just as Kafka exposes the prehistory of the mythical, hollowed, in the mystical, so too does he expose the posthistory of reason, hollowed, in another face of the mystical. The familiarly modern rule of law in *The Castle* and *The Trial* uses the expected language of normativity, but in excess—or what seems like excess because the language of normativity has been detached from practice. The invisible force that maintains the proper relation between the plane of practices and the plane of norms has malfunctioned: norms no longer seem to bare any relation to practice, and the visible effects of norms—the practices of reprimand and praise— are spoken of but never seen. This hollowness is not the banality which goes by the name of the Kafkaesque.

Situations are called Kafkaesque not just when they are absurd but also when they are unavoidable. A diversion is not Kafkaesque, nor is a game, nor a work of art. The Kafkaesque is a rhetoric of the modern that parallels the rhetoric of tradition. In both, the difference between practices and

[handwritten margin notes: IN BOTH "PLATONIC" or TRADITION & "THE KAFKASQUERY", THE DIFF. BTN PRACTICES & NORMS IS COLLAPSED = ? AESTHETIC]

norms is collapsed; what remains is an aesthetic. In one case, this aesthetic is smooth, difference kneaded into continuous substance. In the other case, this aesthetic is sleek, lines and edges cutting this way and that, sharp and pointed. In the former case, what is to be done is so evident from what is done and what has been done that to speak of norms is superfluous. Norms are coterminous with practice, and they only reward. In the latter case, the sleekness is a sharpness; the world is such that violence saturates practice. Norms are coterminous with practice, and they only punish.

The significance of Kafka's works is not that they expose the essence of the Kafkaesque, nor is it that they synthesize the Kafkaesque and the traditional. Rather, Kafka refuses to aestheticize without refusing narrative. His prose is straightforward, clear, quite ordinary. Realism is just as much an aesthetic as the smooth or the sleek, and Kafka is most certainly not a realist. Kafka avoids aestheticizing through sharp breaks that are often shoved in your face—often in the first sentence. Gregor Samsa wakes up as an insect, Joseph K. is arrested, Karl Rossmann arrives in New York. These radical breaks reduplicate the break between the ordinary and the realm of literature, the break that necessitates the aesthetic. In Kafka's works, that break happens again, explicitly, allowing a return from the aesthetic to the ordinary, a special sort of ordinary. His first lines evacuate the worlds he narrates of their histories, disclaiming the project of representation or world creation. The world starts anew: mysteriously, but not mythically. No authority exists from before the time of the narrative. Yet the prose is still ordinary. It is not ordinary prose representing the ordinary world; it is the ordinary cut off from the ordinary, a world with the contours of ours but which has marked its point of departure. It has the contours of an absent terrain: still contours, following an internal logic, doing what is supposed to be done on the level of prose and on the level of the motivation of characters, norms freed from practice—the literary counterpart to the political strategy of tradition. But it is more than a literary counterpart, for it is precisely the relationship between the foci of the traditional and that of the modern that makes this literary practice possible.

Benjamin describes Kafka's worlds as depicting reality's "complement." The enchanted remainder left by the modern swaps its inferior position for the superior. No longer is enchantment the last wrinkle to be ironed, a wrinkle that never comes out, appearing always again in a new location. Enchantment is at the heart of things, at the center of the state, of the family, of the self. This inversion is effected by the breaks of Kafka's first sentences. It produces not a mythical enchanting aesthetic that would fold natural and supernatural, hallowing, an aesthetic that would remind the modern reader of modernity's violence and offer a glimpse of an alternative. Rather, Kafka's doubling breaks produce a mystical enchantment that is perfectly ordinary—ordinary but invisible and so mystical. The modern and the premodern are refused along with the aesthetic; the modern and the premodern attempt to understand normativity, while the ordinary makes no such pretense, accepting rather than contesting the status of Law. Benjamin's image of the ellipse can now be clarified. The foci are not the modern world and the premodern world; they are mystical experience and the contemporary ordinary—"the experience of the modern big-city dweller." Kafka's work is animated by ordinary modern experience and mystical experience—Law hollowed, not hallowed.

Kafka tells an American tale. How provocative this is has often been overlooked. The structure of *Amerika* is the same as *The Castle* and *The Trial*, the same as the structure of some of Kafka's most memorable stories. The first sentence of *Amerika* initiates a new world in the redoubled sense that Kafka has mastered not a literary world but an ordinary world without history or community, an ordinary untethered from the ordinary: "As Karl Rossmann, a poor boy of sixteen who had been packed off to America by his parents because a servant girl had seduced him and got herself a child by him, stood on the liner slowly entering the harbour of New York, a sudden burst of sunshine seemed to illumine the Statue of Liberty, so that he saw it in a new light, although he had sighted it long before."[5] In Kafka's more familiar writings, what orders the reduplicated world is an enchantment at its heart: the castle, the law, the frightening insect. The enchantment at the heart of *Amerika* is America (materialized in the Statue of Liberty), an idea as mysterious and splendid and frightening and inaccessible as the castle, the law, or the insect. If Kafka's other works are ellipses, *Amerika* is a circle, for in this work the experience of tradition and that of modern life converge. The ordinary that is depicted in many of Kafka's other works is a generic ordinary of modern life, bureaucracy, regulation, order, administration, individualization. The ordinary depicted in *Amerika* is at once modern and traditional, for this is the character of its animating enchantment. Karl arrives on a giant ship, he works in oversized hotels with elevators and restaurants and modern conveniences. But this is not all: the underside is also visible, the servants and miscreants and laborers. Moreover, his story is thoroughly American. The European immigrant escapes old-world worries and begins anew, adventuring, finding fortune, losing it, heading West. Because the foci of the ellipse coincide, Kafka permits period detail, which is, in his other works, stripped away. The result is a facade of realism easily mistaken for more than a facade.

To read *Amerika* together with Kafka's other works is to see an alternative to those triumphalist accounts of a reconstructed American democratic tradition, and, more broadly, an approach to the strategic use of tradition. The new partisans of tradition turn to a community's exemplary writers and orators to find the values which a tradition holds dear, and which are constitutive of that tradition. In *Moby-Dick* the values of perseverance, curiosity, naturalism, ambition, and courage, which are implicit in American democratic practice, are made explicit.[6] The practice of politics, for such partisans of tradition, is the practice of articulating, and contesting the articulation of, such values as they affect the practices and institutions of social life. In other words, politics is always the politics of tradition, not of the rhetoric of tradition but of the explication of tradition. *Amerika* poses multiple challenges for such critics. Written by a European who never visited the United States, it seems a strain to characterize it as an intervention in American politics. More significantly, when *Amerika* is read together with *The Trial*, *The Castle*, and Kafka's shorter prose, it brings into question whether it is accurate to characterize exemplary literature (and oration and critique) as explicating community norms. The sources of normativity in Kafka's work are phantasmal. There is no reason to treat America differently than the castle or the law in this regard. It is as if these sources of normativity provide reasons for action—but they do not.

That *Amerika* appears in many ways to be a typical work of American literature, explicating American practices, should be troubling for the triumphalist partisan of tradition. The novel floats free: it is built not from American experience but from the literary representation of American experience. Rather than being ashamed of this, the novel flaunts it, dallying in the realm of representation and refusing the aspiration to represent rightly, to secure the represented to the presented. Kafka's humor, more evident in this work more than almost anywhere else, marks this joyous refusal, as do the occasional moments of excess (the dozens of elevators in Karl's hotel, the senator's wealth, the array of foods). The fantastical ending, where Karl joins the Nature Theater of Oklahoma, confirms this reading. There is no shift in Kafka's matter-of-fact style as Karl embarks for the West, as the ordinary, untethered from itself, has drifted nearly beyond recognition.

Desire does not fuel Kafka's prose. The objects at the center of his texts do not have libidinal force, they simply structure. If this were not the case, his writing would show exasperation—in its characters and in its prose. This is how a novel about America can escape triumphalism: when it is a novel not animated but structured by America. Melville, Thoreau, Emerson, and Ellison are read by the new partisans of tradition as animated by America, their desirous words revealing the nation's truths. American letters ascend from the mundane to the noble, spiraling upward toward that which is most dear. But this love is childish; tradition, as its object, is an object of fantasy. Kafka's work helps us to traverse the fantasy, to release its hold on us without abandoning its critical potential. For *Amerika* does have critical potential; indeed, it has all the more critical potential because it is not viewed with smitten eyes. Its critical force is not exercised by depicting the many facets of its beloved, urging the reader to share in its passion, but by coolly loosening representation and showing where it quickly becomes comic, and where it equally quickly turns tragic. This is the critical power of the ordinary, not represented but doubly represented so as to return to itself in a critique neither immanent nor transcendent.

Amerika is written in such a way so as to disabuse the reader of her aspirations for erotic reading without abandoning narrative. The reader's desire is not displaced, it is attenuated. Perhaps this refusal of the erotic helps make sense of Kafka's understanding of hope. When asked if, beyond the world he inhabited, there might be hope, he responded that there is "plenty of hope, an infinite amount of hope—but not for us."[7] Here, Kafka's world and the worlds of his novels seem to converge, for the refusal of hope accompanies the refusal of libidinous fantasy. In a sense, Kafka's three uncompleted novels would seem to be entirely about hope: the quest to find the castle, to win the trial, to live the American dream is at their core. But, again, it is at their core in a structural sense, it does not motivate their protagonists, at least not in the sense that one would expect. It motivates their actions simply in the sense that it determines what the thing to do is. Joseph K. must stand trial, K.'s job is to work for the castle, Karl Rossmann must begin a new life. The protagonists have no extraordinary motive; they are just doing what is to be done. When they meet setbacks, as they inevitably do, they may be frustrated but they are not exasperated. They continue. It is not a quest that they continue; they continue their jobs, their lives. They have faith. They do not have hope. As Kafka indicates, this does not mean that the world is devoid of hope; it just means that hope is "not for us." Who "we" are is expansive. None of Kafka's characters hope. Some, such as the aspiring businessmen in *Amerika*, say hopeful things, but those are the things they are supposed to say. Where is the "infinite amount of hope," then? Perhaps that is it, in what one is supposed to say, and what many do say—the pervasive but ephemeral language which, when our focus turns away from the ordinary, quickly disappears. KAFKAESQUE = BEING TRAPPED IN A

Understanding Kafka's worlds as worlds without hope is not altogether surprising. Is this not precisely what makes the Kafkaesque: the condition of being trapped in a never-ending maze? There is no hope in the Kafkaesque, there is alienation. The individual human being finds herself trapped in an MAZE impersonal, lifeless world. Worse, this world was constructed by humans and for humans—it is manmade, not natural—but its creators are absent. Inhabitants are stripped of their humanity. Fellow inhabitants offer no comfort; their dehumanized bodies are frightening indicators that the only humanity left in the Kafkaesque world is my own. The experience of the modern city—and, just as much, the experience of the mystical—treat the individual as alien to herself, and make her aware of this alienation. This is the Kafkaesque world; it is not Kafka's world.[8]

Kafka's protagonists live on the plane of norms untethered from the plane of practice. What it means to live in such a world is unfamiliar, for life consists in navigating norms and practices, in judging norms, acting according to that judgment, revising one's judgment of norms according to experience. When the plane of norms has been untethered, this process is static, there is no feedback. Norms are fixed; no amount of practice will change them. There is no reason to carefully judge them if they will always be the same,

KAFKA'S PROTAGONISTS LIVE ON THE PLANE OF NORMS UNTETHERED FROM PRACTICE

and if they will never affect practice. The current is too strong to permit individual navigation of norms and practices. But the current is mysterious; it
appears that norms are less fixed than absent, the castle and the law providing no guidance at all. That is precisely correct: for norms to be absent and
for them to be static is the same thing. Recall Gauchet's image of the pre-
Axial world, a world where norms were set by ancestors supposed to have
lived *here*, fixing normativity and closing off contest. If the absent nexus of
the normative was outside the spatial and temporal bounds of the world, it
would be contestable, it would need interpretation, it would be the object of
fantasy. Because it is *here*, at the center of things, in the castle, in the courts, in
the nation, not a fantastic remainder, it can only be repeated.

What Kafka's protagonists experience is not alienation because alienation
requires fantasy, an absent object animating one's actions. The objects in
Kafka's novels are not absent but present, they structure rather than animate.
Undeniably, there is something unique about the protagonists of Kafka's
novels. As they are thrown into the world, they are perplexed by the absent source of normativity. The other inhabitants of the worlds are not perplexed; they continue doing what they have done from time immemorial.
The perplexity of the protagonists is not the perplexity that results from
being treated as someone other than what one is. K. is a surveyor, and he
is treated as a surveyor; Karl is a European immigrant, and he is treated as a
European immigrant. The perplexity comes about because the protagonists
see the ordinary, not recognizing that it is the simulacrum of the ordinary.
They do not recognize that, in this simulacrum, normativity is structured
differently, it is mystical and present instead of being marked by fantasy and
lived through navigating practices and norms. The protagonists still have
the skills of living, the virtues of faith and of love, but these virtues are unnecessary and so misapplied in the worlds in which they find themselves.
The agents of the castle or of the law do not have faith, for it is unnecessary. Faith is unnecessary when there is not even an aspiration that norms
and practices would match and so no need to worry when they mismatch.
They lack the virtue of love because there is no occasion when their own
norms and practices would be put in question by those of another. When
Kafka's sincere protagonists try to be faithful and loving, their efforts are
frustrated. The women they love do not respond appropriately. K.'s assis-

tants, in *The Castle*, are faithful and loving in the sense a dog might be so described. The protagonists' faithful commitments to their jobs appear, ultimately, uncomfortably similar to the faithless commitments of the world's other inhabitants.

Let us turn to Kafka's renowned and much discussed parable "Before the Law." This parable was meant to be part of *The Trial*—indeed, the centerpiece of *The Trial*—but was also published separately within Kafka's lifetime (Kafka's novels only saw posthumous publication).[9] "Before the law stands a doorkeeper," the parable begins. A man from the country approaches. He asks to enter, but he is told by the gatekeeper that he cannot. The man from the country asks if he will be able to enter later; the gatekeeper says, "It is possible." Oddly, the door to the law is open, and the man from the country looks inside. The gatekeeper tells the man that he can try to enter if he likes—"But note that I am powerful. And I am only the lowest doorkeeper. From hall to hall, keepers stand at every door, one more powerful than the other." The man from the country had not been expecting this, thinking that the law "should be accessible to every man and at all times." The man waits for years, giving all he has brought with him to the doorkeeper thinking that it might secure entry to the law. He has become focused on this doorkeeper and no longer thinks of the others. His condition degenerates: he grows childish, loses his vision, his hearing, approaches death. He asks the doorkeeper a final question: why hasn't he seen others approach the doorkeeper, seeking the law? The doorkeeper responds, "No one but you could gain admittance through this door, since this door was intended for you. I am now going to shut it."

Some have read this as a story about the way that law is constituted through fantasy. The man from the country initially desires Law, and the strength of his desire grows in proportion to Law's inaccessibility. Necessity and prohibition grow together. They can grow together because neither is decisive: the doorkeeper does not say "no" but "not yet," the man from the country's need is blended with desire. It is this indeterminacy, perpetuated through fantasy, that gives Law its force. As Judith Butler writes, "The anticipation of an authoritative disclosure of meaning is the means by which the authority is attributed and installed: the anticipation conjures its object."[10] It is our search for a deep, true meaning, and the materials and practices that we use in that search, which produce the semblance of depth, of truth. The Law is not an object, it is not a list of dos and don'ts. It is the force that animates a practice. On this reading, norms are not imposed, practice does not follow norms. Rather, a nexus of normativity solicits practice, a practice of anticipation, which in turn gives force to the supposed (anticipated) nexus of normativity. Life is about navigating norms and practices, fueled by desire.

This reading of the parable ignores its conclusion. What is to be made of the doorkeeper's final words, his disclosure that this door to the law was made only for one person, only for the man from the country? Other readers of the parable, such as Giorgio Agamben, have focused entirely on this conclusion, suggesting that the specificity of the man from the country, rather than the perpetual delays and anticipation, is what reveals the animating logic of Law. The Law is strongest when it is pure, without content, when it does not offer specific prohibitions. The parable offers a glimpse of Law in this pure form because this pure form, this core logic of Law, has this structure: "The open door destined only for him includes him in excluding him and excludes him in including him."[11] The Law includes the man from the country because it has a doorway only for him; it excludes him in banning him from entering that doorway. When the only content of law is this exclusion-inclusion, we have Law in its purest form. All other content that law has is subsidiary to this logic. This fundamental logic is also exposed in the legal exception: when the sovereign suspends the law and decides directly on a specific case. According to this reading, Kafka's works explore a perpetual state of exception where a mysterious sovereign force can reach out and act on anyone, at any time. *The Trial* begins with a knock on a door for no reason, a suspension of the law that incorporates into the law.

Both readings take Kafka's parable to be exposing the animating logic of Law. The first reading takes this logic to involve repeated practice animated by desire for an object of fantasy, constituted by and constituting that repeated practice. The second reading takes this logic to involve the simultaneous exclusion and inclusion that animates law. What if we set aside the notion that Kafka is presenting a parable that, once deciphered, would expose what Law is really like? After all, is this not precisely the sort of deep meaning that is supposed to be constituted by its anticipation? Advocates of the first reading would perhaps counter that there is no escape from

In the world of untethered norms, virtues that allow one to navigate ordinary

the labyrinth of desires and their constituted objects, in life or in literature. But might it be the case that the man from the country, in his naïveté, poses a challenge to this position? Might he be the ordinary man, faced with Kafka's reduplicated ordinary in which the fantastical has been displaced from the edges to the center? Faced with a world where the plane of norms is untethered from the plane of practice, he is faithful and loving but to no avail. Rather than conjuring the Law through his desire, perhaps he has found himself in a land of Law where his country virtues—virtues that allow him to navigate ordinary life—lead to self-destruction. Love and faith degenerate into libidinal attachment. Perhaps that also is what happens when the ordinary man from the country, and the ordinary more generally, is "theorized."

The man from the country is virtuous but naïve. He is trying to navigate the world of practices and norms, as he is used to doing, but he is not in a world of practices and norms. He is on the plane of norms detached from practices. To look at the words and actions of the doorkeeper, a representative of the Law, an explicator of the Law, and to see some practice in which it is rooted is naïve—as naïve as readers of the parable who take the parable to explicate some fundamental truth about the workings of the law. The man from the country does not realize—as his interpreters have not realized—that the world he exists in is not ours, it is simulacral. It is a manufactured copy, produced strategically. It is not a world where Law is superseded by the Grace that aspires to demystify the fundamental logic of Law. Here is the strategy of tradition: the ordinary reduplicated not to expose its own fundamental truth but to advance quite ordinary interests.

CHAPTER 5

LITURGY

ON THE LAST FRIDAY OF EVERY MONTH, IN MORE THAN THREE HUNDRED cities on six continents, a swarm of bicyclists moves through the streets. They ride without leaders or organization. The flavor of the rides varies from city to city. They ride according to their own rhythm, without respect for traffic laws or the honking horns of motorists. It is "a revelatory, celebratory ride." Through the movements of the bicyclists, a foretaste of a car-free world is performed. From the cyclists' perspective, cars not only harm the environment, they atomize social space, abetting a culture focused on the individual, the consumer, the bourgeoisie. The monthly reminders that another sort of world is possible provided by Critical Mass have not been met kindly by local governments. Between 2004 and 2006, more than six hundred Critical Mass participants were arrested in New York City. Dozens of cyclists and police around the world have been injured in attempts to enforce the rule of law on the bodies of cyclists whose gatherings perform an alternative to that law.[1]

In front of courthouses, government buildings, and media offices during the Pinochet regime, scores of Chileans would emerge from anonymous crowds. For five or ten minutes, they would block traffic, holding banners, singing songs, chanting. To each of a series of statements, the group would respond, "and the justice system is silent":

They arrest Juan Antonio Aguirre	—and the justice system is silent.
They lock him up in Precinct 26	—and the justice system is silent.
They torture him	—and the justice system is silent.
They make him disappear	—and the justice system is silent.
His mother requests habeas corpus	—and the justice system is silent.
The *Carabineros* say "we don't have him"	—and the justice system is silent.
The Minister denies his arrest	—and the justice system is silent.
All Chile is a land of torture	—and the justice system is silent.

Then, the Sebastian Acevedo Movement against Torture would return into the anonymous crowds—unless, as was often the case, the police arrived before they finished. At the time, Chileans lived in fear of being disappeared, of being tortured. This fear poisoned social space; it atomized society as individuals retreated into themselves. Only in events such as the Sebastian Acevedo protests was an alternative made visible. As one participant noted, "They can beat us or attack with water and gases, but there we are to anticipate this new society."[2]

William Cavanaugh interprets the Sebastian Acevedo Movement as a "critical mass"—literally: "The members of Sebastian Acevedo become Eucharist by uniting their bodies in sacrifice with the body of Christ."[3] The body of Christ was tortured by the authorities, and its consumption in the Eucharist anticipates a totally different world from the one in which we find ourselves. Christ's body is "re-membered" in the Sebastian Acevedo protests, a harmonious unity temporarily existing in a fragmented, atomized world. Protest is liturgy: ritual and myth anchored in Christ that counters the "antiliturgy" of the Chilean state—a state which, for Cavanaugh, is the logical conclusion of the *mythos* of liberalism.

There is something very compelling about the connection between the Sebastian Acevedo protests and Christian liturgy, and this affinity is reinforced because priests and pious Catholics were active and vocal participants in the Chilean protests. But to suggest that Critical Mass—say, in Berkeley or Santa Fe—is somehow "liturgical" seems like much more of a stretch. Yet the parallels between Critical Mass and the Sebastian Acevedo Movement are obvious. Calling each political ritual says too little, but calling each liturgy in the sense Cavanaugh describes it says too much. Moreover, the notion that liturgy offers a foretaste of the sort of social and political arrangements that we truly desire, and for which we ought to be striving, would seem to rely on precisely the sort of supersessionist logic that the previous chapters have been castigating. It suggests that the atomized world of modernity is in need of redemption, and that a glimpse of that redemption can be had in moments of protest, of liturgy.

The task of this chapter is to recover a nonsupersessionist concept of liturgy. Understood in a chastened sense, liturgy can offer valuable resources for theorizing political activities such as Critical Mass and the Sebastian Acevedo Movement. To do this, we must carefully distinguish ritual from liturgy—a distinction overlooked both by secular theorists of political ritual and by theological enthusiasts of liturgy. The vocabulary of ritual, like hope, is often used rhetorically. Ritual reinforces social norms, and calling something a ritual is a bid to reinforce particular norms. In contrast, *liturgy* refers to moments when it is as if social norms do not hold sway, and these moments may inflect the social norms that do hold sway. Liturgy opens new possibilities, not by revealing an antinomian future, but by loosening the always already present pull that social norms have on us, thereby broadening our political imaginations. As we will see, there are rich resources for such an understanding of liturgy within the Christian tradition, but these resources have been overlooked by recent theological enthusiasts of liturgy.

Calling Critical Mass a political ritual seems like common sense. It is a regularly scheduled event partitioned off from ordinary life. Yet in ordinary usage *ritual* implies formality, strict adherence to a specific pattern. While the parameters of Critical Mass (and the Sebastian Acevedo Movement) are formal, meeting at a particular time on bicycles and riding together without regard for traffic laws, within those parameters a great deal of variety is possible. In many Critical Mass rides, there is no set route and no set destination: these are spontaneously chosen along the way. To call Critical Mass political also seems obvious: heightening the visibility of bicycle riders is a clear political goal. But it also seems problematic, in that each Critical Mass rider has her or his own goals, ranging from persuading the local government to add more bicycle lanes to combating liberal atomization to just having a good time.

Canonical theorists of ritual offer little help. For Durkheim, ritual brings society together through shared focus on a divine object—an object which is ultimately phantasmal.[4] Just as supporting a football team, and the practices of watching, cheering, and discussing that constitute that support, brings a city or university community closer together, so do religious rites unify and solidify a society. But how would Durkheim's theory make sense of oppositional political rituals like Critical Mass, rituals that are intended to call into question precisely the unity that rituals, in Durkheim's theory, promote? While it might be tempting to suggest that Critical Mass and the Sebastian Acevedo Movement unify and solidify a "counterculture," both understand themselves as only offering a momentary glimpse of what an alternative society might look like.

Victor Turner's theory of religious rituals seems more promising.[5] For Turner, rituals are strongly associated with times of transition, times when individuals in a society step outside of their normal social roles. As boys become men in "primitive" societies, a group of them is taken away into the forest for a few weeks of initiatory teachings and practices. During this period, all of the initiates, regardless of their parentage, are treated as equals. They are dressed the same, they endure pain and hardships together, they learn humility. Initiates learn that human beings are essentially the same; this knowledge inflects their actions in the world to which they will return. Like Critical Mass, the rituals that Turner focuses on take participants temporarily away from society and into a state of equality, which is a state of "antistructure." But to adopt Turner's perspective would be to take a cynical view of Critical Mass and the Sebastian Acevedo Movement, for Turner is committed to a dialectic of structure and antistructure. Moments outside of society ultimately reinforce social bonds, just as rituals reinforce social bonds on Durkheim's theory. St. Francis ultimately strengthens the church hierarchy.

Perhaps the inadequacies of these accounts of ritual are symptomatic of a more general problem with the concept of ritual: that it is built on theological foundations. Durkheim, Turner, and other theorists of ritual participate in a continuous tradition that has its roots in Christian theology of late antiquity—so it has recently and persuasively been argued.[6] Indeed, early medieval historiography sounds remarkably similar to modern scholarship on ritual. Medieval historians wrote about rituals producing order and consensus, but a more careful reading of these historians' accounts shows that they are partisan polemics. Rulers supported by medieval historians were said to use rituals to create order and consensus; rulers disliked by medieval historians were said to use sham rituals which were inefficacious, even though the actual ritual practices in both cases were largely the same. In the tenth century, there was a widespread royal practice of feeding the poor. The practice was adapted from clergy and monks with the intention of showing the king's holiness as an imitator of Christ. Contemporary historians looked favorably on this practice: having paupers at the king's banquet table brought the kingdom together, and made the king saintly. But the practice was only favorably depicted when the kings involved were already favored. The historian Liudprand depicts the disliked Lombard royalty as chameleons, faking identification with the poor by darkening their hair and feigning disabilities in order to achieve, through manipulation, an undeserved aura of sanctity.

The rhetorical employment of the language of ritual in medieval historiography has its origins in the attempts of early Christians to distinguish their own, true rituals from false, pagan, and secular rituals. Augustine describes how secular political leaders use rituals to control their subjects. These leaders "taught men as true under the name of religion [beliefs and rituals] things they knew to be false" and so "bound them tighter . . . to the citizen community." These secular rituals are simulacra of true rituals, invented by humans for the purpose of controlling other humans using "private desires for temporal things." There is an alternative: rituals "divinely instituted as if for the common good, for the love of God and of one's neighbor." From rituals such as these true consensus and social harmony could flow.[7]

This is the context against which discussion of ritual in medieval historiography must be read. But it is also the context against which modern discussions of ritual should be read. Protestant reformers claimed that Catholic rituals were just as phony and manipulative as ancient Roman rituals, invented with the same intent: social control. In colonial encounters, native rituals were understood as false and manipulative, merely utilitarian. In the aftermath of the French Revolution, the Revolution's self-consciously invented rituals were similarly dismissed as false and manipulative. Sociologists and anthropologists now repeat this maneuver: they call rituals in the exotic societies they study manipulative and utilitarian; they just suppress the normative judgment that these rituals are "false." This pattern has spread to popular culture. While television commentators without hesitation would describe Soviet practices as rituals, there is a certain unease that accompanies discussion of, say, voting as an American ritual. In the latter case, we feel as if we need to emphasize that we are speaking *metaphorically*. Where the language of ritual was used by medieval historiographers to commend and sanctify those they favored, now we use the language of ritual to implicitly discredit those we find illegitimate.

There is a widespread intuition in the academy that *ritual* and *liturgy* refer to the same things; the former is an outsider's term and the latter is an insider's term.[8] But this intuition is discredited if we acknowledge the rhetorical use of the vocabulary of ritual. If the naming of rituals—by Augustine, by Durkheim, or by Tom Brokaw—is used to legitimize certain understandings of social cohesion and to delegitimize others, ritual is always an insider's term. Indeed, it is through strategically employing the vocabulary of ritual that the distinction between insider and outsider is marked. With this distinction blurred, can we still understand liturgy as an insider's term?

There has been much excitement in the last decade about using the language of liturgy in a broad sense, discarding conventional wisdom that liturgy is an insider's term. In the face of postmodern culture and philosophy, liturgy seems to offer an alternative. One scholar has recently proposed a "liturgical consummation of philosophy"; another has proposed a "liturgy of citizenship" composed of faithful, hopeful, and loving practices; a third has emphasized the transformation of liturgical reverence from religion to aesthetics.[9] Even scholars of Judaism have been caught up in the excitement for liturgy, one recently suggesting a turn "after postmodernism to liturgical reasoning" as a way of understanding Jewish thought.[10] Yet many of these attempts lean on the same Christian theological heritage as the concept of ritual. This is not just any theological heritage; accounts of ritual and liturgy often lean on a supersessionist logic.

The new enthusiasts of liturgy use the term in a particularly broad sense. Liturgy, ritual, and tradition all blend into a fuzzy mixture without remainder. In this blend, both worldly and otherworldly, there is supposed to be an antidote to the ills of modernity. More precisely, modernity itself is understood as liturgy in this expansive sense, though modernity is taken to be an "antiliturgy liturgy."[11] The culture of modernity is a "parody" of liturgical culture, a degeneration of liturgical culture, a heresy. By recognizing the (anti)liturgical nature of modernity, characterizing its aesthetic, and contrasting it with an alternative aesthetic corresponding to an alternative form of liturgy, a choice is forced: either remain in antiliturgical culture or switch to liturgical culture. The criteria for this choice are aesthetic. To put it crudely, liturgical culture is beautiful, antiliturgical culture is ugly. The right choice is obvious.

What is liturgy for its enthusiasts? How can they understand it so broadly as this, as characterizing an entire culture? To begin with what it is not: liturgy is not ritual in the pejorative sense, it is not mechanical repetition. In liturgy, action and story, practice and meaning are tied together. Liturgy is a story enacted, though narrative and action cannot be detached. Liturgy is not guided by reason, or at least not a reason external to liturgy. Reason does play a role in liturgy, but reason is internal to liturgy in the same way that reason can be internal to a story. When characters in a story find themselves in a particular situation, the reason of the story, the story's internal logic, guides the characters; their actions can be predicted by the reader. In liturgy, reason is aesthetic. An art instructor can look at her student's partially completed painting and assess the reasonableness of proposals for its completion. The claims made by the enthusiasts of liturgy are even stronger, as there is no "outside" of the painting: we are artists of our own worlds.

Put differently, there have been moments when it has been fashionable to characterize the human condition as primarily linguistic, or primarily social. Recent enthusiasts of liturgy propose that the human condition is primarily liturgical. As one writer puts it, "All cultures begin in liturgy which fuses the repetition of ideal values, with physical inscription upon bodies, places, times and motions."[12] Liturgy, as a foundational category, uniquely brings together self and world, ideas and actions. Such concepts are themselves hypostases of liturgy, pinched out of the amorphous, opaque, multiform, harmonic substance of liturgy. We act as if there is a distinct self, a distinct external world, a distinct realm of ideas, a distinct set of actions, whereas actually, when these fictions are set aside, we are left with the throbbing substance of liturgy.

Liturgy is fundamental, even in modernity. Modernity is characterized by a double false consciousness regarding liturgy. In modernity, if liturgy in the broad sense, an underlying rhythmic unity, is recognized at all, it is imagined to be a realm to be reached through our own effort, through transcending our selves. That is the attitude prevalent in modernity, not how those in modernity act. The world of late capitalism, of virtual reality, is a world in which all boundaries, all categories, are fluid. Self and world, ideas and actions again become hypostases of this all-encompassing plane of the virtual. Businesses operate twenty-four hours a day, seven days a week, every day of the year. Each town, small or large, near or far, has the same businesses. Individuals and information (and capital) travel instantly from place to place. All intervals of time collapse into an instant, all intervals of space can be traversed in an instant. The manufactured and the natural are one and the same. This is the antiliturgy liturgy that underlies modernity. Like liturgy, it fuses values with their inscription on bodies, places, times, and motions. Unlike liturgy, there is no depth: everything is fused into a point, an instant. This is the second aspect of the false consciousness of modernity, because this underlying unity, too, is just an act. It refuses to recognize the human condition: the liturgical condition. Nature (in a special, broad sense) still obeys its own rhythm, but modernity attempts to deny this rhythm, to conflate it with the artificial and so to pretend that it is controllable, divisible as we please.

What would it look like to refuse this double false consciousness, to return to a liturgical culture? It would look rather like the Middle Ages. The calendar would be heterogeneous, marked with different festivals. Life events would take place in the context of a community, where experiences of birth, death, marriage, and coming of age would be integrated into the community's understanding of itself, across time and space. Kinship networks beyond the dyadic would regain importance, connecting individuals with others in many ways, on many levels, at many times. There is always mediation; there is nothing other than mediation. Yet cities would be, both literally and metaphorically, "focused around cathedrals," centered on something that points beyond themselves.[13] This last feature of liturgical culture seems discordant at first, but it is quite the opposite, a counterpoint that integrates the whole—or, an element of the whole which marks the whole. The cathedral stands for the mystery of the beautiful, the impossibility of expressing the organizing principle of liturgical culture in propositions, or in any form of transparent representation.

To understand liturgy in this way is to collapse the gap between practices and norms. In a liturgical culture, what is done is what ought to be done; what ought to be done is what is done. In the aesthetic, the descriptive and the normative are one and the same, and liturgy, understood in this way, is just beautiful practice. Certainly, practices are represented, but these representations are themselves beautiful practices. Each practice is always already a representation, a mediation; there is no outside of liturgy. Yet there are cathedrals, there are signifiers of the transcendent. Uncertainty and mystery is located within the plane of representation, not orthogonal to that plane. Representations always slip into each other, they never signify perfectly. Every signifier signifies the transcendent because it simultaneously succeeds and fails, because it signifies imperfectly. That imperfection introduces an aesthetic element: it is only through aesthetics that this uncertainty is transformed, not into certainty but into beauty. This may not be evident from any particular position, but if liturgical culture is acknowledged, it is just a matter of aesthetic discernment—looking for the image in the apparent chaos, looking from different angles, in different ways—that will, eventually, allow the beauty to be discerned, will allow right judgment to prevail.[14]

A liturgical culture is a peaceful culture. Each component has its place, and each moves together. The beauty which characterizes liturgy results in what enthusiasts of liturgy term peace, an absence of violence. Peace and violence seem to be harnessed primarily for their rhetorical force, as the claim made on behalf of liturgy is certainly not that bad things do not happen. Rather, when bad things happen, a liturgical culture has the resources to make sense of them. There is a story—and neighbors, friends, family—to sooth the pain. Moments when, seemingly inexplicably, something goes wrong, when a dear friend dies, when the economy goes sour, when a house is robbed, liturgy incorporates these. Or, more precisely, it is the double false consciousness of modernity that makes such events seem inexplicable in the first place. Tragedies are felt acutely because they seem to be personal afflictions from out of nowhere. Science and reason are supposed to explain everything; when an event occurs which they cannot explain, the suffering it causes is bottomless. All the more so in the postmodern world of the virtual: when time and space collapse, when the artificial and the natural are one, the conceptual space that would make sense of tragedy is evacuated. This is violence at its very worst, for it cannot be acknowledged. Paradoxically, violence which is acknowledged becomes peace while peace that is proclaimed becomes violence.

Enthusiasts of liturgy encourage the slippage from the rhetorical to the ontological to the physical. When liturgy is called peaceful it brings with it the everyday connotations of peace, to which are added the apparently more profound claims of ontological peace (aesthetic harmony as that which fundamentally characterizes the human condition), to which are added examples of actual existing peace. Chile, under Pinochet, exhibits the culmination of modernity, the ultimate rejection of liturgical culture.[15] It is because of, and through, the atomization of individual Chileans that totalitarian rule was possible. Disappearances and invisible torture are the natural underside of modernity, the most brutal violence perpetuated in the name of maintaining peace. It is because the conceptual space for suffering, whether state-sanctioned or not, is absent that suffering must take place in hiding—or beyond the borders of the sovereign nation (peculiarly, it is the Middle Ages that turn out to be the most peaceful for some of these enthusiasts of liturgy).

Another way to understand the ontological peace proclaimed by enthusiasts of liturgy is as a refusal of norms, as practice without norms. What is a norm except a potential for reprimand, for punishment? There are no violations of a game without rules. Liturgy makes a game where rules are unnecessary, where practice is always right, where there is no threat of reprimand. Yet there is still judgment, aesthetic judgment.[16] This judgment does not bring with it the threat of violence because it is uncontroversial—at least to everyone who recognizes that aesthetics are the sole criteria for judgment, to everyone who has shed illusions (illusions which are nothing more than hypostases of liturgy). But might this picture of a world without norms bring with it precisely the sort of false consciousness of which modernity stands accused? Liturgical culture and virtual culture offer competing aesthetics. Each has a way of dealing with what we might call the tragic. Partisans of liturgical culture claim that the way virtual culture deals with tragedy is less efficacious than the way liturgical culture deals with tragedy. But this argument hangs on the assumption that dealing with tragedy is something that ought to be done, and that ought to be done well. The enthusiasts of liturgy criticize virtual culture because, by cleansing the violence of norms from visibility, this violence is displaced to invisibility, lurking in the basements of Chilean police buildings and in journeys of extraordinary rendition. Should there not be a worry that a story—an all-encompassing story, an aesthetic—that is more effective at presenting a picture of peace than modernity's story, of cleansing the visible of violence and incorporating even more into the visible, would have an all the more frightening underside? If a choice has to be made between aesthetics, where the choice is a Gestalt switch between the virtual or the liturgical, how can the suppression of violence from the visible count in favor of the liturgical, given that the liturgical is actually better at suppressing violence from visibility? This is the paradox of all supersessionist logics. The forgotten option is always the middle, the place where the discussion began, the ordinary. Enthusiasts of liturgy are right to suggest that the enchantment of the virtual magnifies rather than mollifies the tragic—but that is the effect of every enchantment.

A few decades before the recent enthusiasm for liturgy, a previous generation of theologians injected new energy into the concept. These theologians, working in the wake of the Second Vatican Council, agreed with more recent enthusiasts that liturgy is practice without norms. But, unlike recent enthusiasts, these earlier theologians did not have such a broad view of liturgy. They focused on specific liturgical activities, from baptism to song to communion. They also argued that liturgy does bear a relationship to norms. Theological doctrine—that is, the norms of religious practice—would have to be revised if it is found to conflict with liturgical practice. Liturgy is *theologia prima*, first theology. This view offers a way to avoid the supersessionist logic inherent in recent accounts of liturgy, for liturgical practices could be understood strategically, as a means of inflecting, or righting, or humbling, specific norms.

Drawing on patristic sources, liturgical theologians in the 1970s and 1980s shifted from studying liturgy as an object, liturgical practices as data classified and analyzed, to studying liturgy as "the living source and the ultimate criterion of all Christian thought."[17] This movement was captured in the slogan *lex orandi est lex credendi*, the law of prayer is the law of belief.[18]

Of course, it is not exactly the "law" of prayer, for liturgy is a practice with-out norms, without law. Where more recent enthusiasts of liturgy conflate liturgy and ritual, earlier liturgical theologians take this distinction as cru-cial. Ritual is understood as a community practice, reflecting or growing out of social norms. Liturgy offers a foretaste of a world to come, and as such is not governed by social norms. Not only that, liturgy has the poten-tial to alter norms. Put another way, liturgy is authoritative while ritual is reflective. Taking liturgy to be the activities of the Church, studied as an ob-ject, a sort of institutional excrescence, is one way the distinction between ritual and liturgy has tended to collapse. When liturgy is treated in this way, liturgy becomes law; it is just a matter of following the rules set out in the denominational handbook. Another way for the distinction to collapse is when liturgy is treated as pure affect, unrepresentable. In this case, liturgy becomes an individual feeling, personal devotion. Liturgy might help cope with stress, or might be performed because the congregant enjoys its beauty. In such cases, there are no rules at all, or the rules are made up along the way for the benefit of the practitioners. Liturgical theologians reject both of these options—which map clearly onto a supersessionist logic. Neither liturgy as ritual nor liturgy as feeling allow liturgy to *do* anything, to affect the Church.

Anyone can participate in liturgy, from "charwomen and shopkeepers" to "pontiffs and professors."[19] Liturgy is authoritative, and this makes re-ligious authority democratic. Authority resides in practice rather than in people, or in doctrine. Certainly, the relationship between doctrine and liturgy is bidirectional, each influencing the other. But it is also asymmetric. This is because the act of liturgy "is not reducible to conceptual proposi-tions," it always retains an "ambiguity."[20] In other words, there is always a gap between liturgical practice and any representation of it. The job of theologians is to take meaning from liturgy; liturgy does not give mean-ing. This meaning will, obviously, vary depending on the place and time in which liturgy is performed, but it is not free-floating. This meaning is con-nected to liturgical practice, accountable to liturgy. Every attempt to speak the meaning of liturgy, to translate liturgical practice into theological dis-course, will necessarily get liturgy wrong to some degree. Yet this is a nec-essary risk; the theologian must refuse to "wait upon absolute certainty."[21]

In this account of liturgy we find an acknowledgment of the unavoidable gap between practices and norms, a gap absent from the account of liturgy provided by its more recent enthusiasts. Yet this is a special sort of gap between practices and norms: liturgy is a practice that does not aspire to match norms. In ritual practice there is also a gap between the norms governing ritual and the actual practice of ritual, but the aspiration is to close this gap, for ritual practice to be as close as possible to ritual prescription (this gap in ritual is itself productive, introducing an important dynamism).[22] Liturgical practice is practice as if there is no norm. Of course there is a norm, whether it is explicit (say, in a prayer book) or implicit (say, in the imitation of previous liturgical practices). But because liturgy is recognized as authoritative, not only for the norms directly relevant to it, the norms of how to perform the liturgical practice, but also to another set of norms, norms at a distance—the norms of theological discourse—it appears temporarily severed from the plane of norms. Eventually, effort must be made to bring them back together, effort that involves risk. Before this can happen it must be as if liturgy were on its own, as if the plane of practices floated free from the plane of norms in the liturgical moment.

This view clearly holds potential for understanding liturgy as a theopolitical strategy. It presents a means of refusing the hegemony of the visible, of refusing to be limited by the options that present themselves. While liturgical theologians sometimes attribute the authority of liturgy to its status as a foretaste of the world to come, there is no reason that this description cannot be bracketed as a rhetorical flourish, leaving simply a certain practice which, when employed, has the potential to alter a certain set of norms. What might liturgy in this generic sense look like?

Jean-Yves Lacoste writes of experiences that "bracket the petitions of history" and "thwart all the laws of topology."[23] In a night vigil, the laws of the day no longer hold sway. Obligations to employer, family, and government are not in effect, "our daytime duties have been fulfilled" (79). But vigil is not vacation; it is not a leisure time free from work (obligations to family and government would still hold). One is not asleep, nor is one suffering from insomnia; this would again be subject to biological laws. Even though worldly laws are bracketed, they are still present. But it is as if they have been set aside: liturgy is practice as if there were no norms. A vigil is a practice that one can bring about but cannot determine the outcome of. A vigil does not bring with it "certitude" or "affective verification" (143). If it involves knowledge it is experiential (knowledge how) rather than propositional (knowledge that).[24] Indeed, liturgy is "the 'soul' putting consciousness into question"; it is one's habits being subject to "the critique conducted by the soul."[25] More broadly, liturgy is a critique of history from within history, an instant when the force of the invisible makes itself felt within the world. Whether the time of a vigil is spent on poetry, philosophy, or prayer, it has a necessarily subversive effect on social norms.

One of the founders of Critical Mass describes the event's "beauty" as "the chance it provides for people to face each other in the simmering cauldron of real life, in public, without preset roles and fixed boundaries."[26] It is a space where social norms are suspended, where the need to do what one is supposed to do feels as if it no longer holds sway. That space of suspended norms does not have a fixed meaning; its meaning is opaque, in need of interpretation. "Each person is equally capable of offering a perspective, a definition, a manifesto, a purpose," but this freedom is not absolute. It is accountable to the practice itself, and to the community of practitioners: "Our sense of what's possible and what we do about it is shaped in action with each other."[27] However much agreement there is about what Critical Mass is, it remains an "unpredictable space, with unpredictable consequences and unpredictable reactions, both for people in it and people outside it."[28] While Critical Mass participants, like participants in the Sebastian Acevedo Movement, understand their activity as offering "a window into a different world," this window is always blurry—a fact that participants acknowledge.[29] Indeed, it is not a blurry window but a blurry mirror, offering a different way of seeing not a hoped-for future but the possibilities of the present.

Perhaps such an account of liturgy can be found in the writings of Simone Weil. Like liturgical theologians, Weil is careful to distinguish religious practice from social convention. Understood as a social entity, the Church is no different than a nation or a sports team; the Church is most often understood as a social entity. But among these social entities, the Church has a privileged position: it is an aspect of the social labeled divine, and so it brings with it particular dangers. Weil considers the Roman Empire and Nazi Germany, where worship of the state was foundational, to be "almost certainly" the Beast of the Apocalypse.[30] This, in fact, is the reason Weil states for refusing to consummate her long flirtation with Catholicism. Unless the sacraments are understood properly, they involve ritual rather than liturgy. They reinforce a feeling of attachment to the social world; they do the work of interpellation. Weil suggests that she is particularly susceptible to such work, to patriotic fervor (her writings on France certainly support this), so she must be especially wary. "A collective body is the guardian of dogma," whenever many gather a "collective language begins to dominate."[31] This does not have anything to do with the "supernatural," the term Weil uses in contrast to religiosity as patriotism. Of course, Weil does write extensively about what this experience of the supernatural would involve. It is, perplexingly, a simulacrum of the social experience of religiosity. For Weil, ritual and liturgy may look, from the outside, identical, but it is only in the latter that the heart is moved: "The action of grace in our hearts is secret and silent."[32]

Yet Weil repeatedly distances herself from Pascal's contention that first one kneels and prays, then one believes. The ability to make this distinction is crucial for an account of liturgy, for the Pascalian picture has been used to describe the social at its most potent and insidious: as ideology. In Louis Althusser's appropriation, ideology is not a set of beliefs that are taught to citizens. Indoctrination does not come about through lessons. It is through practice, through doing what a good citizen is to do, that one acquires the beliefs that a good citizen is supposed to have, the beliefs of ideology. Ideas derive from "material practices governed by material rituals which are themselves defined by the material ideological apparatus."[33] An ideological apparatus defines rituals, rituals define actions, and the subject so acting feels as though she is acting according to her own belief. That is what her consciousness tells her: I am doing this because I believe it is true, it is right, it is just. A free-floating realm of ideas is but a powerful illusion. Its analysis will necessarily lead to faulty conclusions. Ritual is where everything starts. Institutions, such as churches, but also legal systems, family structures, educational institutions, trade unions, media, and much else, create and sustain ritual. In this way, there is no need for the state to directly exert its will on citizens; these institutions form citizens in such a way that they already agree with the state.

If this is correct, it is unclear what role liturgy could possibly have. By opposing the priority of practice to belief, Weil opens up a distinct space for liturgy and its critical potential. But it is not the original thesis—the contention that practices are expressions of beliefs—to which Weil returns. Weil's worry is precisely that, if practice is given priority over belief, there will be no way to escape the grip of the social. For Weil it is intelligence, rather than belief, that offers an alternative to the "power of suggestion" that is the social. Intelligence is not holding particular propositions to be true, or having particular capacities. It is also not a practice that is created or perpetuated by an institution. It is not precisely intelligence that Weil lauds, but the cultivation of intelligence through what she calls attention. Intelligence is "fed" by attention, and intelligence makes possible the grasping of truths otherwise indiscernible. It is by focusing the intelligence, then bracketing intelligence, that faith comes about.

Here is an example of what Weil is talking about, of what might be termed her account of liturgical practice: focusing intently on a piece of music. Normally, when the intelligence focuses, it works hard, trying to understand what is happening. But in a piece of music (or other work of art), there is intent focus but no adjudication, no affirmation or denial. To judge a work of art by historical or social standards is to refuse to focus intently enough. The art object itself provides no knowledge, either propositional or experiential. If you think you know that a painting is x, or that you know how to look at a painting, like how to sail a boat, your intelligence is not sufficiently focused. Further, there is no obligation to focus your attention on the art object. Social obligations (say, at a dinner party or in an art history course) compel us to acquire or state knowledge of an object, to cut short attention.

Attention is an exercise of intelligence. After focusing attention on the artwork, the intelligence is better able to grasp worldly truths more generally. This is not because of any feature of the artwork, but because of the practice of attention itself. It is the practice that matters, not the object. Weil is not shy about associating attention with the liturgical: "Attention, taken to its highest degree, is the same thing as prayer. It presupposes faith and love."[34] At its lowest degree, its most elementary, attention quite literally involves exercises, school exercises. Geometry is a privileged example: everyone remembers the attention focused on a problem, a theorem that needs to be proved by means of intelligence. At first, and sometimes for quite a long time, the intelligence feels like it is of no use. The best help a teacher can provide is to say, *Just stare at the problem for awhile.* When one stares, the intelligence is focused, not distracted by other thoughts. It is not calculating or testing, it is just looking. Eventually an insight will come about, from no-where, which will provide something to work with. But the insight would not have come about had there not been that period of attention with in-telligence at once focused and disengaged.

The insight that arises from attention is provisional. However, it must be taken as if it is true in order to test it. The example of a geometry proof makes this clear: after focusing one's attention on a problem, a solution seems to present itself, but it is only by working out the proof that it will become evident whether or not the proof works, and whether or not the theorem actually is true. It is only by taking the proof to be right that it can be shown to be right. In other words, Weil inverts Pascal's privilege of practice over belief. We must start by believing, then act as if we believe, and only then will the belief become certain. More precisely, this is what happens in the practice of attention, a practice which brings about new truths outside of itself, a practice which brings into question the social order, what Weil calls the "great beast." When the institutions of the so-cial and the beliefs that they create pervade, what is subversive is *to believe too much.* It is by taking the risk of believing something to be true on a hunch, as it were, that certainties not countenanced by prevailing social norms can come about.

Attention is the only genuine source of obligation, according to Weil. It is as if there are obligations created by the social world, but only as if. Obligations cannot be forced on oneself from the outside, nor can they be forced on oneself from the inside, through efforts of will. The practice of attention is nearly the opposite of will: it is the subordination of will to something other than oneself, but it is a subordination that still engages the intelligence. If it is not the will that focuses attention, then what is it? Weil suggests that it is supernatural, that it is God. But it is easy for Weil's rhetoric to distract. For her, God is just that which makes attention possible; other uses of the term have been corrupted by the social.

Does this not still leave in place a clearly supersessionist logic: worldly obligation opposed to divine obligation, the latter made visible through attention? But such an understanding is misleading. Attention *trains* the intelligence, increasing its capacity for discernment. It makes truths appear that were invisible before, but these are worldly truths. They were invisible before not because they were in some spiritual realm but because they were obscured by the social, by enchantment. Put another way, attention is humility. It teaches us that our view of the world is largely wrong, and so prepares us to see the world more clearly.

Like the practices discussed by liturgical theologians, attention is a practice which alters norms. Unlike the practices discussed by liturgical theologians, attention does not alter a subset of norms, not even a privileged subset such as those concerning theological discourse. Rather, attention has the potential to affect any norms. Perhaps this begins to suggest how Weil, often thought to tend toward supersessionism, sometimes directly labeled a self-hating Jew, is neither. "Within the sphere of the intelligence," she writes, "the Church has no right of jurisdiction whatsoever."[35] What is the importance of the Church, then, if it is largely consumed by hollow patriotism and does not govern the practice which can move beyond patriotism, the proper use of the intelligence? Its importance is simply that it "imposes on the intelligence a certain discipline of the attention."[36] In other words, the Church does what school exercises and geometry do, just at a higher level, with respect to a broader domain.

There is something perplexing about liturgy understood in this way, practice as if there is no norm. The examples that Weil provides, ranging from Latin exercises to geometry theorems to contemplation of artwork to prayer seem incongruous. There is a tendency to affirm the latter two as practices as if there are no norms, but to think of the former two as rigidly governed by norms. Might it be the case that practice radically underdetermined by norms resembles practice radically overdetermined by norms? When the plane of practices is temporarily untethered from the plane of norms, living no longer involves negotiating between practices and norms. It no longer involves acting and checking and recalibrating. What this looks like, from the outside, is strict adherence to an indiscernible rule. For someone untutored in geometry or Latin, who sits in on a class in one of those subjects, it is clear that there is a rule being followed, but what that rule is seems wholly mysterious. From the perspective of the outsider to prayer or to the tourist in a museum who passes by someone whose attention is focused on an artwork, might there not be a similar appearance of an indiscernible rule? It may appear even more absurd, as though the artwork, or some unseen being, is issuing commands which only the viewer or the worshiper can hear.

Is this not precisely the situation which Kafka presents? In his worlds, there are rules seemingly without reason, individuals strictly following the rules which cannot be made sense of. Might it not be that this is liturgical practice viewed from our outsider's perspective? Or, more precisely, might the worlds of *The Castle*, *The Trial*, and *Amerika* be liturgical cultures, worlds pervaded by liturgical practice? It seems as though there are only norms, but could it equally be said that there is only practice? Characters suspend their intelligence, no longer adjudicating or calculating. Instead, they focus their attention solely on one object: the castle, the law, the American dream. Out of this attention come truths, ways to make sense of the worlds, ways to act. There is an excess of belief: things are taken as true, put into practice, and then they become true. The man from the country, approaching the law, does not stand in a libidinal relationship to the law. The law is the object of his attention. He waits patiently. The object of attention does not matter; it is the belief that matters. It is not the man's practice that produces his belief, for what is his practice? He does not *do* anything, he simply waits. He takes the gatekeeper's words to be true, he believes that there are increasingly fierce gatekeepers at the inner gates, and his actions follow this belief—he gives everything he has to the first gatekeeper. How else, other than by this excess of belief, could we explain why the man never enters the open door to the law that is right in front of him? And how else could we explain his arrival at that gate, from the country, in the first place?

But Kafka's stories are frightening. The man from the country is increasingly grotesque, his eyesight weak, his back bent, his collar filled with fleas, his life coming to an end. Is this the quintessential liturgical culture? Perhaps here we have encountered the underside to that beautiful aesthetic that recent proponents of liturgy have trumpeted, the harsh realities of the medieval. The law (or the castle, or the American dream) is most certainly a transcendental signifier at the center, a cathedral in the middle of town. The aesthetic of which it is both a part and the whole organizes time and space. These worlds are frightening not because violence is arbitrary—for we are continually assured that the law is applied systematically; nor because these worlds are atomized—for there is rich community joined by their central transcendental signifiers. These worlds are frightening precisely because the planes of practice and norms have become untethered, and the tragic has been so thoroughly suppressed. Now, everything is tragic and nothing. There is no longer a brutal underside, as there is to modernity; now, in a liturgical culture, everything is beautiful and everything is brutal. Yet what is frightening is liturgical culture, not liturgical practice. The protagonists of the three novels are crippled because they are incapable of liturgy.

CHAPTER 6

SANCTITY

SANCTITY SEEMS ANTIPOLITICAL. IT SEEMS ANTIPOLITICAL WHEN IT describes an individual, for the individual's sanctity comes about precisely in her ability to keep her hands clean of always messy politics, and it seems antipolitical when it describes institutions, for this sort of aggrandizement is what leads to the suppression of always messy politics. But this view of politics distorts. A better approach, one that avoids supersessionism, says: politics, at its best, is motivated by the desire for justice, not the desire for innocence.[1] The more that innocence becomes the focus of personal or institutional political activity, the more harm is done. Innocence is near-sighted; it cleanses what is proximate at the expense of one's neighbors. In contrast, politics is, or should be, about living together, not living here. The desire for innocence is always accompanied by a confused depth perception, mistaking what is proximate and what is far. It is not the proximate that is cleansed; that which is perceived as clean comes to seem proximate. Sanctity is associated with the distorted view of politics as a desire for innocence.

Justice, in contrast, involves seeing rightly and treating rightly; it involves giving each her due. Political figures associated with struggles for justice are sometimes called saintly, but are more often called prophetic. Rarely are they associated with sanctity. When they are hallowed it is through metonymy, through proximity to a commended cause, although this mechanism is quickly forgotten. When their personal misdeeds come to light, this mechanism is quickly remembered: we say that it is the leader's deeds which are great, the leader himself was only human. In cases where saintliness comes first, where the saintly individual becomes involved in politics, excuses are necessary to explain away perceived political failures. It was a mark of the saint's personal holiness that she did not compromise when she intervened in political matters. The strangeness of her interventions should not cause worry, for they are otherworldly. Grace is the business of the saint; the business of the politician is Law.

Understood in this way, the saint is the exception that proves the rule. To be recognizable as a saint, she must reject norms—in a particular way. Sainthood complements pathology: each is a systematic divergence from norms. It is misleading to say that hagiography is stylized; it is no more stylized than a medical case study. An explanation for anomaly is necessary: a story must be told, whether it relies on pathogen or on holiness. Ultimately, the saint does not call into question social norms, she reinforces them. It is not the saint but the prophet—or the messiah—who threatens the status quo.

Perhaps sainthood and sanctity need not be understood synonymously. They are not used synonymously. Supererogation is associated with saintliness, not sanctity. Saintliness describes doing more than one's duty; sanctity describes doing one's duty naturally, as if it were not an obligation at all. Sanctity brings with it a quieter sense, a certain steady dignity that does not necessarily accompany the sometimes showy saint. Sanctity can never be outlandish; saintliness sometimes can be. Where saintliness is associated with innocence, sanctity is associated with justice. This is the justice neither of dirty hands nor of clean hands, but a justice so single-minded that it is oblivious to the natural responses prompted by grime or glisten.

The saint is a person, and saintliness is her character. For sanctity, there is not an easy correlate to the person of the saint, so it is tempting to associate sanctity with character or with specific actions. These are all quite common usages, but they obscure sanctity as a political strategy. The everyday language of sanctity commends actions; it is an attempt to persuade an audience to view certain actions in a more favorable light. When sanctity describes a person's character, when the label hallows her soul, it suggests a site at which the Law has been perfected, Law refined into Grace. Sanctity becomes something to which all should aspire, a goal which some can hope to obtain. The politics that correspond to sanctity understood in this way is, once again, subject to the hegemony of the visible, for the character sanctity is ascribed to is one who does things we do, or wish we would do. Restoring sanctity to an office despoiled is to return that office to its proper function, to the function which all acknowledge and recognize. Similarly, to long for a return to sanctity in the character of citizens is to long for them to act properly, as they are supposed to act—based on the norms that are presently acknowledged.

Indeed, this view of sanctity resembles a certain view of tradition. To bring sanctity to the performance of a role is to act in accordance with the norms that accompany that role; to do what is to be done, no more, no less. Tradition is to a community as sanctity is to the individual. Where a call to tradition can be understood as a call for a community to act in accordance with the values implicit in its practice, a call to sanctity can be understood as a call for an individual to act in accordance with the values proper to a good citizen—no more, no less. That is how the citizen becomes holy. Both tradition and sanctity can be understood as strategies—and the two strategies are complementary. Both, for a political purpose, untether the plane of norms from the plane of practices. Tradition makes use of the plane of norms; sanctity makes use of the plane of practices. With different imagery: tradition makes use of norms hollowed out; sanctity makes use of a hole after the shell of norms has been stripped away.

The strategy of tradition necessarily is rhetorical, necessarily because the plane of norms is a plane of representation. The strategy of sanctity is practice stripped of rhetoric, presentation without representation. In this way it rejects the hegemony of the visible. Sanctity in this sense does not discern norms and then bring practice in line; it acts as if there are no norms. This is where the political potential of sanctity lies: by acting as if there are no norms, new practices can be born that are unpredictable from the perspective of norms. The hegemony of the visible is broken. And this is why sanctity is a strategy and not a lifestyle: to make it a lifestyle would inevitably give rise to norms, tethering the plane of practices again to the plane of norms. Yet sanctity is also distinct from liturgy. Where liturgy involves specific, exceptional practices in which one acts as if there are no norms, in sanctity it is as if there are no norms at all.

What is challenging, of course, is that one cannot just decide to act as if there are no norms. There must be certain techniques which provide the necessary leverage to get to this point. What one thinks of first are the clichés: yoga, meditation, silent retreats. These are unhelpful for our purposes precisely because they are clichés: they are governed by norms, so much so that their use even as a lever to thrust apart the plane of practices from the plane of norms is compromised. An alternative model is to be found in an unexpected locale: the Lacanian diagnostic typology. Psychosis, perversion, and neurosis can be distinguished precisely through the relationship they involve between practices and norms. This typology corresponds to a chronological story about maturation: in the psychotic, psychic development was stinted the earliest, the pervert's later, and the neurotic has fully matured psychically—she just needs to go through psychoanalysis to become a healthy individual. Those writing about psychoanalysis and politics have often used these diagnostic categories as means to explain undesirable political actors and structures. Fascism is group psychosis; to move beyond capitalism we must traverse the fantasy and so shake our neurosis; and so on. But perhaps these categories also can provide a way to think through the strategy of sanctity, a strategy that harnesses the psychic structure of perversion.[2]

Here is the Lacanian story. A baby begins like an animal or a rock. Biology describes its behavior completely: in circumstances such as *these* it will act in *this* way. The baby must acquire a second nature, human nature. She must be taught the Law of the Father. What she is supposed to do she may not want to do but she should do. Before induction into the regime of the Father, the baby simply does. Mother and infant form a closed circuit of desire. Infant fulfills the desire of the Mother, Mother fulfills desire of her infant. The infant hungers, the Mother provides milk; the Mother frets, the infant brings her joy. The baby has no consciousness of Law. Whatever the baby does, its Mother approves. When it cries, it is fed; when it makes a mess, it is cleaned.

This closed circuit of desire is broken by the Father. He imposes himself between Mother and child. Mother desires Father; Father fulfills the desire of Mother in a way that the child cannot. The infant has a desire, the oedipal desire, which its Mother cannot (must not, according to Law) fulfill. With this first prohibition, with the "no" of the Father protecting his rights over the Mother, the infant realizes that the closed circuit of desire is broken. The infant begins its formation into an adult stance toward Law, a stance in which there is a "yes" and a "no," a right and a wrong. Father brings Law. He introduces the normative. There are things that one is supposed to do. If one does not do what one is supposed to do, Father will punish. Mother does not punish. Mother says yes to whatever the child desires. But it is only through punishment that one can become conscious of Law. One is not born into Law, one is formed into Law; one is subjected, one becomes a subject to Law.

If subjection fails, if it is short-circuited at some point, there is grave psychic disorder. If the child never becomes conscious of Law, she becomes psychotic. She does what she likes; her unfettered desire constitutes her own Law. Her Law is in no way accountable to the Law of the world, to Law as such. Her Law is hers and hers alone. Her behavior is not random, it is a regime. She is following a Law, deciding cases, acting *this* way in *these* circumstances each time they arise. But her Law is not subject to correction. She can be told that she is not Napoleon but she still acts like Napoleon, she still believes that she is Napoleon, she still absorbs the world into Napoleon's world.

If subjection succeeds and the child becomes conscious of Law, desire condenses to a point, an object which has infinite value, the value of the Mother. This is the case with the neurotic: she goes about her life doing what one does, following Law. But she is animated by fantasy. The object of her fantasy is an object in the world just like any other, except this object is given infinite value: the lover, the spouse, the dictator, the eccentric hobby. The object itself is mundane. It can never fulfill her fantasy. So she loves the idea of the object and she hates the object itself. She must never approach too near the object. If she does, she will see that it is just like any other. Surely this ugly, fat, snoring thing cannot be the man I love!

Between the psychotic and the neurotic is the pervert. The pervert acknowledges the presence of Law. She knows that, in *these* circumstances, there is something that she is supposed to do. She understands the privilege and authority of the Father, yet she refuses to set aside the closed circuit of desire that she had with her Mother. Instead, she reproduces the space of that closed circuit in her perversions. The Mother has been replaced by an Other. The pervert longs to be what the Other desires, but she is not: the Other is not the Mother. Second best, the pervert tries to identify the desires of the Other and to desire those desires in turn; the pervert identifies with the desires of the Other. Whereas the neurotic enters analysis because she does not know what she wants, the pervert knows precisely what she wants. She wants to be with the Other, to please the Other and to be pleasing to the Other.

The neurotic is Harold; the pervert is Maude. Harold has a well-developed fantasy; he wants to kill himself. And this is a proper fantasy: it always stays at a safe distance from the subject. Harold stages his death over and over again, but it is always just a show. Maude says yes to life and to everyone and everything in it. When Harold and Maude speak of their love, they are speaking in two different languages: Maude loves Harold like she loves everyone, like she says yes to everyone; Harold's love is his fantasy redirected toward Maude and only Maude, Maude as the object of fantasy. At the end of *Harold and Maude*, it is Maude who actually kills herself (a final "no" after a lifetime of "yes"), Harold just continues his fantasies.

In the Marquis de Sade's fantasy, each individual agrees to put himself fully at the mercy of each other. The relationship with the Mother has expanded to cover the whole world of Sade's fictions. Everyone says, "Do with me as you please," in other words, "I desire to fulfill your desire." When the sadist does harm to an Other, it is because the Other desires that harm to be done to her. The world has become one giant circuit of desire. Outside of Sade's worlds, in cases of perversion encountered in analysis, the circuit of desire with the Mother becomes a restricted space, an exceptional space outside of the regime of the normal. The pervert's partner may take the role of the Mother and the pervert may strive to fulfill all of her desires. Or, as Slavoj Žižek has suggested, Sade's world may become the church or mosque—as in the cases of George W. Bush and Osama bin Laden.[3] In those spaces, the pervert believes he directly accesses the desires of the Other—and always responds with a "yes."

Indeed, this is how perversion may be characterized: the ability only to say yes. Law involves decisions. In circumstances such as this, how is the court to rule? In the simplest terms, yes or no? There are right and wrong answers. If the judge makes a wrong decision, it will be overturned on appeal; if a subject acts wrongly, he will be corrected by his peers. He is part of a network of accountability, initiated into it by the first "no" of the Father. While the pervert acknowledges the Law—acknowledges that there is a correct decision of the court, there is something proper to do—he cannot himself make that decision. He cannot choose. Within the circuit of desire of the Mother and child, there was never any need for choice. Confronted with a set of circumstances demanding a response, the pervert can only answer with a constant "yes" (or, equivalently, a constant "no").

This inability to say anything but yes, this structure of perversion, is found in politicians, in criminals, and in saints. Bill Clinton is imagined to say yes to everyone—it is up to his subordinates to grapple with the realities of the Law (if we say yes to welfare reform, and yes to poverty relief, and yes to tax relief, how do we legislate?). The pathological criminal does not simply break the law but disregards it, affirming all of his desires. St. Francis was saintly because he said yes to everyone, from the pope to the pauper to the birds. He was not a representative of God's Law; he was a representative of God's Grace, of God's perpetual affirmation.

Lars von Trier's film *Dogville* presents an example of a character whose perversion pervades her entire life—within the town of Dogville. Grace, the heroine, says "yes" to everyone in town. A wealthy outsider, she finds herself hiding out from seemingly menacing mafiosi in the small, insular community. She enters the life of the town with high hopes, trying to help out the locals however she can. As time progresses, their demands increase. She works harder and harder and eventually descends into physical, and sexual, slavery. All of this is entirely the result of Grace saying yes to everyone. Any doubt about how voluntary Grace's affirmations are is taken away in the final sequence when Grace's pursuer is revealed to be her father (the father figure who is always the greatest fear of the pervert, the father who intrudes into the primal harmony of the infant-Mother relationship).

There is one space in which Grace does not say yes. In her interaction with Tom, the man she fancies, and who fancies her, she always says no to the ultimate question. They will never have sex. They talk and sleep next to each other in bed, but when he wants more, she always says no. The pervert can never alternate, never decide, this time yes, this time no. Judgment is in the jurisdiction of Law. The pervert must have rigid boundaries. In Grace's case, there are two spaces, the space of interaction with everyone except Tom, and the space of interaction with Tom. In the former, it is always yes; in the latter, it is always no. At one point, Tom is particularly persistent. Grace says that he is welcome to have his way with her, but if he does she will consider him like all of the other townspeople. She, still, would only be saying yes, since for the pervert to only say no is structurally identical to only saying yes. In both cases, the law is disregarded and there is no longer a choice made. The coupling of a yes domain and a no domain is common, perhaps necessary. Consider the ascetic saint, saying no to the world and yes to God (or, rather, to His earthly representatives: the poor, the ill, the downtrodden). The domains are rigidly set once and for all. Within their bounds there is no choice.

The space of saying yes is usually an exceptional space. Outside of this space, the pervert follows the Law precisely. Not having been brought up into the Law, the Law always feels alien. To follow it takes effort, the result is exaggerated precision. Consider Luis Buñuel's film *Belle de Jour*. Like Grace, Buñuel's protagonist, Severine, loves a man (her husband) but refuses to consummate their marriage. With him, Severine always says no, she always remains at a distance. At the same time, she fantasizes about having (sado-masochistic) sex. This is a perverse fantasy, not a neurotic fantasy. Severine does not keep it at a distance. She goes to work at a brothel. There she must accept every client who comes in, she must say yes to each—even the Korean with his mysterious and frightening little box. Yet Severine continues to subject herself to the Law most of the time. She acts the part of an upper-middle-class Parisian, dressing properly, going on the proper outings with her husband, speaking refined words. She rigidly separates the space in which she can only say yes and the space in which she is subject to the Law. In the former, she accepts her new name, Belle du Jour. She only works during the day and insists on leaving by five in the afternoon so that she can meet her husband when he comes home from work and play the part of the ordinary housewife. When her husband's friend, Pierre, makes advances toward her, they are decisively rejected. Pierre is part of her social network, part of the regime of the normal rather than the exceptional. In her normal life, Severine must follow the Law, must choose what is proper; she cannot only say yes.

Perversion is a psychic *disorder*, a pathology in need of cure. It also marks social perversion, the state of the social world when the distinction between Law and Grace animates politics. This is shown by both Buñuel (through satire) and von Trier (through pedantry). Buñuel exposes the absurdities and banalities of bourgeois life in contrast to the common sense of the working man. As Severine rides in a taxi carrying large gifts, the taxi driver shares his worldly knowledge of brothels and volunteers that he has been "robbed twice, if you care to ask." Bourgeois pseudo-order is juxtaposed with proletarian grime and grit. This recurring class conflict (or, rather, contrast) in *Belle de Jour* mirrors the conflict between Severine and Belle. The one is committed to following the Law in all its seriousness, the other is committed to impossible escape. Von Trier has made a career out of telling the stories of saintly women. But the saintliness of Grace is undermined in *Dogville* (and *Manderlay*). The protagonist aspires to be Grace, but she fails. She must be rescued by the return of her father, the return of the Law. There is no Kingdom of God on earth. The pervert's false belief that there is such a Kingdom leads to destruction—think Grace in *Dogville*, Jim Jones in Jonestown, George W. Bush in Iraq.

So it is not perversion as such that is promising as a theopolitical strategy. Perversion can manifest itself in a politician, a criminal, a saint. When the pervert gains power, destruction often results. But perversion also offers a glimpse at what it is like to live as if there are no norms. At first this sounds confused. Isn't it just the source of normativity that has changed—no longer the Law, but the Other? But that would be to misunderstand the Lacanian account of perversion, for the pervert seeks a realm without norms, where every practice is sanctioned without judgment, as it was by the Mother before the intrusion of the Father. The techniques generated in order to achieve this as an adult, to find such a place where it is as if there were no norms in a world of norms, are theopolitical resources. Perversion is a disorder in need of remedy when these techniques are taken to provide an exit from the difficult world of Law and to entrench a supposed antinomian realm: this is what happens in the case of the politician, the criminal, and the saint. But when these techniques are used for a specific political purpose, they can make a potent strategy. This strategy is theopolitical—that is, it refuses the hegemony of the visible—because it opens up new options not present in the landscape of Law. By allowing the plane of practices to drift from the plane of norms, the logic of practice can work itself out in ways that are impossible when tethered to the misrecognition of practice by norms.

This is a strategy of sanctity because it has the appearance of quiet dignity, of acceptance. It involves only saying yes, but not in the flamboyant manner of von Trier's Grace or Buñuel's Severine, not in the pathologically perverse manner that only says yes because it is incapable of judgment. The strategy of sanctity involves training. Acceptance takes work, for it first involves seeing rightly, hearing the appropriate question to which the answer is always yes. In the writings of Simone Weil, particularly her so-called spiritual writings, we find resources for sanctity of this kind. In some ways, Weil seems to fit very easily into perversion as a diagnostic category; she writes that she would obey any order she is given: "The most beautiful life possible has always seemed to me to be the one . . . where there is never any room for choice."[4] It is in her descriptions of how such a life is achieved, in the techniques Weil details for acting as if there were no judgment, only practice which does what is to be done so naturally that norms are superfluous, that we find resources for the strategy of sanctity.

It is tempting for those interested in writing about the political import of Simone Weil's work to turn first to her writing about politics—tempting, but counterproductive. The political writings are interventions in particular debates: the exhausting polemics of early twentieth-century Marxist and socialist theory. The tension between this rhetoric and Weil's own constructive thought produces the occasional anomalous excrescence (for instance, the seemingly out-of-place discussion of obedience to God in the final pages of *The Need for Roots*, a largely political text). Weil's political writings are political rhetoric, not political philosophy. In the brilliant rigor of her "spiritual" letters and notebooks she writes philosophy that can be political.

Weil's "spiritual" texts are as simple as they are opaque, for in a sense they refuse representation. They do so without wallowing in this fact; she is not an early advocate of deconstruction. Instead of representation, Weil aspires to presentation. This aspiration becomes possible when presentation is not thought of, pejoratively, as a linguistic or epistemological illusion. If presentation is understood positively, as practice, then the linguistic and the epistemological become illusions—what Weil calls, pejoratively, imagina-

tion. Imagination is more than representation; it is ideology, a rigid, because power-infused, self-perpetuating set of representations. To stay closer
to Weil's own terminology, it is the collective that "chains us to the earth."[5]
Imagination not only pervades (and creates) our worlds; it constitutes our
selves. We imagine our selves to be what we are not. Weil's pithy example is
this: the ugly woman is better off than the beautiful woman, for the beautiful woman is tempted to think that she is as she appears while the ugly
woman knows that she is different than she appears.

Practice is contaminated by these representations: we are always saying or
thinking what we are doing. This soothes us, soothes us like a drug. Imagination makes this or that seem reasonable, obvious. It seems as though without these representations there would be chaos; Weil suggests that without
these representations there is grace. This is grace in a special sense, grace
that simply describes action undistorted by representation. Weil urges us to
abandon the false comfort of representation, and she offers a rich repertoire
of techniques to make this possible.

Forgiveness is one such technique. When one does not do what one
is supposed to do, a wrong is committed; it must be righted. This is what
constitutes the normative order, the law. This is what maintains equilibrium. When practice does not match norm, there is potential for reprimand;
when it does, there is potential for praise. To forgive is to refuse this, to take
the force away from law. Penalty is deserved but withheld. Such a characterization obscures forgiveness as a technique of sanctity, as Weil describes it. It
is not that a reprimand is deserved but, through an act of grace, not administered. Nor is it that a reprimand is not deserved, that the norm violated
is not recognized. Rather, it is that the practice of forgiveness is an exercise
that helps shake the hold that imagination has on us. The point is to give up
the worry about norms, whether they were violated or not; this can only be
done indirectly, and it can only be accomplished through work. Put another
way, the rejection of equilibrium through forgiveness does not establish a
deeper equilibrium, a harmonious community of forgiveness. This would
be equally imaginary; it would establish a new set of norms in the guise of
antinomianism. The problem is to reject the imagination.

Complementary to the technique of forgiveness is the abandonment of
reward. When one acts rightly, when one acts as one is supposed to act, one

is eligible for praise. Reward is explicit when one is learning the Law, as a child or as a student. When one has been acculturated, brought up into the Law, reward more often takes an implicit form, self-satisfaction, the delight in a job well done, a task carried out appropriately (penalty, of course, is also internalized). This is what must be abandoned. It is the strongest adhesive by which the plane of norms is attached to the plane of practice, and to tear it is undoubtedly painful. To refuse what one "deserves"—the raise, the promotion, the anniversary festivities, the proper compensation—that is an exercise in sanctity. The life of sanctity is a life without penalty or reward, for it is a life of practice without norms. To say that what is done is done rightly or done wrongly does not make sense; one just does what one does. To say that it is what one is to do would be to say too much.

A third technique for cultivated sanctity that Weil discusses is dispossession. Central to imagination is an understanding of the world as our world, of some things as our things, of some bodies as our bodies. Our possessions are our loves, the things to which we are most attached, with which we are most comfortable. These attachments must be destroyed. At birth and death there is nothing that is ours. We have no possessions. During our lives, we acquire things, and ideas, and familiarities. We become increasingly entrenched in imagination, which is to say, in enchantment. Moments of tragedy remind us how hollow it all is, how easily we can be dispossessed, how it is only *as if* we possess. To renounce possession, or, to duplicate the hypothetical—to live as if we do not possess—this is a technique of sanctity. As Weil writes, "To possess is to soil."[6]

Famously, Weil commends affliction. By affliction she means not merely pain, disease, or despair. Affliction involves physical suffering, but suffering and affliction are not synonymous. Affliction is a psychic condition, one in which the possibilities of representation are removed. What the afflicted individual is enduring is not possible to represent in speech. The afflicted individual can only think of one thing: the affliction. Affliction is slavery, for representation is freedom, and affliction eliminates the possibility of representation.

If affliction is consoled, it loses its potency. Consolation is the work of imagination; it reincorporates the afflicted into a comforting story, an enchantment. It must be refused. "We must not weep so that we may not be comforted," writes Weil (14). The imagination functions by comforting our tears.

The more we weep, the more we are comforted, the stronger the imagination. When affliction is potent, when it goes uncomforted, it leads to detachment. For the only things left in a state of affliction are "the most wretched," and finding ourselves attached to such objects reminds us of the insignificance of all attachments. One who is afflicted is only attached to survival. Weil suggests the image of a man "stripped and wounded by robbers," one who has "lost the clothing of character" (25). Affliction trains for the hypothetical: to be able to live as if there are no possessions, as if there are no norms.

One could call what is revealed by affliction the exposure of our essential humanity, but this would have to be understood in a special sense. Stripped of "the clothing of character," whether in affliction or in dispossession more generally, in many ways the human appears just like an animal. But there is an essential difference. When faced with affliction, humans have a choice. Affliction creates a void. The void can be filled or accepted. For the void to be filled is for it to be filled with new imagination, a particularly invidious imagination. Someone or something must be blamed for affliction (is this *particularly* invidious, or is this, as Nietzsche would suggest, the foundation of all morality, of all imagination?). When the void created by affliction is first filled, we find imagination at its simplest: "doglike devotion," Weil writes, or "naked, vegetative egoism" (23). The gap in the normative universe, exposed by the moment of affliction that showed the inadequacy of a normative regime, is patched by deferring to some readily available normative authority: that of someone else, or that of one's own basest desires.

If one who is afflicted accepts, if she endures the void, refusing to cover it over with imagination, she is opening herself up to grace. Grace does not appear immediately; if it did, there would be no void, and grace would be a product of imagination, like so many gods. Indeed, the uniqueness of Christianity, in Weil's eyes, is its refusal of imagination at its root. There is nothing alluring or comforting about its meek savior, particularly when the story of Christ is stripped of all accouterments.

But is this not supersessionist logic in its most blatant (and explicit), with an ideal of otherworldly Grace opposed to a denigrated, this-worldly Law forming the crux of Weil's thought? From the very first pages of Weil's notes collected in *Gravity and Grace*, this image of her thought is complicated. Yes, there is gravity and there is grace; gravity has to do with the lawlike character of the world; grace has to do with evading this lawlike character of the world. A key image is the downward movement of gravity. Indeed, Gillian Rose associates Weil with Levinas, calling the two "angry angels" who oppose ethics to law.[7] But careful attention to Weil's thought shatters this caricature (though the caricature may well apply to her rhetoric). Grace, for Weil, is not located outside law; it is law shorn of its mystique, of the enchantment which holds it fast, which ties us to it. Like Kierkegaard's workaday saint, the ideal Weil commends is one in which the ordinary is disenchanted, not unlawful; indeed, it is fidelity to the very lawfulness of the ordinary that disenchants.

This is easy to misread. Weil's initial discussion of gravity and grace begins, "All the *natural* movements of the soul are controlled by laws analogous to those of physical gravity. Grace is the only exception" (1). An anomalous movement of the soul. Unnatural. To follow what is natural, to obey gravity—that is "the greatest sin" (3). However, while gravity goes down, grace does not go up. Grace goes down "without weight." To understand this is to understand Weil's thought. Grace is not, in fact, anomalous. It is a law, or rather the simulacrum of a law—or, rather, gravity is the simulacrum of the law of grace. It is grace that is true, gravity that is false. In the language of practices and norms, it is norms that are imperfect representations of practice. Strictly following norms will create the appearance of correctness, but only the appearance.

Forgiveness, refusal of praise, dispossession, and accepting affliction are exercises to aid in making the switch from living according to gravity to living according to grace. More precisely, they aid in switching to a life open to grace, for grace is an added component, something that cannot be forced by human action, according to Weil. But what does this life look like? Surprisingly enough, it looks like a life of doing one's duty—doing one's duty not motivated by feeling compelled to obey the law. "Obedience to the force of gravity," Weil writes, is "the greatest sin" (2–3).

The heart of imagination is the self, specifically the self as imagined—the beautiful girl thinking that she is the person she sees in the mirror. To crush the imagination of the self is to crush imagination, and the means to crush imagination of the self is slavery. Slavery, that is, to an impersonal master, to duty, to social norms. One does what one does, that is what is to be done (to say anything more about what is to be done is to employ imagination). This crushes the self because it makes withdrawal possible. There is no longer any choice, no need for judgment, nothing left for the self to do, so it withdraws. Necessity rules all. This is not the necessity of laws, which is the simulacrum of necessity. This is pure necessity, unrepresentable. It is for a human being to be like inanimate matter, propelled only by external forces. The self only introduces distortions, falsehoods. As soon as we are conscious of a choice that needs to be made, we have left the realm of necessity. Even if we choose rightly, if we make the most reasonable choice, we will be acting wrongly. Knowledge of necessity is not achieved through reason or through desire, nor through access to inner feelings. It is not knowledge at all. It is what happens when imagination is suspended; it is "inactive action" (39). This we find in ordinary heroes, the fellow heading home from work who would jump onto the subway tracks to save another man. It is not because of reason or desire. It is simply doing the thing to do. Holiness is a life of such inactive action.

Not only to do one's duty, but to do one's duty and to desire no more. To do one's duty because one desires reward, or because one desires to please, is to slip into imagination. What, then, motivates sanctity? It is not desire for an object, but what might be called, somewhat misleadingly, a desire for truth. For imagination is false. Affliction demonstrates that imagination is false, since from the perspective of affliction what seemed to be most important and most obvious no longer seems so. The only thing left is persistence in life, doing what one does, practice without norms. Weil characterizes this persistence as "waiting." It is not empty waiting, but waiting filled with "attention." It does not involve "desire," at least not in any ordinary sense: "It is only effort without desire . . . which infallibly contains a reward" (106). Indeed, Weil urges that we submit to our desires, but we must submit to them like we submit to any other necessity. We must desire without attachment to the object of desire, or to the desire itself.

Interpretation is heresy; the appearance is what it is. Acknowledging contradiction is a marker of sanctity. There is no contradiction in imagination, it is smoothed over. Through persistence, through what Weil calls attention, imagination can give way, contradictions are let be. This is what acceptance is all about: accepting contradiction. The order of the world is contradictory. Accepting affliction is but a special case: affliction is an affective contradiction. Accepting chance is another special case. Fortunes rise and fall: to offer an explanation is, again, to resort to the imagination, and to refuse sanctity. With acceptance, joys and sorrows are each treated similarly, just as the way things are, what happens, nothing more.

Simone Weil has been accused of anti-Semitism, of Jewish self-hatred. And it is easy to read her rhetoric this way, just as it is easy to read her as a supersessionist. She contrasts the "supernatural" God of Christianity to the "natural" God of Judaism. She considered worship of the Jewish God as idolatrous as worshipping Napoleon. She writes, "Israel is the Great Beast of religion" (146). But Weil never converted to Christianity. Might it be possible to read her thought, even more than Rose's, as too Jewish to be Christian and too Christian to be Jewish? Weil criticized both Judaism and Christianity for idolatry. Her praise of Christ is not Christian; it is not praise of the individual worshiped, or of the individual, or even of what the individual, Jesus Christ, represents. It is praise of a structure, one that prevents imagination; Christ is simply the label for that structure (and a tool for exploring it, and how it can be corrupted). At one point, she suggests that there is no difference between Christian virtue and Stoic virtue.[8]

The prose of Weil's works demonstrates their content. She employs an aesthetic of sanctity, as it were. Declarative, almost mechanical, austere, the steady advance of Weil's short sentences destroys and constructs at once. The steady advance bulldozes: it smashes and clears the terrain that enchantment has populated with manmade dwellings. In the rigor, the tightness of the construction, no space is left for that which would be outside. The words that enchant us, that comfort us, both thought and unthought, find themselves exposed, their dwelling places gone. Exposed, they die, at least in the space carved out by Weil's work. Yes, something is said, but what is said cleaves so close to the newly cleared landscape that it evades the risk of exposure. Something is said, but it is not words that can be toppled by the elements; it is barely words at all. The more words that are said, the fewer words there are—the more closely they cleave to the landscape, a landscape present but not represented. The words are simple. They are simple, but not obvious. The obvious provides shelter and comfort, which Weil refuses. Her words form a system, but this systematicity is not claustrophobic. Claustrophobia results from the chaos of new construction, but the new construction of Weil's writing is not chaotic. It is austere. Nor is the systematicity analytic. It does not take apart, it does not rearrange, it does not classify.

To use one of Weil's own terms, her prose refuses equilibrium. It is in the balance of our enchantments that equilibrium appears, not in the world itself. We create systems to make sense of the world, representations, approximations, heuristics. To appear plausible, these systems must maintain balance, lest their grotesque, constructed nature is exposed. Weil's prose does not maintain that balance, nor does it demystify through imbalance. It refuses affect in favor of straightforward declaration. Representation cannot be refused, but it is shorn of its identifying markers. This is not done through a realistic representation that would match as closely as possible our own, everyday representation. It is done through an austerity that refuses both the realistic and any imagination that would take its place—it is a prose that self-destructs.

To commend that which self-destructs is to refuse time. Weil aspires "To stop time at the present instant."[9] The techniques of sanctity Weil describes break the hold of past and future. Forgiveness and refusal of reward set aside what has been done, and destroy motivation for future action—motivation that relies on imagination. Dispossession and affliction cede the accumulations of the past and the promise of future accumulation, both material and psychic. The future no longer matters in the face of grave despair. The past is taken away, dramatically, in the case of the ancient exile. Not only is the exile taken from his homeland and enslaved, but his city of origin is destroyed, all of its inhabitants dispersed. There is no past, nothing to which he can return. Again, he is faced with a choice: will he endure the void or fall back on the comfort of some new imagination, some resentment? Imagination discarded, there is no future, no hope.

This stance toward temporality suggests a certain equivocation in Weil's work concerning the duration of sanctity. It is easy to read Weil—with an eye to her biography—as commending a life of sanctity. But, she also writes of "lightening flashes," moments when it is as if there is no law. These are the moments of encounter with the void, when a decision must be reached: is the void to be endured or is it to be reabsorbed into imagination. How are we to understand this? If the void is to be endured, does it not last for longer than the instant of a lightening flash? Endurance suggests that the void does not end, that it stretches out, that one continues to act as if there were no law, continues in practice as if there were no norms. Perhaps, when this paradox is taken to frame Weil's thought, the supersessionist overtones subside. Sanctity becomes strategy. It is techniques that she is describing and commending, not a state. There is a double hypothetical at work. Sanctity is practice as if there were no norms but it is only as if there is sanctity. "God fills the void," Weil writes, but is there anything more than hypothetical to fill?

To live a life of sanctity is "to cease to make the future our objective."[10] This is the technique and the result, once the void, filled by grace, has been narrowed to an instant. Techniques no longer are aimed at creating a void, and the grace-filled void no longer creates detachment. The void can be bracketed, leaving sanctity. In a phrase that was later reformulated by Gillian Rose, Weil links time, eternity, and devastation: "Time is an image of eternity, but it is also a substitute for eternity."[11] The question of an afterlife is moot. Once the pull of the future and the past, the pull of imagination, the pull of norms, once this has been set aside, then the fantasy of the eternal is also transformed into the preeminence of the blank concept of time. Not before, not after, not even now, but time pure and simple. Holiness is hidden from the world; if it is not hidden, it is not holy.

Reading Weil against herself, perhaps it would be more proper to call this holiness openness to holiness than to call it holiness itself. Holiness and the profane are equally concerned with fulfilling duty, but it is the reason that duty is fulfilled which distinguishes profane from holy. Or, rather, it is that the profane person needs a reason; the holy does not. Because of this, it is the holy person who is willing to employ the strategy of sanctity. She is already acting as if there are no norms, but it is only in specific moments when this becomes visible. When circumstances arrive to which norms cannot speak, the holy woman is the only one who remains calm. And this is the political relevance of the strategy of sanctity, prepared through exercises like those Weil described. In times of turmoil, in the midst of storms, the calm island of sanctity reveals.

CHAPTER 7

REVELATION

REVELATION, NOT RELIGION, IS A CONVERSATION STOPPER.[1] IN THE face of revelation, as it is used in everyday language, there is no need for persuasion, or judgment, or deliberation. It is perfectly clear what is to be done. Revelation brings clarity because it is extraordinary, supernatural. To know a truth of the natural world requires investigation, discernment; a truth revealed is transparent. A voice sounds from the heavens, stone tablets contain words engraved with a divine hand, pages of a sacred text set out the way things are. There is no need for interpretation: the booming voice is heard by all; the engraved stone is seen by all; everyone has a copy of the book with "holy" on the cover.

Revelation is authoritative, providing an indisputable reason for action that has the ability to trump other reasons for action.[2] This is the same way that a doctor is authoritative: in the fray of reasons competing to motivate actions regarding my health, the reasons offered by a doctor will trump nearly all others. Such is the case with any expert: we defer to their expertise, even when it runs against our own intuitions, against conventional wisdom. But the reasons of experts have the ability to trump only with regard to specific domains; revelation can trump our intuitions or conventional wisdom in any domain. Revelation is a conversation stop-

REVELATION IS
A CONVERSATION STOPPER —
A "POLITICS" OF REVELATION" IS
TO THE UNKNOWN

per because it is transparent and authoritative. There is no possibility for exegetical debate, and there is no possibility for debate about the relative weight of the reasons provided by revelation as compared to other reasons.

A politics of revelation is totalitarian. The decrees of the state are understood to be transparent and authoritative. There is no need for interpretation; interpretation would be contamination. There are no competing authorities; the state provides reasons for action that can trump any other reasons. There is no need for deliberation. To do more than regurgitate state decrees is, more likely than not, to challenge the state itself—it would be to implicitly contend that the revelation on which the state is founded is not transparent or not authoritative.

RELIGION IS WITH CONVERSATION BEGINS

Religion is where conversation begins. Religion brings structures of authority, layers of interpretation, and for both of these conversation is essential. Revelation is now at a distance, spatially and temporally. Distance distorts. Interpreters are needed. Conventional wisdom misleads. Interpreters are authorities; they offer reasons that trump. But these reasons no longer trump absolutely. They are not qualitatively different from other reasons under consideration; they are not above the fray. It is the words of authorities that matter, and these words themselves need interpretation. The distant point of revelation is itself empty, a black hole constituted by the material that it draws around itself, the matter of religion. So it is for the political analogue, when members of an aristocratic class set themselves up as the guardians of the genuine, timeless values of a society, as authorities who can see what is obscure to *hoi polloi*.

How convenient this ordinary usage of revelation and religion is! It felicitously brings us to the present: democracy is politics after revelation, and after religion. There is no absolute source of normativity, just the revel of conflicting and contested norms. There are no absolute normative authorities, as each citizen can, with her own capacity of discernment and of judgment, identify and weigh norms. Democracy comes at the end of political theology, after politics has been freed from analogy with theology. But might the opposite be said? If the logic of the language of revelation and religion is taken seriously, might we find in democracy an uncomfortable return to revelation? Is it not now the will of the people that is transparent and authoritative? If an election is "free and fair," there is nothing that can trump its results, and no need for interpretation. A state that fails to respect the will of its people is deemed rogue, illegitimate. This is the case if it suppresses demonstrators, the violent images of which exemplify heresy against democracy: the people's will is ignored. It may be the case that only a small fraction of the population participates in a "free and fair" election, only a tiny fraction may take to the streets in protest—but they are still *the people*, still the site of revelation. They may vote or march for myriad reasons, but these have no bearing on the content of the revelation they produce. God's motives are bracketed (even though we are sure they are good).

This is to say nothing beyond the rhetorical, to toy with everyday language. Enchantments secure themselves in many ways, sometimes with the language of revelation, sometimes with the language of religion, sometimes with the language of atheism. But enchantment itself has the character of revelation in the extreme: so transparent as to be invisible, so authoritative as to not seem like an authority at all. It is just the way things are. Everyone can see *that*, to question *that* is to be automatically wrong, opposing reasons are preemptively trumped. Historical accounts of secularization and political theology are misleading because they make it seem as though the character of enchantment is changing—for instance, from revelation to religion to democratic atheism. But the character of enchantment is not changing; only the effects of enchantment change. The effects are above the surface, visible. The enchantment of democracy privileges the people (a mythical entity if ever there was one); other enchantments privilege gods or their earthly interpreters. From this perspective, too, revelation, now no longer in the everyday language sense, seems politically impotent. It would refer to nothing more than enchantment itself. Revelation would just refer to the source of normativity—norms themselves—no more.

Perhaps there is another way to think about revelation, one that is neither taken from everyday language nor simply refers to enchantment as such. What if revelation is an event? Revelation would, of course, be a special sort of event. It would not be an intraworldly event, like the event of a train arriving, or snow falling, or a birthday party.[3] These events seem impersonal: "It happened." Although they seem impersonal, they do happen to someone, to many people. But the person to whom such events happen is not affected in any profound way. The self is not put in question; it remains fundamentally the same before and after the intraworldly event. And the world is not put in question; the intraworldly event is inscribed in the world, taking a place in a network of causality. Such an event is part of the course of ordinary life, part of what one finds when navigating practices and norms.

There is a second sort of event, one for which the label of intraworldly is not sufficient. There are events that shake things up. There are events that are not inscribed in a world but which are located in a world, and which make that world opaque. In light of such an event, the world is not as comprehensible as it once seemed. At the same time, such events put the self experiencing the event into question. The self is required to interpret the event—to make sense of the event in light of the now confusing world. The world and the self change, together, in the wake of the event. The event itself does not receive its meaning from the world; the world receives meaning from the event.

Claude Romano suggests that an example of such an event might be the arrival of the first automobile to a small town in the American South.[4] The event does not arrive from nowhere—the town has a context, and townspeople are aware that cars exist and are becoming increasingly prevalent. But the world of the town is made opaque by the first car's actual arrival. The car does not fit in: it travels awkwardly on the dirt roads. Individuals are unsure how to treat it (the car is traded for a racehorse). Individuals living in the town take part in a hermeneutical enterprise brought on by the event. They must interpret it, and in doing so they change their worlds and themselves. In this process, doing this hermeneutical work, tensions within the community are revealed, as well as larger tensions, such as those between rural South and industrial North. These tensions had been smoothed over in the world before the event, in the world where enchantment was transparent. The event makes enchantment opaque, its workings are exposed, and enchantment must be reworked.

Yet another type of event seems even closer to revelation. This third sort of event, like the second, is not intraworldly. It does not receive its meaning from the world; it makes meaning. Like the second type of event, this third type of event makes the world seem awry. But unlike the second type of event, jointly adjusting the world and the self through reinterpretation, it is not a possibility. The only way to make sense of the event is to radically alter the world—so radically alter it as to make the new world incomprehensible from the perspective of the world beforehand. This event has the potential to bring about an all-encompassing Gestalt switch. What was previously impossible becomes possible, what was previously invisible becomes visible. Such an event only creates the possibility of such a shift: it is up to the individual to decide whether or not to be committed to it. Alain Badiou, offering a detailed description of this sort of event, terms commitment to it fidelity, and he argues that fidelity is constitutive of subjectivity.[5] The subject is subject to an event. The capacity to be faithful to an event is what differentiates humans from animals.

Badiou points to the French Revolution, Galileo's scientific innovations, Haydn's musical innovations, the Chinese Cultural Revolution, and the love between Héloïse and Abelard as examples of events in this sense. Each affects a radical shift in the possibilities available to those who embrace it. The world looks different after the event. In love, the roses never smelled so sweet; in a revolutionary situation, the family doctor becomes a representative of the oppressive intelligentsia. From the perspective of one faithful to an event, the babble of all others is mere opinion, idle chatter devoid of truth (pseudoscience). One who is devoted to an event is committed to something outside of himself and outside of his community, something not recognized by those around him. It is a lonely vocation.

Confusion about events, on this third view, is common. Their simulacra abound. Fidelity to a simulacral event, on Badiou's view, is evil. Such simulacral events are not genuine because they do not involve a complete switch away from the situation in which they arise. They are recognizable from the perspective of the world before the event because the event privileges some aspect of that preevent situation, organizing the postevent world around that aspect of the preevent world. Nazism is a simulacral event because, while the worlds of those faithful to it do radically shift, they shift around a predetermined axis. Jews are made the enemy, but "Jew" names an aspect of the situation before the event; after the event, "Jew" names the same group. There has not been a Gestalt switch, just a reconfiguration. A genuine event brings a new universalism. The old social standing of every individual is lost, and in their commitment to the event they share a common humanity.

If revelation is to be associated with the third sort of event, it would only be transparent and authoritative ex post facto. From the perspective of the world beforehand, the event is merely a glitch. But from the perspective of the subject faithful to an event, the event takes on the familiar characteristics of revelation. It is authoritative: indeed, everything else is reduced to opinion, trumped by reasons produced by those faithful to the event. It is transparent: from the perspective of the faithful, it is in need of no interpretation. Abelard and Héloïse take their love to be perfectly obvious, as do proponents of the Cultural Revolution, as do composers working in the wake of Haydn.

This third account of the event clearly makes possible an understanding of revelation that does more than authorize the status quo. It does quite the opposite. Revelation understood as this sort of event is precisely that which rejects the status quo, that which rejects enchantment. Does it not inaugurate a new enchantment? On Badiou's account, events are rare, and it is fidelity to the event that matters. Past events may haunt, but these are ghosts, not live events to which a subject could be faithful. Reenchantment only begins once the single-minded devotion, and the attendant universalism, of fidelity to the live event passes.

But isn't this third understanding of the event clearly, blatantly, supersessionist? Badiou writes of St. Paul as a prime exemplar of fidelity to an event. Paul is faithful because of his rejection of the particularity of Jewishness and his embrace of the universality of the Christ-event. The specificities of Jewish law are replaced by the all-encompassing embrace of Christian grace. What could be more supersessionist than this? An echo of this supersessionist impulse is found on the philosophical level in Badiou's work. Being and event are understood as disjunct, equiprimordial. Badiou characterizes the structure of being in terms of set theory: some elements are included in sets, some sets are subsets of other sets, and so on. The event, represented as a null set, is different in kind than being.

Is there a way of describing this third sort of event that avoids supersessionism? Perhaps what might be involved in doing so will become clearer if we return to the second account of the event, the one that associates the event with the work of hermeneutics. In that case, the event suggests a novel practice for which there is not yet a norm. Something new *is done*, but there is not yet a thing *to be done*. A car arrives in town for the first time, but there are not things that one is supposed to do with a car. Existing norms do not adequately apply. The norms concerning what one ought to do with a carriage or a buggy are clearly inadequate. A new norm must be developed, and in the process existing norms that have been taken for granted are brought to light. They may need to be modified in the process of altering the normative plane in such a way as to cover the newly expanded territory on the plane of practice.

The second account of the event describes this renegotiation as the work of the subject, as constitutive of the subject. But this seems to elide the social nature of norms, as well as their primacy. The subject is constituted by norms. Focus on the subject's hermeneutical labor subordinates practice and norms to something quite mysterious. Indeed, there is a supersessionist logic at work. On this second account of the event, a choice is forced. Subject and world can be understood naïvely, as wholly subject to a causal network. Or, they can be understood as dynamic, changing in relation to each other. The advance from the former to the latter view is made possible by the event. By means of grace escape is possible from the stifling realm of law. Yet this account of the event retains interest once we have set aside a supersessionist logic and restored practices and norms to primacy. The event still makes the world opaque, but this is not due to the agency of the subject. Autonomy is restored to the event as well: it is the event that has agency, in a sense, not the event that gives the subject agency. Revelation happens; it does not happen *to us*.

The direction in which the second account of the event is being revised brings it quite close to the third account. It is the event that happens, and individuals may embrace it or not. Translating into the language of practices and norms: as in the second account, in the third account what happens is a practice which norms do not speak to, which thus thins enchantment. But in the third account, latent in this new practice is an entirely new set of norms. *Entirely* new: the problem with the simulacrum of an event, on this account, is that it is a new practice which brings about new norms, but not entirely new. This translation into the language of practices and norms rotates Badiou's language ninety degrees clockwise, shifting its alignment from the ontological axis to the temporal axis. Where Badiou dis-

[Handwritten margin notes, left side:]
E.G. CAR MANRS FOR 1ST TIME

(TOO MUCH) FOCUS ON HERMENEUTIC LOSES SIGHT OF PRACTICES & NORMS THAT SHAPE THE SUBJECT

REVELATION HAPPENS? 7

INSTEAD A PRACTICE ARISES THAT THINS ENCHANTMENT EVEN AS IT BRINGS ABOUT AN ENTIRELY NEW SET OF NORMS

cusses what there is, this translation presents what one does. Badiou refers to presentation and representation as modes of being; these are translated into practices and norms. Sometimes something is presented but not represented; sometimes something is represented but not presented—just as it is with practices and norms. Out of this mismatch comes the possibility of the event. The worry about supersessionism translates into a worry about the possibility of replacing all norms at once, in a Gestalt switch. To be committed to this possibility does require faith—but not the virtue of faith. The faith it requires is a faith in the impossible, the unknowable, faith in another world as yet unseen. This is not the virtue of faith, the disposition to persevere in worldly life; it is supersessionist faith.

Both the second and third accounts of the event are ostensibly opposed to an understanding of the event as strategy. On the third account, if it were possible to use the event strategically, what seemed to be an event would actually be just a simulacrum of the event, for the shift it affected would be motivated by some aspect of the situation before the event. The second account is more amenable to strategic use, since the event is understood as an occasion on which subject and world are reconfigured. But the second account gives the event a primacy more fundamental than strategic. According to this second account, life, understood rightly, consists of interpreting events, each opening up a new realm of possibility following from the previous, beginning with the initial event, birth.[6] It might seem as though an event, then, would always be used strategically, appropriated by the subject in ways advantageous to the subject. But once the social nature of the hermeneutical process is taken into account—that it is social norms that must be reformed in light of the event—then the possibilities for strategic usage evaporate. The event is then simply the engine that animates social life, turning norms and practices from static to dynamic; the motivation to interpret the event is categorical, the choice against stasis is not hypothetical.

Perhaps there is a way to appropriate elements from the second and third accounts of the event in order to put together a nonsupersessionist account of the event—an account of the event as revelation and as strategy. When there is a protuberance of the plane of practices to which nothing corresponds on the plane of norms, an event is the reconfiguration of the plane of norms so that the two planes again correspond. This reconfiguration may be radical, but it cannot be total. Such a transformation is in the interests of those disadvantaged by the current configuration of the plane of norms. There are many of these: people whose lives are barely livable because the practices most dear to them are deemed contrary to the normative order. For these, the strategy of revelation offers the potential for that mismatch to be righted—or rather, for its violence to be dissipated, although its violence can never disappear.

How could a protuberance in the plane of practices come about? Certainly an event is one way, one occasion for revelation. But there are other occasions: for instance, sanctity. As the previous chapter discussed, sanctity is practice as if there are no norms. The plane of practices, untethered from the plane of norms, spreads out according to its own whim. Its shape no longer matches the shape of the plane of norms. There are protuberances, occasions for revelation. Here, again, the difference between sainthood and sanctity is manifest. Sainthood never involves revelation. The saint imitates; her behavior is authorized by supposed revelation. She confirms enchantment. In Lacanian parlance, the saint believes that she has direct access to the voice of the Other, to revelation. In the case of the corresponding politicians, both Bush and bin Laden chat with God. The saint, or politician, or criminal thinks that she has set aside the plane of norms, but in fact she is inscribed at its very heart: she hears the words of enchantment undistilled.

Sanctity does not intend to reveal, but that is its effect. The practices of sanctity—forgiveness, refusing reward, acceptance, and so on—untether practices from norms, leading to novel practices not covered by norms. Sanctity is not total, it is strategic. When sanctity is supposed to be total, there is never an occasion on which the untethered practices must again confront the plane of norms. It is this confrontation that produces revelation. Words of revelation come from the lips of one who employed the techniques of sanctity and who is then confronted head-on with the plane of norms.

Here appears a tempting error. If sanctity is practice as if there are no norms, and revelation is the reconfiguration of norms that results from sanctity, then is it not the effect of revelation to narrow the gap between the plane of norms and the plane of practices? The reconfiguration affected by revelation, since its provenance is the plane of practices, would seem to bring the two planes closer than they were before. Indeed, is this not the point of revelation as a strategy: for those whose lives are made nearly unlivable by the current configuration of the plane of norms to have some relief, for their practices to be authorized by the plane of norms? Everyday usage would suggest that the life lived in light of revelation is a life with more sanctity (not necessarily a life of sainthood). Or, put another way, if sanctity is a life of acceptance, is not revelation all about sharing the good news that acceptance leads to a better life with the world?

Such a view is not only erroneous, it is pernicious. It is yet another guise of supersessionism. Its aspiration is to hallow the world, to bring the holiness that appears in the techniques of sanctity to everyone. To call the space between the plane of norms and the plane of practices a distance is to speak metaphorically. The space is not measurable; it cannot grow or shrink. It simply marks the fact that the very nature of norms is to misrepresent practices; the very nature of practices is to misperform norms. But acceptance sounds pleasant, like the sort of thing that everyone should aspire to, not only those appropriating it for a strategic purpose. How clever it would be if the content of revelation were just to accept life as it is! How "Buddhist"! And how wrong! The error hinges on an equivocal understanding of acceptance.[7] As usual, this is an equivocation between the everyday usage and the usage that refers to practices and norms. The everyday usage, which takes revelation as acceptance to mean the collapse of the distance between the plane of norms and the plane of practices, affirms that whatever is done was the thing to do, the thing to do is whatever will be done. Acceptance in terms of practices and norms is precisely the opposite: it is the acceptance of the distance between norms and practices, acceptance that what is to be done will not be done, what is done is not what was to be done. Acceptance in the latter sense may be used strategically, as a technique of sanctity. Acceptance in the former sense is an acknowledgment of the way things are, an acceptance of the hegemony of the visible.

In the writings of James Baldwin, we find an example of revelation as a theopolitical strategy. Baldwin has been read by some political theorists as quintessentially democratic.[8] In typically sophistic fashion, academic advocates of radical democracy regurgitate Baldwin's work and find in it an exemplary way for radical democrats to talk about race. That is, they find a language with which they are comfortable, which does not challenge their convictions—all the more troubling because they proclaim their admiration for the way in which Baldwin disturbs. They write that Baldwin does not take anything for granted, he interrogates categories, he acknowledges difficulty, he does not offer easy solutions, he affirms American democracy but at the same time is very critical of it. He champions the powerless but he is also cosmopolitan, he affirms human worth but also human particularity. He wrote that "all theories are suspect." In short, Baldwin is supposed to affirm what goes by the name of radical democratic political theory, a postfoundationalist pluralism that comforts those with a vague idea that leftist politics is desirable but with no desire to get their hands dirty. A very comfortable position, indeed—for the reader of Baldwin who does not want to read.

For to read Baldwin is to find an intricate textual practice, one in which a drama featuring the plane of norms and the plane of practices is played out. A writer who has achieved excellence, as Baldwin has, necessarily avoids easy answers. Excellent writing is writing that is equivocal, equivocal all the way down. There is no firm base, no shared beliefs or concepts on top of which a narrative is constructed. Excellent writing works in the opposite direction, starting with shared beliefs and concepts and working them, not until they transform into something else, or until they are exposed for what they really are—not until anything. There is no terminus. This is an effect, one achieved through literary conventions. These conventions are also taken as the starting point. They are worked, without end. The descent from convention to the depths of equivocation does not proceed along with the time of the narrative. It is an effect of the literary work as a whole. Every component of the literary work—the wording, the phrasing, the ending, the tempo, the voice—is a tool used to effect the end of equivocation. Of course, this is just to say that literary excellence persuades the reader to return to a commitment to the ordinary by shattering enchantment, refusing any sanctified alternative. It is just to say that literary excellence cultivates the virtue of faith. It is not a world without norms that the excellent work extols; it is tension between practices and norms, and the work of navigating that tension, that the excellent work both performs and commends.

This is why it is confused to read a politics from Baldwin's literary style or from the content of his writings. Many of his essays and stories are excellent, not because they state that "all theories are suspect," or because they show that "all theories are suspect," but because they *perform* the proposition. To perform it cannot be reduced to saying it. To say it is a heuristic, an abbreviation, an unequivocal marker of equivocation. But it quickly becomes more than a marker when it is associated with a politics. Troubled norms become new norms; norms have transformed. To say this is to refuse to read, for to read is to work, it is to open oneself to equivocation and to see how far down it goes. To read is to discern the norms at play, to track their play, and to search for its terminus. Excellent literary work can be read and reread because the search for a terminus is endless. Baldwin's worst writing refuses precisely this, using language to say something rather than using it to do something.

There is an obvious peculiarity involved in considering James Baldwin as part of an antisupersessionist canon. Perhaps he is post-Christian, or has what is banally called a *complex relationship* with Christianity, and perhaps this qualifies him as antisupersessionist in a certain sense. But does he stand in any way between Judaism and Christianity? In a way, yes. False religion (of the church) is juxtaposed with genuine religion (of the loving and suffering ordinary)—but of course such an easy contrast would not permit equivocation. False religion, the god of the father, the god of law, is not erased by a new god, a god of the son, a god of love. The god of the father is put under erasure. It is present but impotent. The father is a failure, but allegiance to the failed father is the only option available. What the son must do is to fail better. The son must be committed to a god that will fail (the son is often portrayed as a stepson, structurally a failure in the father's eyes).

Baldwin's worlds are infused with the rhetoric of religion. The word *Lord* fills the ears. There are sinners and there are saints, and everyone knows which are which. This is the axis along which all of Baldwin's narrative oppositions lie, or seem to lie: an axis religious and familial, and much else. The rebellious son must be brought up into the law, into the realm of the saints. Father and mother complement each other's efforts to do this. But the center of the narrative is askew, set off this axis but not perpendicular to it. The center of the narrative is often the stepson. In "The Rockpile," the father's role with respect to the children is "to end their freedom."[9] He is the pastor. He brings religious law. Another order tempts. It is not the secular, for there is no secular in Baldwin's worlds. There is true enchantment, false enchant-

[margin note: FALSE ENCHANTMENT of FALSE RELIGIOUS TRANCES]

[margin note: The son]

ment, and the work of disenchantment. The rock pile that gives its name to Baldwin's story is the locus of false enchantment. Neighborhood children give it mythical significance. This false enchantment tempts the son, the pastor's son, who "felt it to be his right, not to say his duty, to play there" (15). The son's commitment is not just to the false enchantment; it is to master the false enchantment, to fight (and fail, like his father) in order to stand on top of the rock pile. Yet the stepson, torn between the enchantments of his half-brother and stepfather, is the center of the story.

[margin note: YET THE STEPSON IS THE CENTER OF THE STORY]

Paternity askew is everywhere in Baldwin's work, from his first novel, *Go Tell It on the Mountain*, to the letter to his nephew, named James, that opens *The Fire Next Time*. Near the start of Baldwin's collection of essays *Notes of a Native Son*, he writes, "The most crucial time in my own development came when I was forced to recognize that I was a kind of bastard of the West."[10] It would be easy to take the title as ironic, describing precisely what the author is not. It is also tempting to take the title of the collection as exploring a tension: Baldwin both is and is not a "native son." But perhaps it is better to talk about a tension worked—worked, not explored: writing, good writing, is not writing *about*. It posits, pushes, reaches an impasse, reformulates, posits again. Irony halts this work. It is from the position of the son askew that this tension can be worked, for he is both bound by paternity and rejected by paternity.

One of the first essays in Baldwin's *Notes* is a dismissive discussion of Richard Wright's *Native Son*. The trouble with Bigger Thomas, Baldwin charges, is that he is created in response to a portrayal of blacks as devoid of humanity, and that Bigger himself is portrayed as devoid of humanity. His actions are overdetermined by the system of racial oppression in which he finds himself. His core is hollow. Yes, he is human, and he is black; and in portraying a black human Wright has gone further than his predecessors. But he has not portrayed black humanity. Bigger is narrated into the white story because he is stripped of his own story: "Bigger has no discernible relationship to himself, to his own life, to his own people, nor to any other people—in this respect, perhaps, he is most American."[11] Bigger is not part of a black tradition, of a history-bound community of shared practice (significantly, his father is absent). Baldwin compares him unfavorably with the Jew, a figure who "left his father's house" but retains distinctive practices. The Jew would never consider himself a "native son." It is not that blacks do not have tradition, according to Baldwin, but that blacks' tradition has not been articulated—a distinction without a difference. A tradition is the expression of "the long and painful experience of a people," it is their "struggle to survive" made articulate (28). Wright's failure to depict Bigger as part of a distinctive tradition is a failure, not only because it gives the misleading impression that there is not a tradition of which he could be a part, but all the more because tradition is constituted in its expression, its representation. The failure to represent is a performative failure that *does* harm by representing harmfully.

Bigger's name no longer starts with an *n*—he is not that, but he is not something different. "Bigger's tragedy," according to Baldwin, is "that he has accepted a theology that denies him life" (17). Perhaps we could say that Wright betrays the superficiality of his critique in the superficiality of the switched letters, *b* for *n*, while the structure—the theology, as Baldwin puts it—remains. *Native Son* displays precisely the structure of paternity which Baldwin so despises. If the rock pile is the son's enchanted counterpoint to the father's vapid theology, Bigger's theology of rebellion is the native son's counterpoint to the generic white oppressor's equally vapid theology. Father and son share a theological axis, and this is what must be set askew: theology, but also paternity.

Native Son, a book notably lacking in reference to kinship, is a book about family dysfunction; Bigger's theological shortcoming is at the same time a shortcoming of paternity. Paternity is the quintessential gift, for it is a gift that gives itself—and so, according to Jean-Luc Marion, it displays the theological essence of the gift.[12] It is not reducible to scientific, or social-scientific, data. Paternity may be connected with politics, with economics, with biology, but none gives a sufficient explanation of fatherhood; such an explanation does not even come from the aggregation of insights of all of these disciplines. Fatherhood is a gift—that is, something given from one to another. But this giving cannot be wholly anticipated or controlled. Nor can it be wholly explained: cultural and religious values underdetermine birthrate. It is a gift that begins in possibility rather than fact, the possibility of a child; that child itself is underdetermined, its future unpredictable. Moreover, the possibility of giving the gift comes from the gift itself: it may

be given only by one who himself has a father. There is no way to reciprocate for the gift of paternity. The son was given by the father what he
could not give himself; any attempted return would be worthless. A man
may have a child, but this does not repay the gift of paternity given to the
man from his own father. As a result of this analysis, Marion concludes that
paternity is not reducible to the conventional understanding of a gift, one
that can be broken down into giver, givee, and object given. Instead, fatherhood is a phenomenon that is given just in its giving. Paternity "marks the
sole indisputable transcendence that all human life can and must recognize
in its own immanence; with the result that if we ever have to name God
with a name, it is very appropriate to call Him 'Father.'"[13] Paternity opens
up a space before ethics (reciprocity, on which ethics is founded, is impossible between father and son); it negates the principle of noncontradiction
which founds metaphysics (paternity is a gift not equal to itself, for if it was
it would be reducible to exchange); in short, paternity is the worldly marker
of "unconditioned possibility," securing the legitimacy of theology even in
a culture where metaphysics and ethics are under fire.

What is most striking about the way Marion folds paternity into theology is that both theology and paternity are said to open up a region immune from worldly critique. This is not a realm of reason, this is a realm that
gives reason. It is "never wrong, but always right" (134), it "renders to reason
its full validity" (133). It is unconditioned; reason is its effect: immanence
and transcendence are one. And we have arrived here through reflection on
fatherhood. The duplication in the phrase *native son* does not indicate du-
plicity; it signals the unbounded excess of fatherhood that envelops the son
as always already native. Wright attempts to harness such a rhetoric to re-
store Bigger to his proper status as son; Baldwin's critique, put starkly, is that
Wright is ironing a wrinkle when it is the cloth itself that is the problem.
For that cloth presents itself as paternal-theological, unconditioned possibility, immanent-transcendent. To realize that this theo–paternal object of desire
is conditioned, *is* limited, and *limits* possibility—that would be revelation.

The alternative to the theological-paternal axis sounds at first like a
quaint humanism. Baldwin writes, "The failure of the protest novel lies in
its rejection of life, the human being, the denial of his beauty, dread, power,
in its insistence that it is his categorization alone which is real and which

cannot be transcended."[14] It sounds as though Baldwin is affirming that there is something that cannot be transcended: the human being, which Wright has misdescribed. It sounds as though it is the human being in its multiform complexity which cannot be transcended, and which transcends "categorization alone." It is still through reflection on the immanent, on human life recognizing its own immanence, that transcendence is reached—the difference is just that for Baldwin human life recognizes its own immanence in the ups and downs of life rather than in life itself, in affect rather than in flesh. Indeed, Baldwin writes that "the finest principles" that do not match up against what happens in life must be modified. He loudly refuses sentimentality. Indeed, he suggests that sentimentality distorts and prevents understanding. White people don't understand black music because of sentimentality. What is the portrayal of "beauty, dread, power" if not a trigger of sentimentalism?

It is an invitation to acceptance. In the sentence before the representation of "beauty, dread, power" is affirmed, Baldwin writes, "Our humanity is our burden, our life; we need not battle for it; we need only to do what is infinitely more difficult—that is, accept it" (17). There is a tendency to both run away from and toward "reality." This is how theology, and injustice, are maintained. Everyone is excited by reality, no one looks at reality, no one accepts reality. By reality, Baldwin is not making a claim about the external world. He is talking about the ordinary. Baldwin uses "beauty, dread, power" as appositives to "life." They are used rhetorically to describe the substance of life, the substance of the ordinary. Baldwin understands his own work to describe just this: life. Or, more precisely, the goal of his work is to lead readers to acceptance of life. Describing ordinary life is not always (indeed, is never) the way to achieve this goal. Stylization is necessary. Life is disorderly; the artist is to bring order to it. But it is stylization that is in the service of this end: stylization that grips the reader and shakes the reader, shakes her free of distortions, of enchantments of the ordinary. Baldwin urges, and practices, rhetoric, but it is rhetoric rooted in philosophy, in a deep understanding of practices and norms. The writer, he writes, rhetorically, must "go beneath the surface to tap the source."[15]

For the privileged, acceptance is a luxury; for the disenfranchised, it is a necessity. It is a necessity, but it is far from certain. Acceptance is all that can

be hoped for, and it is not really a hope at all. Other hopes are enchantments; they purport to offer solutions to disenfranchisement but their effect is to further entrench disenfranchisement, to perpetuate horrors. The
problem with most literature depicting blacks (Baldwin takes particular aim
at *Uncle Tom's Cabin*) is that it refuses acceptance—not unexpected if this
literature is written by the privileged, or their imitators. In such literature,
stark choices are posed: "For or Against." These choices, Baldwin counsels,
must be refused. But this is difficult, especially for the disenfranchised. The
reason is obvious: *to stay alive.* Discernment is impractical in the face of
life-threatening dangers. Living an enchanted life is understandable for the
disenfranchised; it is inexcusable for artists purporting to represent the interests of the disenfranchised. Writing enchantment on behalf of the disenfranchised often incorporates them all the more securely into enchantment.
Implicit in Baldwin's reflections on the work of the artist: the sense that for
the disenfranchised to become enfranchised, it is necessary to persuade the
privileged to do the difficult work of acceptance. The disenfranched are
continually exposed to the ugly underside of enchantment; they have tremendous motivation to urge on critique, but none of the resources.

Writing autobiographically, Baldwin identifies the moment that he became a writer: it was the moment when he acknowledged that he had hidden from himself and began the work of acceptance. He realized that he
"hated and feared white people," and that he "despised" black people (4).
He did not accept the world, he was afraid of the world—that is what
the world had taught him. Writing is the process of unlearning. In no
sense was this acknowledgment a "coming out." He did not realize that
he was hiding and then accept who he was. Rather, he began the work
of acceptance. Sentimentality marks those who remain fully enchanted.
It reduplicates enchantment in its representations. Enchantment mystifies
the ordinary by smoothing it over through affective investment. No longer is a person doing what she does; now she is comfortable doing so,
she is attached to doing so, to do otherwise would be a loss. And we are
comfortable with her doing what she does. Aesthetic sentimentality takes
the enchanted ordinary and doubles the enchantment. It is "the ostenta-
tious parading of excessive and spurious emotion," and it is symptomatic
of what Baldwin refers to as "inhumanity" (10). Again, the category of

*BALDWIN
ONTOLOGY*

"humanity," like that of "reality," does not bring with it, in Baldwin's usage, the metaphysical baggage with which many critics saddle it. Inhumanity is "dishonesty," "fear of life," "aversion to experience." In other words, to be human is to live, to navigate the world. To be inhuman is to be alive without living. It is no longer to live in the enchanted ordinary, but to live in pure enchantment. What is done no longer matters. The violence of the world is hidden: sentimentality is "the mask of cruelty."[16]   *BALDWIN'S own writing + thinking style*

The quite obvious suggestion made by Baldwin's choice of title—calling his essay collection *Notes of a Native Son*—is that his writings will fill out the missing humanity of Bigger Thomas. Baldwin's authorship will fill in the "beauty, dread, power" that is missing from Wright's portrayal. Baldwin's writings are not intended to portray black men, they are to portray black humanity. Perhaps there is a better word than they portray: they *reveal* black humanity. The actions of Bigger Thomas show infelicitous revelation. They display something new, seemingly incomprehensible from the perspective of the present, from the hegemony of the visible. They show a figure with the potential to be authoritative. It is clear *what* he is but not *who* he is. To find such an individual in one's world, even in a fictional world, would hold the potential to force a shift both in oneself and in one's world—so it would seem. But it does not. This is the failure of the protest novel, the failure at which Baldwin takes aim. The question—of *who* pitted against *what*—is foreclosed by a rhetorical failure. What makes *Native Son* so captivating, the affective force of its narrative, is what hobbles its political efficacy, what makes its revelation infelicitous. It is the question of who pitted against the question of what that gives the narrative its affective force, which drives it relentlessly because it drives Bigger. Ultimately, the question is ignored. It does work, animating the narrative, but it is not worked. In the place of his soul, a void; in the place of revelation, satisfaction. To see the black soul bared: that would be frightening.

Baldwin's work is intended to do just this. It can be done best, it seems, as specific interventions, "notes," reflections on particular, quite ordinary, incidents. A black musical group goes to segregated Atlanta; Baldwin is absurdly caught in the Parisian bureaucracy; Baldwin travels through a Swiss village where the children have not seen a black man before. These events are recognizably ordinary, and they are stylized in such a way as to bring

out that familiarity. No one is going about starting protests or acting in
ways that run against norms. But these are notes *of a native son*. Every black
man, Baldwin suggests, has a bit of Bigger Thomas in him. This is Baldwin's
revelation, the revelation that his aesthetic practice is intended to affect. It is
affected by the uncomfortable juxtaposition of "notes" with a "native son."
The native son can write! And in the strongest sense: he can do the work
of writing. The "notes" depict life itself, all the silly little things. But they
are not silly, they are tragic and comic, not because of stylization—the stylization only renders them familiar—but because they involve native sons,
black folks just acting in ordinary ways. We are shown practice—and then
the norms come crashing in. Practice spread out so naturally in the narratives, so recognizably, that the brute force of the norm is put in sharp relief.
The black musicians are just young people doing what they do, playing and
singing. At first, their hosts seem to be acting as good hosts—until the stark-
ness of racial norms is enforced (they are refused work and are tricked). An
ordinary trip to the Swiss countryside turns bizarre as children who have
never seen a black man tug at Baldwin's hair.

Baldwin's prose, like Wright's, is animated by the disjunction between
who one is and what one is. While Wright's prose directly harnesses this dif-
ferential, Baldwin's prose proceeds more subtly. For Baldwin, in his "notes,"
the question is first repressed, then revealed. It is first as if the black man
is living in the ordinary, navigating practices and norms. Then, suddenly, it
becomes clear that this was not the ordinary at all, this was practice with
norms set aside. Practice has spread out in unauthorized directions. Eventually, inevitably, there is an event, a confrontation with norms—norms now
revealed to be much less natural than they seemed. The son is reminded that
he is a stepson, that the father's authority is unnatural. But the son cannot
leave the family: he is native.

Revelation
reminds
the son he
is a
stepson

CHAPTER 8

PROPHECY

THE PROPHET, IT WOULD SEEM, HAS UNIQUE ACCESS TO THE FUTURE. She uses that access, informing others what will happen—prompting those she tells to act differently today. The prophet does more than predict the future. Anyone can do that. Everyone does that. Unlike everyone else, the future has been revealed to the prophet. Her knowledge is unequivocal and authoritative. So it prompts action.

The words of the prophet need not be specific. She has access to the future, not necessarily knowledge of the future. It could just be a feeling that she has, not a feeling about the future but access to the feeling of the future. The future will be bright or gloomy, jubilant or uncomfortable. Feelings of the future, just as much as knowledge about the future, prompt action. Knowledge or feeling—or, the prophet could have access to something in between, to something opaque which refers to the future but which is incomprehensible now. In such a case (which is, perhaps, every case), the work of interpretation is the clearest. The prophet is authoritative, undeniably, and her words motivate—but not always decisively. They need interpretation, though the prophet is her own best interpreter. Interpretation is inextricable from the contest of reasons. The words of the prophet do not necessarily provide a decisive reason for action, though they do prompt action. There is another mode of prophetic speech: the prophet may speak in the conditional, accessing multiple futures. If certain actions are taken, a certain future will, certainly, follow.

A false prophet does not have unique access to the future, but acts as if she does. She is motivated entirely by the same reasons as everyone else, but cloaks them in the guise of prophecy to lend them authority. She takes advantage of the office of prophecy, the tropes and vestments of prophecy that make one who uses them recognizable as a prophet. Though its distinguishing features change, it is a permanent office. From John Winthrop to Martin Luther King, Jr., prophecy transformed, but the office of the prophet remained: authoritative, unequivocal even if conditional, providing a counterpoint to the mundane.

Or so it would seem. The enchantment of the ordinary makes prophecy plausible. Enchantment can be mastered; the ordinary cannot. Enchantment is smooth, unified, comprehensible. The ordinary is jagged, coarse, atonal. Prophecy is a counterpoint to enchantment, entrenching enchantment by means of a time outside of time. In this way prophecy is, as one would expect, closely associated with hope and melancholy. Secularizers of prophecy, those who would shake off religious enchantment—in favor of secular enchantment—cannot stomach knowledge of the future, much less authoritative knowledge. The concept of prophecy must be made comprehensible, so these secularizers conclude that prophecy is actually not about the future but about the past.

Talal Asad describes prophets as "creative poets who expressed a vision of their community's past—the past both as renewal of the present and as a promise for the future."[1] What distinguishes the prophet, for Asad, is not a predictive ability but a creative ability. The practice of prophecy is an aesthetics of representation, where the object represented is the past and the means of representation is whatever can make its object speak to contemporary concerns. We are stuck in certain ways of thinking about our current situation, and these ways of thinking limit the options available to us and the places we can go from here. Prophecy is to be understood, according to Asad, as a specific technique to shake up these ways of thinking, to see problems in a new light, and so to have a new set of options. This shaking is done by accessing the reservoir of history, presumably because history has prima facie rhetorical force (because people think that there is some value in history, if not in its replication then in its "lessons") and because it is relatively unfamiliar; the somewhat strange concepts and experiences provide leverage on the all too familiar concepts and experiences of the present.

Similarly, Greil Marcus writes, "Predicting the future is soothsaying; prophecy has more to do with the past than the future. America's prophets prophesy one thing: as God once judged the Children of Israel, America has to judge itself."[2] Here the emphasis is quite different than it was in the case of Asad, but their shared refusal is clear. The prophet still draws on history, but history no longer opens up new possibilities: it judges. "America's prophets" perform a clever rhetorical maneuver, displacing God at the same time they draw on His authority. The impetus to judge comes from mimicking God, but the basis of judgment is historical. God's actions are historical so they both provide a basis for judgment and its impetus, the judgment that judgment is necessary. The jeremiad makes perfect sense, is perfectly rational—whether it is spoken by Abraham Lincoln or by Allen Ginsberg.

In these secular translations of prophecy, the prophet's authority comes, not from privileged access to the future, but from privileged access to history. In the same way that, in the everyday view of prophecy, anyone can predict the future but only the prophet has authoritative access to the future, in these secularizations, anyone can read history books but only the prophet has access to history, access that can make it authoritative for the present. The prophet has not read more history books than anyone else, but brings to the enterprise of prophecy, the office of prophecy, a certain je ne sais quoi.

There is another option for the secular purifier of prophecy. Prophecy may be understood as critical rather than historical; the prophet's powers are in her ability to cut through barbershop babble and speak to the heart of things. Future or past may be invoked, but doing so is part of the office of prophecy, not of its content. The prophet retains unique access, but now it is access to a realm of the pure normative, outside of time and outside of place. Its only characteristic is that it holds the mysterious force of an "ought."

Prophecy, according to Emmanuel Levinas, is the voice of ethics in a world concerned with justice. To do justice is to give each his due; that is, to allocate fairly to all, providing none with more than he deserves, and none with less. Justice has to do with institutions, with laws, with administration. Ethics has to do with singularity. Ethics is the birthplace of normativity. When confronted with one human being, stripped of all social roles, uncategorized—in his nudity, as Levinas puts it—then everything is owed to him. In such a situation, this other human being, this Other, is entirely vulnerable, and I must provide. Indeed, that is all I must do; encountering the Other is the root of justice. As soon as I see another human being in his nudity, I see another, and yet another, and yet another—I see the world. They are all vulnerable, they all demand; the only thing to do is justice. But in doing justice, we forget its origin, we forget ethics. On occasion, we are reminded of ethics, reminded by "prophetic voices reverberating imperiously beneath the profundity of established laws."[3] The relationship between justice and ethics is asymmetric; ethics is infinite while justice is finite. Prophecy is the voice of the infinite in the midst of the finite.

Our everyday concepts and calculations, where only remnants of ethical substance remain—this is what prophecy moves us beyond. Where it takes us, for Michael Walzer, as for Levinas, is a realm of the pure normative. But for Walzer this realm is within ourselves; it is our community purified, its most basic values exposed. The prophet calls out practices that differ from that normative core. A natural feature of humanity is to tell lies to oneself and to others, to use "everyday evasions" that create a "veil . . . over the more ugly features of the world."[4] Removing that veil is the work of the social critic—and of the prophet, when that office is understood rightly. In ancient Israel, priests were concerned with ritual requirements, prophets with ethics, and, on Walzer's view, ethics always trumps ritual. Prophets were not "ecstatics or visionaries" who would find a domain of ethics entirely outside Judaism (as Levinas might have it); they looked within, to the most basic commitments of the community, commitments often neglected but never totally forgotten.[5] On this view, the prophet is like the Renaissance madman, a figure without reason who is the most rational—that is, who cuts through the distortions of reason to display to us who we really are. What she says may be shocking, but it is recognizable and it prompts action.

When prophecy is understood as critique, as Levinas and Walzer suggest, it remains a counterpoint that secures the polyphonic beauty of the whole. The melody is nothing without the harmony, the guitar nothing without the bass. It is, of course, that aesthetic desire that exposes secularization as secular enchantment. It is the desire to surpass the ordinary that exposes these accounts of prophecy as supersessionist—which is to say the same thing another way. But there are hints in Walzer's account of prophecy of a nonsupersessionist alternative. For are those dearest values of a community that the prophet recalls any different than norms, than those norms implicit in the practices of a community? But Walzer says a little too much. He speaks of community, of norms of a community. For him, norms and practices do not go all the way down; communities are the rock bottom. Communities have norms, for Walzer, but on the nonsupersessionist alternative communities are constituted by norms. The political consequences are obvious: a community can change, its values at one point in time greatly differing from its values at an earlier time, but it retains its identity as *that* community (it is tempting to attribute Walzer's political views concerning Israel, and its "defense," to this view).

Walzer should be focused on the audience of the prophet, not the community of the prophet. The prophet is a rhetorician; she speaks to an audience and attempts to persuade that audience. A prophet, understood in this way, may look as though she is invoking the values of her community, but actually she is invoking the values of her audience—an audience which may understand itself as a community (the prophet, of course, may promote this self-understanding as part of her attempt to persuade). But the prophet is more than a special rhetorician who favors certain rhetorical techniques, those that belong to so-called prophetic language. How the prophet is more than this is contested in the competing understandings of prophecy—is the supplement historical or critical?

The choice between the historical and the critical understandings of prophecy is forced only because the secularizers of prophecy do not understand prophecy as a rhetoric, do not appreciate the prophet's vocation to persuade. Cornel West understands rhetoric. Indeed, according to some of his critics, that is all that he understands. And West writes at length about prophecy. He writes about the prophetic voices of others, about the role of prophecy, and sometimes—seemingly unaware of the appearance of hubris—of his own work as prophetic. Indeed, when West is writing of "the prophetic critic," he seems to be describing his own chatty and opinionated alter ego. He extols his listeners and readers to keep alive "prophetic thought and action," but he associates so much seemingly disparate content with such thought and action that it is easy to dismiss West's invocation of prophecy as, at best, rhetorical in the pejorative sense.

In his most direct discussion of what prophecy is (in this case, "prophetic thought"), West offers four characteristics associated with it: discernment, connection, tracking hypocrisy, and hope.[6] Discernment involves "the capacity to provide a broad and deep analytical grasp of the present in light of the past" (3). West goes on to emphasize the necessary consciousness of hybridity involved in discernment: when talking about jazz, although thought of as Afro-American, we must not forget that it is made possible by European musical instruments. Connection, the second element of prophecy, is another way of talking about empathy, about the "attempt to remain in contact with the humanity of others" (5). By tracking hypocrisy, West means that prophecy involves critique of ourselves and others when there is a mismatch between what is said and what is done. Hope, according to West, is a component of prophecy because the world is unfinished and the future is open-ended. However, West's commitment to hope is nuanced (or, perhaps more accurately, he uses hope rhetorically). Giacomo Leopardi, one of West's favorite poets, who he describes as presenting "deep-sea diving of the soul," writes, in a line West singles out for admiration, "I refuse even hope."[7] Prophecy, on West's view, has nothing to do with unmediated access to God. Rather, it has to do with the historical (discernment, finding resources in the past to open up possibilities for the present) and the critical (tracking hypocrisy to expose the mismatch between practices and norms). It also has to do with rhetoric (connection and hope, both evoked in the audience to which the prophet speaks). For West, the historical moment and the critical moment are not sharply distinguished. By offering a historical account of privilege, drawing on a "subversive memory," it is revealed as contingent and so opened to critique.[8] The rhetoric of hope is critical, it calls into question the necessity of the current arrangement; the rhetoric of connection is historical, bringing people together based on a shared past. There is a sense in which discernment and tracking hypocrisy are just as much rhetoric as connection and hope. The former pair also are intended to persuade, just by different means. West is worried about the world tearing people apart;

PROPHET HAS VIRTUES OF FAITH & LOVE

prophecy, even in its critical moment, brings people together by appealing to their history, their values, their collective existence, their possibilities.

At the end of the day, prophecy, for West, is "democratic" because it is situated "in the midst of the quotidian, the commonplace, in the midst of the messy struggle in which one's hands are dirty."[9] In other words, prophecy does not have unique access to the pure future, the pure past, or the pure normative. The prophet could be anyone. All that is necessary to become a prophet is commitment to "moral convictions," and for one to attempt "to convince others that [these convictions] ought to be accepted even though these moral convictions themselves can still be subject to criticism."[10] While the prophet could be anyone, she is not everyone. The prophet has a certain character, a commitment to her convictions and a willingness to bring those convictions into the fray, to try to persuade others of them and to allow herself to be persuaded. In other words, the prophet has the virtues of faith and love: she is disposed to navigate the ordinary, to negotiate tension between norms and practices without settling for easy answers. *True (Western) prophet v. false prophet*

The distinction between true and false prophecy now becomes a distinction between those prophets who do or do not have the virtues of faith and love. The false prophet may assume the office of the prophet, employing its language and techniques, but the false prophet lacks the willingness to wrestle with the practices and norms of the ordinary. This is the critique that West levels at much institutionalized religion. While it may use language that sounds like prophecy, when its ultimate concern is either pure "management" or pure "vision," what results is the simulacrum of prophecy; that is, to be more blunt than West is, false prophecy.[11] The potential for genuine prophecy is everywhere, and the work of the prophet is to shake things up, to redescribe what seems dominated by management or vision in terms that blend the historical, critical, and rhetorical moments of prophecy, grounded in the virtues of faith and love. *WEST PRESCRIBES THE...*

Genuine prophecy is contagious: the rhetoric of prophecy lays the groundwork for more prophecy by breaking up the impediments to prophecy, purely managerial or visionary ways of approaching the world. West redescribes the American democratic tradition by underscoring the contributions of Emerson, Melville, Morrison, and Baldwin, figures whose "penetrating visions and inspiring truth telling" combine appeals to history,

DEMOCRATIC TRADITION

critique, and the function of rhetoric to bring together community, open new possibilities, and, ultimately, to persuade.[12] West, writing prophetically, redescribes American democracy by emphasizing the centrality of prophets; in doing so, he opens the space for future prophecy, space that would have been foreclosed by the managerial or visionary outlook. When the prophet is understood as a rhetorician, she need not stand in the midst of the community to which she speaks. She only needs to persuade effectively. West speaks to Christians but also to Jews and Muslims, in each case prophetically speaking of prophets and distinguishing genuine prophets from false prophets.

West's account of prophecy refuses to identify a je ne sais quoi that would stand beyond or behind prophetic rhetoric. Prophecy is the public speech of the virtuous; its authority does not derive from somewhere else, it does not speak from on high. The authority of prophetic speech comes about in its own felicitous utterance: it provides a reason for action because it persuades by mimicking the everyday, when the everyday is not smoothed over with enchantment. It is jagged, incomplete, contradictory; these features are harnessed in the rhetoric of the prophet, according to West. Genuine prophecy refuses the hegemony of the visible, which is exploited by the managerial (and, ironically, by the visionary, for the visionary's utopia is nothing but a projection of the present). Yet something is still missing. West characterizes the ordinary as "the quotidian, the commonplace," but he elides the texture of the ordinary, its individuated norms and practices. Without this texture, West's account of prophecy is not qualitatively different from those of prophecy's other secularizers, it is just that West locates authority in the everyday (quotidian, commonplace) rather than in some more mysterious realm. But the everyday is itself wholly mysterious when it is characterized only in the negative, as not enchanted (not interpreted in a managerial or visionary manner), when its only positive characterization is its name. There is a quietist moment in West's thought, and it is seductive. The everyday is simply what remains when we stop theorizing, yet out of the realm of the everyday prophecy gains its voice. The rhetoric of prophecy persuades by mobilizing an ensemble of techniques to strip away distortions, but the movement is motivated by a sense that such a movement is inherently valuable because of what remains—the quotidian, the commonplace.

Perhaps this limitation of West's account of prophecy is most evident in his treatment of the work of Michel Foucault. West argues that the prophet (this time the "prophetic pragmatist") can accept Foucault's answer while rejecting his question. Foucault's question is "Kantian"; it is always a question about the conditions of possibility. Foucault's answer is a genealogical inquiry that makes available "strategic and tactical modes of thinking and acting" (though sometimes Foucault's focus on rebellion as such or the microphysics of power elide this ultimate conclusion).[13] Prophecy is speech that persuades its listeners to take part in such thinking and acting, and genealogical inquiry is one of the means by which that persuasion is affected. The prophet, according to West, is uninterested in the "Kantian" question because "the question itself is inextricably tied to a conception of validity that stands above and outside the social practices of human beings."[14] Here we find the quietist impulse that often seems to animate West's work on prophecy. Concern with validity obscures—indeed, taints—the quotidian, the commonplace ("social practices of human beings" (225)). The problem, of course, is that social practices and social norms—the Kantian questions *quid juris* and *quid facti*—are always already intertwined. That West finds in the everyday a realm free of law is here made particularly clear. Genealogy, for West, is a means to shake off questions of law, to free ourselves from the illusions that prevent us from speaking with the authority of the everyday.

In contrast, Foucault is concerned with both the social practices of human beings and the social norms which constitute and are constituted by those practices. This is precisely the meaning of Foucault's slogan, "Where there is power, there is resistance."[15] Resistance is impersonal because of the primacy of norms and practices; they come before subjects, they constitute subjects. It is by means of genealogy that this interplay between norms and practices, between power and resistance, becomes visible. In Foucault's genealogical investigation of sexuality, he demonstrates how the concept of sex has served as an "anchorage point" for sexuality. Seemingly most natural, sex is conventionally opposed to its various cultural manifestations. The view that the Victorian period was one of great sexual repression is plausible because of this focus on sex. The Victorians talked, and acted, very extensively in ways relevant to sex, but if all of these words and actions were aimed at prohibiting sex, then the Victorian age truly was one best characterized by repression.

If, on the contrary, we set aside sex as the anchorage point of sexuality, if we suspect that the centrality of sex may have been produced as an "artificial unity" by sexuality rather than vice versa, a different picture emerges. Now, all of the varied components of sexuality are on equal footing: "bodies, organs, somatic localizations, functions, anatomo-physiological systems, sensations, and pleasures" (152). When this move is made, the ubiquitous tension between norms and practices is exposed. It is no longer laws that regulate, and repress, sex, but myriad norms that at once regulate and constitute the practices of sexuality. It is only once this genealogical move has been made that we can turn to political strategies and tactics. If this turn is made prematurely, political practice—for instance, the gay rights movement—will take sex as an anchorage point, focusing its fire there. The more that sex is contested, the more deeply entrenched it becomes, and the less the complex texture of practices and norms is at issue. In contrast, if genealogical analysis comes first, it is "bodies and pleasures" (that is, the myriad norms and practices associated with sexuality) that are the necessary site of contest. The means of contest, as Foucault writes: "the strategic codification of these points of resistance that makes a revolution possible" (96). In other words, sex enchants, it hides the points of tension between practices and norms of sexuality. Once those are exposed, the work of politics—or at least one political strategy—is to suggest a new anchorage point, one that enchants in a new way, that affects a paradigm shift, as it were, by making sense of puzzles (points of resistance) present but smoothed over in the old paradigm.

Here we find the key to prophetic politics. Prophecy is a strategy; it employs rhetoric. But to ensure she is using a genuine theopolitical strategy, the prophet must refuse the hegemony of the visible. The quotidian, the commonplace, the everyday, this is subject to the hegemony of the visible—even when it is understood as tragic, unless this tragedy results from the tension between practices and norms. The challenge that the rhetoric of prophecy faces is to make visible the invisible. This is the supplement to rhetoric which constitutes prophecy. While historical and critical moments can both be useful rhetorical tools, they must be employed in the service of this supplement. Foucault's work on sexuality demonstrates two rhetorical techniques to make visible the invisible. One is setting aside a purported anchorage point; in other words, putting the name of the law (what Lacanians like to call the Name of the Father) under erasure. This is not a practice of acting as if there are no norms; it is a rhetoric that persuades by inviting the listener to (temporarily) set aside a view of norms as homogeneous Law. With Law set aside, norms—and the tension between norms and practices—are exposed. To underscore those tensions is the second, though coprimary, technique employed by the rhetoric of prophecy. It is coprimary because it is through exposure to such tensions that it becomes plausible to put the anchorage point of Law under erasure. Such tensions expose the limits of the explanatory power of Law; they are themselves exposed by setting aside the unified view of Law.

Authority of the Prophus7

When prophecy is understood theopolitically, its authority is still derived from its performance, but the way in which that performance resonates with its listeners shifts. Authority is no longer derived from listeners recognizing in prophecy their own quotidian, commonplace experiences (although listeners will certainly hear of such experiences). Rather, authority is derived from what is familiar but unrecognized. The prophet harnesses the authority latent in the tension between practices and norms. There is no way to directly refer to this tension: if there was, it would not be a tension; enchantment would have succeeded completely. However, there are markers of such a tension that the prophet harnesses. An affective remainder, left by incomplete identification, is present in even the most thoroughgoing enchantment. This is how prophecy is authoritative: rhetoric harnesses such affective remainders in order to persuade, whether it be through the names of gods and spirits or through quotidian details of life. The type of rhetoric employed does not distinguish the genuine prophet from the false prophet. In genuine prophecy, the tension between practices and norms underlies prophetic rhetoric. If that is absent, then prophecy is simply a counterpoint to enchantment, making enchantment all the more enchanting. In other words, the false prophet does not put the law, the Name of the Father, under erasure. *Prophut must put Father/Law under Erasure*

Putting the Name of the Father under erasure is characteristic of James Baldwin's prose. In the previous chapter, we saw the way in which Baldwin troubles the conventions of paternity by focusing on the position of the stepson. In his essay "Notes of a Native Son," in the eponymous collection, it is not only the position of the son that is put in question but also the position of the father. The essay focuses on a transformative moment in Baldwin's life, and in its portrayal we find a stylization motivated by an underlying commitment to the instability of law, a rhetoric made possible by the erasure of the Name of the Father. Indeed, that is precisely how the essay begins: "On the 29th of July, in 1943, my father died." Of course, it is not the event of the father's death that is significant; it is the realization that the father (the Father), his authority, was already dead. But that is getting ahead of things.

There are three threads of the essay's narrative, three threads that begin together, then separate, then, together, present a conclusion. They begin together: the father is dead, a child is born, and there is a race riot. The child who is born is Baldwin's brother, his father's child. But in the intersection of death and birth, and social tumult, it is also the author who is formed, who is born. After knotting together birth, death, and social ill in his first paragraph, the second begins, "The day of my father's funeral had also been my nineteenth birthday."[16] The author is the eldest son, and he is coming of age. It is the reworking of this familiar narrative—the son taking the place of the father, transforming the anger he has with his father into identification with his father—that gives Baldwin's essay its force. What Baldwin is to realize is that he cannot take the place of his father because his father did not have a place. That is the problem of race in America: the impossibility, and necessity, of coming of age, of becoming a black man. But, again, that is getting ahead of things.

Where there is a father there is a god. The father was a preacher, a man of God. In his wake, after his passing, the order of the universe is shaken. Outside the window: "the spoils of injustice, anarchy, discontent, and hatred were all around us" (71). From the perspective of the son, of the author, this violence "had been devised as a corrective for the pride of his eldest son" (71). The father had been a believer in the apocalypse; the son, the prideful son, had not. The heavens were to prove him wrong, it seemed. The father is, most certainly, otherworldly. No one is quite sure of his age. He comes from the South, the "Old Country" that his children have never seen. He looked "like pictures I had seen of African chieftains" (72). He had "tremendous power." And he was black, dark, dark black. Unknown, and unknowable, from a different place, a different time, an ancestry from which the son, in the New World, in New York, was cut off, the father was a black deity. The provenance of his authority was afar, but it provided him with an authority which was absolute. Baldwin's essay does not provide his name. His name is always already absent.

The father appeared like an African chieftain, but he was not one. His mother had been born in slavery. He appeared to have unlimited household authority, but he did not. The father forbid playing Louis Armstrong records, but one of his "strong-willed female relatives" hung a picture of Armstrong in their home and stopped the father from removing it. The father appeared to be a man of God, but he moved from the employment of church to smaller church to yet smaller church. There was no demand for his religious services. All of this might have gone unnoticed by Baldwin, the son, had it not been that the father's authority over his own family was undercut. A white schoolteacher offered to bring the young James to a play, an activity forbidden in the Baldwin household. Carefully choreographing the outing, James informed his father when the teacher was already en route to pick him up. The father was expectedly displeased, but "very much against his will," he consented. In that moment, it became clear that this will of the father, which seemed so mighty, with its mysterious, otherworldly authority, was not omnipotent. In the face of the white world, the white teacher, the father could not demur. The immediate result of this incident was that Baldwin would "despise" his father.

It is tempting to read this childhood memory as typical of a coming-of-age narrative. At first, to the child the father seems all powerful, then something happens that makes the child realize that the father's powers have limits. But in this case, although the conventional form is being employed, something else is going on. In the conventional story, the father begins as the all-powerful source of normativity. What is wrong is that to which the father says "no." He is the final authority: in the face of the father's approval or disapproval, there is no appeal. Realizing the limits of that authority does not lead to freedom; it leads to the dispersion of normativity across the social world. There is no longer any one person who, alone, determines what is or is not to be done. For any situation, there remains something that is or is not to be done. But now it is not enforced by the penalties of the father; it is enforced by the penalties of society, penalties more often implicit than explicit. Sovereign power becomes disciplinary power, singular law becomes multiple norms. This transition is nearly seamless for a well-reared child. The father approves and disapproves of more or less the same things that society approves and disapproves of. The father's authority is a heuristic, normativity made explicit for the child so as to aid in proper acculturation.

This conventional coming-of-age story of the shift from the law of the father to the norms of the social world does not explain the paradox of authority encountered by the young James Baldwin. The authority of social norms cannot seamlessly take the place of Baldwin's father; his father's blackness causes a mismatch. To do everything right in the eyes of his father still would be to do something wrong in the eyes of society. And his father knows that. His father is in an impossible position. When the teacher comes to take James to the play and his father consents against his own will, it is not that the father's power is limited. It is that the father's power is put under erasure; it exists in a shadow. He is not one among many fathers; he is one among many black men, but a black man in America can never be a father, can never assume that symbolic role. In other words, the black man can never succeed as a father: even with his very best efforts to inculcate what one is and is not supposed to do, he will never succeed in inculcating social norms. His son will necessarily have to look elsewhere, to another authority—not simply an authority to supplement the father, as the white child would need to do, but an authority that ignores and overrides the father.

Such a situation inhibits the virtues. To be virtuous requires discernment; it requires seeing a situation rightly and responding rightly—all in the same movement, without thought.[17] The virtuous person perceives herself to be in a situation that calls for courageous action and acts courageously, perceives a situation that calls for mercy and acts mercifully: perception and act occur in a single movement. But a single movement is not possible for a black man living in the shade of white authority. Perception must be double, for two authorities can hold sway at once. A situation can, must, be perceived doubly. Those perceptions are held together: at the theater, James still knows his father objects; he still knows that his presence is wrong at the same time that it is right. Action cannot seamlessly follow from perception; thought is always needed. Where am I? Who is looking at me?

In such a situation, faith and love would seem senseless. Why put one's own practices in play in relation to another's when they are not one's own practices at all, when they follow the norms of either the father or the teacher? Is not fantasy—the fantasy of the transcendent object of love or the immanent proximity of love, both the same—is this not tremendously more plausible than the virtue of love? To be subject to two authorities at once, does that not foreclose the possibility of putting myself at stake by providing a slippery escape for the self when it is called into question, an escape which solidifies both authorities? When pressure is put on the authority of the teacher, the authority of the father is there to fall back on, and vice versa. The young James Baldwin, in this essay, masterfully manipulates this situation around the axis of his mother, using her to convey the importance of "education"—that which the teacher brings—to the father. When the father is unemployed, the mother happily accepts help from the teacher, acting black again for the family. The mother, as mediator, calls the teacher "Christian" ("the highest name she knew"). The father, subject to his own authority, "never trusted her"; he always suspected that there was something "cunningly hidden," some "hideous motivation" (92). The tragedy of Baldwin's father, and perhaps his nobility, was that he insisted on but one authority; he refused to navigate between.

It seems as though there cannot be love, and as though there cannot be faith. Faith would involve a commitment to work through the difficulties, to navigate the shoals. But, holding two authorities at once, there is an easy explanation for any difficulty, for any tragedy. It is the work of the other authority. For Baldwin's father, it is the work of invidious whites; for the whites Baldwin encounters, it is blacks' refusal of white authority that leads to their ills (the ills not only of blacks, but of whites as well). The virtue of faith is superfluous, though the language of faith abounds. Indeed, if Baldwin's literary worlds are anything they are worlds of faith; they are saturated with the language of saints and sinners, cries of "Lord," preachers and ecstasies and conversions.

Perhaps supersaturated: Baldwin's worlds exude a language of faith, a language used to mark a crucial distinction. "Whose little boy are you?" was a question posed both by church women and the people of the street, the pimps, drug dealers, and gamblers who lived next to the saints in Baldwin's youth. (It was also the question Baldwin felt he was being asked by Elijah Muhammad when Baldwin visited with the Nation of Islam leader.) This was faith posed as a choice and paternity posed as a choice. The two answers are opposite and the same. To be the son of a minister, a son of the church, to see the world composed of saints and sinners and align oneself with the saints, that is what faith means in Baldwin's literary worlds. Baldwin charges that to align oneself with the church is to align oneself with the principles of "blindness, loneliness, and terror," not "faith, hope, and charity"—the former are the same principles guiding the street lifestyle of the dealers and pimps. The only possibility of black faith, it seems, is reactive, enchanted, a faith that ignores difficulty; in the end, it is a faith of soothing words, not of a life of difficult commitment. Street life enchants with possessions and drugs; church life enchants with comforting words and the illusion of a loving community. The virtue of faith is impossible, in both cases, because there are not one but two normative seas to navigate. Just as one's skills at navigating one sea begin to improve, everything that has been learned is undercut by the authority of the other. It makes more sense to float than to sail; or, to float and imagine that one is sailing.

The crippling affliction faced by Baldwin's father is that, unlike other black man, he refused illusion. Nothing soothed the discord between the two authorities, and he went mad. He descended into psychosis, recognizing no authority outside of himself, making up his own rules as he went along and applying them to the world around him. The psychotic who believes herself to be Napoleon turns the world into her empire, bringing each happening into the Napoleonic story, making her friends generals, her doctors advisors, her children citizens. It is much too simple to say that, as Baldwin's father degenerated into psychosis, he became increasingly paranoid, increasingly convinced that the world was out to get him—to trap him, to poison him, to kill him. Rather, to be black in America in 1943, and to believe that one was black, was as mad as believing oneself to be Napoleon. It was to be committed to an authority which was constantly undermined, and yet to stick with that story, to incorporate the world into that story. It was to refuse to split authorities and elide the self, and it was to refuse to elide the possibility of faith. It was to be faithful when faith was impossible and mad.

To make sense of the world from this perspective, Baldwin's father had to be paranoid. He was always paranoid. He thought the white teacher could only have ill intentions toward his son. He could not understand why she would take an interest in the young James. There was a moment, Baldwin writes, when the family discovered that James's father was ill. Before this moment, he had just seemed unpleasant—indeed, "indescribably cruel" and "the most bitter man I have ever met" (87), according to the essay's narration. That was just the way he was, it was his personality. Yet "the discovery that his cruelty, to our bodies and our minds, had been one of the symptoms of his illness was not, then, enough to enable us to forgive him" (74). At his passing, his children only felt relief. Their father had hated the world, and had hated his children for mingling with the world. Even if this hatred was a symptom, its effects were what mattered to the children, and there was nothing in the father's attitude or behavior to mitigate those effects.

The young James Baldwin was mad, too. That is what he thinks the locals in New Jersey believed the summer he was working in factories there, before his father died. "I acted in New Jersey as I had always acted, that is as though I thought a great deal of myself . . . with results that were, simply, unbelievable" (77). Before that summer he had, of course, heard of segregation and Jim Crow policies, but he had never experienced them. When he experienced them, "I simply did not know what was happening." It did not take him long to understand, but that did not change how he acted. His coworkers and supervisors disliked him; he was fired from jobs. And the townspeople "really believed that I was mad" (78). The metaphor of illness recurs: the year in New Jersey is likened to contracting "some dread, chronic disease," a disease that is sometimes in remission but at any moment can return. Every black man in America, Baldwin suggests, has this disease. There are two options: "living with it consciously or surrendering to it" (94). Like his father, he refused enchantments that would make sense of two authorities, that would surrender to the disease. He was committed to one authority, committed to his blackness, committed to living consciously with the disease; the white world was no more than an impediment, at most a pseudoauthority.

James would go to all-white restaurants again and again, waiting for service. This habit led to the moment when James's madness reached a point at which he snapped, and so differed from his father's madness. It led to revelation, which made prophecy possible. One evening in Trenton, after watching *This Land is Mine*, Baldwin and a friend went into the "American Diner." After being told "We don't serve Negroes here," Baldwin went into a rage—his madness boiled over. On the crowded street, it seemed that everyone was "moving toward me, against me, and that everyone was white" (95). The madness became physical: "I felt, like a physical sensation, a *click* at the nape of my neck as though some interior string connecting my head to my body had been cut" (80). Ignoring his friend, he headed into a restaurant. When a waitress appeared to tell him that black people would not be served at that restaurant, Baldwin planned to take her neck in his hands—or so he writes. But she did not come near enough, so he hurled a glass of water at her. He ran, and escaped.

Afterward, Baldwin realized that he could kill, and he could be killed. He realized his life was in danger. And he realized that this danger was caused by "the hatred I carried in my own heart." Here is revelation in the theopolitical sense, in a peculiar configuration. There was practice as if there were no norms; or, rather, practice as if there were no norms of the white world. The plane of practices spread out according to its own whims—until it violently encountered the plane of norms. Out of this collision came a reconfiguration of norms, a reconfiguration for Baldwin with the potential to catch more broadly. He discovered that he had, within him, the same bitterness as his father, and the same bitterness as every black American. This, not the encounter with the white teacher, is the moment at which Baldwin comes of age, becomes a man. He realizes that his father is not unique, neither uniquely powerful nor uniquely impotent. He is like his father and both are like all other black men. Is this more like acculturation than revelation? Baldwin refuses to be acculturated, at least not in the standard way. He refuses to be dominated by the bitterness he shares with other blacks, either by descending into madness as his father did or by salving it with enchantment, as church goers and street folk do.

Another option appears, one which was not visible before Baldwin's revelation. The option involves acknowledging the difficulties of the world and refusing the domination of hatred. This option has two sides. First, "acceptance, totally without rancor, of life as it is, and men as they are" (113), acceptance of a world in which injustice is commonplace. Second, "that one must never, in one's own life, accept these injustices as commonplace but must fight them with all one's strength," a struggle that begins "in the heart" (113). Conventional wisdom has it that struggle against injustice can only be fueled by hatred and despair. Baldwin suggests quite the opposite: that struggle against injustice ought not to be fueled by these damning emotions, yet the fight must continue "with all one's strength." How can such a fight, a total war, arise out of acceptance?

It is tempting to take the final paragraphs of "Notes of a Native Son" to culminate when Baldwin recognizes the legacy of his father as offering resources for him, as opening opportunities for a future that remains open-ended. On this reading, Baldwin's alternative to all-consuming hatred, to bitterness of heart, is a combination of piety and hope, a combination of looking backward and forward, critically appropriating the past in light of the challenges of the present in order to move toward a future that we participate in determining.[18] This is what religion does, Baldwin seems to be saying, a possibility that is neither to be abandoned nor embraced. When Baldwin meditates on one of his father's favored biblical passages—"But as for me and my house, we will serve the Lord" (Joshua 24:15)—the religious language can be given a deflationary meaning. Baldwin can embrace this passage as a legacy of his father to which he can give his own meaning. This is possible because of acceptance, because of his even-tempered view of his situation, a view that is not skewed by hatred or fixation on artificial (for example, racial) divides. The struggle against injustice is to be motivated by this paternal legacy; fidelity to that legacy means struggling against that which would compromise it, and that would mean struggling against injustice.

But this reading is unsatisfactory. It is a reading that succumbs to the hegemony of the visible, fixing its terms in relation to what is remembered and what appears possible. Baldwin's father lived "like a prophet," he was "in such unimaginably close communion with the Lord that his long silences which were punctuated by moans and hallelujahs . . . never seemed odd to us" (74). The legacy of the father was a call to faith, a call to total commitment never fully justified. The scriptural passage favored by his father on which Baldwin meditates as he travels to the cemetery is posing a choice: "And if it seem evil unto you to serve the Lord, choose you this day whom you will serve; whether the gods which your fathers served that were on the other side of the flood, or the gods of the Amorites, in whose land ye dwell: but as for me and my house, we will serve the Lord" (94). There are false gods and there is one true God, the Lord. This Lord does not deflate into the rhetoric of piety and hope. Heralded by the father, it is faith in Him, in the God of the father—when the father is put under erasure, when the God of the father appears impotent, when faith is truly unjustified—this is the faith which can fuel a struggle against injustice "with all one's strength." Baldwin gives Scripture a different interpretation than his father. For Baldwin, commitment to the Lord involves the virtue of faith, for it is premised on acceptance. It begins with an understanding of the ordinary, of practices and norms. Faith comes about in the intersection of the ordinary and the invisible; prophetic rhetoric names and performs that intersection.

Does this not mean a refusal of the commonplace, a refusal of acceptance? Acceptance need not mean taking things as they appear. Indeed, the work of Baldwin's essay is to bring about acceptance by means of refusing to accept things as they appear. At the start of the essay, Baldwin's father is cruel and quarrelsome, the race riots are chaotic and apocalyptic, and the birth of Baldwin's new sibling is a pure blessing. Acceptance means stripping oneself of these easy images. The preacher at the funeral spoke of "a man whom none of us had ever seen—a man thoughtful, patient, and forbearing, a Christian inspiration to all who knew him." This image, so absurd to those who knew the deceased, was, at the same time, "in a sense deeper than questions of fact, the man they had not known, and the man they had not known may have been the real one" (88). At the funeral, surrounded by his father's children, children James had helped raise, memories and fragments of popular culture pass through his mind. These memories do not form a legacy onto which James intends to build; instead, "I thought I was going mad." In these "Notes of a Native Son," it is not the father's legacy that brings reason. With the father under erasure, his name missing, the father brings madness, which is at the same time a call to faith. Not faith in madness, but faith that things need not be taken as they are given, they may be more than they appear. The race riots surrounding the funeral were themselves caused by misperception, on scales large and small. Rumor had it that a black soldier had been shot in the back protecting a black girl from a white policeman, but in fact the soldier was not shot in the back and the girl was a prostitute. "They preferred the invention because this invention expressed and corroborated their hates and fears so perfectly" (92). Prophecy not only calls out enchantment, it calls to commitment. By directing commitment to an unrecognized God, the prophet is not primarily concerned with prediction, history, or critique; she is concerned with the systematic violence of norms, and she addresses that concern with her rhetoric.

Prophet talk is concerned with systematic violence or norms

CONCLUSION

Politics of the Middle

[handwritten: "politics of the middle" vs "politics of law & grace"]

THERE ARE TWO KINDS OF POLITICS: ON THE ONE HAND, THE POLITICS of Law and Grace; on the other hand, the politics of the middle. Buttressed by the virtues of love and faith, employing the strategies of tradition, liturgy, sanctity, revelation, and prophecy, a politics of the middle <u>toils in the</u> ordinary. It does not wallow in the ordinary, nor does it vegetate in the ordinary, although these are powerful temptations. Refusing a politics that would claim authority from beyond the world or from the beyond located within, a politics of the ordinary is tempted to content itself with this refusal. The ordinary can saturate; it can offer a feeling of completion. There is no need for the "big words" of theorists when everything one needs, and needs to know, is right here, present in the everyday conduct of life. Here, right here, we have joys and pains, sorrows and triumphs, and the wisdom to make sense of them all. It is familiar, reassuring, beautiful. Why bother with politics at all?

To answer that question we need to think through the representation of everyday life. We need to distinguish between the ordinary and the obvious. The obvious saturates, the ordinary does not. Years of experience make the everyday obvious. Surprises and failures no longer shock. There are things to do and things that one does, norms and practices, and there is a tension between them that constitutes the work of living. A capacity

[handwritten: The ordinary doesn't saturate everyday life]

of judgment develops, the virtue of practical wisdom. It may take years; in some who are precocious it may develop much more quickly. In the obvious, practical wisdom displaces the virtues of faith and love. Everything does not hang together well, but with practical wisdom there is a capacity to deal with it, to make difficult, even excruciating decisions calmly, without a feeling of distress. The virtuous person—with practical wisdom as a marker for all of the virtues—lives tranquilly in the obvious. The risks of the ordinary may be acknowledged, but they are not felt. And so politics in a robust sense is abandoned.

The possibility of disambiguating the ordinary and the obvious rests on the representation of the everyday. There is a way of representing the everyday as obvious that seems to refuse to subordinate itself to the immanent or the transcendent, but still rests on a supersessionist logic. The contemporaneous popularity of the American sitcoms *Seinfeld* and *Friends* clearly demonstrates this. Both shows are, proudly, about nothing. Or, more precisely, they are about nothing special, which is to say they are about everything, every little thing. Every thing is little because it does not mean something big. The most mundane activities of everyday life are on display not in order to demonstrate how they lead to something more profound, nor to take on any profundity themselves. They are just there, or so it seems. Every thing is the same size, just a different shape. There are things that ought to be bigger than others—on *Seinfeld*, George's fiancée dies; on *Friends*, main characters marry and have children—but these are treated with the same levity as the little things. Weddings and funerals do not receive due weight. They do not raise questions of human existence. They involve silly little norms and practices like everything else, like work, like neighbors. They may be called the biggest moments in one's life, but that is just what one is supposed to say. They still fit in four segments separated by three commercial breaks.

Seinfeld is about law, *Friends* is about grace. Each is animated by a hermeneutics which begins with the everyday and processes it in a different way. The characters in *Seinfeld* take a trip to the laundromat, order Chinese takeout, or tell a little white lie. They discuss what, in that situation, one is supposed to do. There is always something that one is supposed to do, and it is always opaque. Each new piece of evidence presents the situation in a new light, and calls for a reevaluation of what the proper thing to do is, maintaining the opacity of the answer. Moreover, reasoning goes wrong; it is too rational. What the characters decide is called for in a situation is understandable, but is just beyond the edge of the reasonable. As long as what is done is proper, it is acceptable—the (unwritten) letter, not the spirit, of social norms is what matters. And the law has a compelling force: if it is discerned, or if it seems as though it is discerned, characters feel compelled to act.

Friends is also about a hermeneutics which begins with the everyday, but in *Friends* the goal is to discern affect. Does one character "like" this man or that woman? Is he still angry? Are they "in love"? This last question, the question of love, is central, and frames the series. From the first episode to the last, Ross and Rachel work to figure out whether or not they are in love (after ten years, they finally are certain that they are). Norms are acknowledged, but only because they aide in discerning affect. When Chandler kisses Joey's girlfriend, the superficial problem is that the "rules" have been broken, but the actual problem is what the transgression says about Chandler's feeling of friendship for Joey. Chandler, Joey, and Ross are always ordering their friendships among each other: is Joey or Ross Chandler's "best friend"? Rules are used instrumentally: when Rachel no longer feels in love with Ross, she uses a dispute about broken rules (whether or not they were "on a break" when Ross slept with another woman) to end their relationship. Spirit is stripped of the letter. In one episode, Phoebe knows she is angry with Ross but she cannot remember why—which does not deter her from remaining angry.

While both shows are ostensibly about nothing, they are actually about hermeneutics animated by desire. The characters of *Seinfeld* aim to maximize their profit: in money, in things, and in women (in Elaine's case, men). That is what discerning the law will allow them to do, and that is what they want. The characters of *Friends* desire true love. They want to live happily ever after, and discerning their true feelings will make that possible. Desire also holds together the unlikely assortment of friends at the center of each show. In the case of *Seinfeld*, this is desire generated by comfort. George, Elaine, Jerry, and Kramer get along because they are comfortable with each other, and so attached to each other through inertia (there could be no other reason). The relationship between Jerry and Elaine, formerly romantic, betrays no desire. Even when the relationship becomes romantic again for one episode, it is for pragmatic reasons, and whatever desire comes about is portrayed as artificial. The desire that holds together the six central characters of *Friends* is more nearly sexual. There is consistent sexual tension between the characters in a way that is unthinkable in *Seinfeld*. Besides the framing relationship between Ross and Rachel, there is the relationship, and eventually marriage, of Chandler and Monica, and a brief relationship between Joey and Rachel. There is the sexual innuendo between Chandler and Joey (even when it is indirect, their homosocial bonding over, among other things, "free porn" is unmistakable). There are romantic, though staged, kisses between Rachel and Phoebe, and between Monica and Phoebe. The male friends comfortably josh about the female friends' sexual desirability, and vice versa. Even between the siblings, Monica and Ross, there is prohibited desire rather than lack of desire. Is this difference between desire in *Seinfeld* and *Friends* not the difference between immanent love and transcendent love discussed in Chapter 1?

It would be too easy to attribute the popularity of *Seinfeld* and *Friends* to their depiction of everyday human life, to our identification with characters who are dealing with the little things. It would also be too easy to attribute their popularity to characters who display our essential humanity. This is clearly wrong, because the essential humanity that the two shows depict is in direct conflict. Each of the main characters in *Friends* is essentially a "good person," which is to say they are passionate and compassionate, they love and they suffer, and they do so together. They each have their quirks, but deep down they are the same. If we met them in real life, we would like to be their friends. If we met the characters from *Seinfeld* in real life, we would want to have a beer with them—and then we would want them to go away. There is no indication that, deep down, they are capable of passion or compassion. Yet, deep down, beneath their quirks, they are all the same, and in that similarity is something essentially human. To be human, according to *Seinfeld*, is to work at discerning social norms.

While the characters in both shows display something essential about humanity, neither portrays what it is like to be human. They are comedies, not tragedies. They begin with the everyday, then they move beyond it and so make sense of it. They do not depict the tension between practices and norms, the risk, the surprises, the rewards, the failures. Once the hermeneutic is understood, once the viewer is practiced in ascending from the everyday to law or grace, the apparent surprises all make sense. To call these shows formulaic would be to underappreciate the richness of their respective animating hermeneutics, but it would point to the sense in which those hermeneutics order and enchant.

Others have represented the everyday in such a way that affect and norms, law and grace, are both at the center, and are indistinct. The films of Robert Bresson, the mid-twentieth-century French director, are entirely concerned with representing the everyday stripped of any hermeneutic. Indeed, Bresson's characters do not have the capacity to discern, or even to understand. They speak and they act without thoughts, either conscious or unconscious. This is a result to be achieved, it takes discipline, and Bresson works hard to make it happen. To represent the everyday, on Bresson's view, is to refuse representation. It is to fight against representation. The theater is the enemy of film because the theater is founded on representation. Film (what Bresson calls cinematography, using the term expansively) makes it possible to present without representing, although he asserts that this possibility is almost always overlooked. To its detriment, on his view, film is made to tell stories, to show images that captivate—in other words simply to upgrade and mass produce the theater.

Theater uses actors: individuals who strip away their personality and replace it with another, that of their character. To present, rather than represent, Bresson refuses actors. He calls his performers—typically nonprofessionals—models. He works with them to strip away their personalities, but he works even harder to prevent another, that of a character, from taking its place. Bresson has his models rehearse endlessly, repeating their lines and actions until the models are so familiar with them that the performance takes on a quasi-hypnotic quality. What is desired is not naturalness, not an appearance, but nature, reality. This reality has the quality of necessity; acting of contingency. An actor could play any part, could put on any mask. A model could only play one (Bresson usually worked with them only once). On the screen, a successful actor entirely conceals his interior, only displaying his exterior. On the screen, the successful model does exactly the opposite. It is her interior which is on full display, an interior that is unrepresentable even as it is present. This is truth on film. It is life, "the enigma peculiar to each living creature."[1] It captivates: theater involves simultaneous belief and unbelief, cinematography involves pure belief.

The truth that Bresson's films display is the truth of human nature, or so he argues in his writings on filmmaking. It is a truth that is not only concealed from the outside, in appearances, but even from the individual herself. The model does not know the truth that she displays on film. Indeed, she hides it from others and from herself, and she does not even suspect it is there. What is displayed in Bresson's films, or what he intends to display, is life without explanation or analysis. He urges that effects should come first, causes later. The effect is where the truth is; the cause is a heuristic to make sense of it. Truth is in habit, automatism; willing and thinking are unusual, and in these exceptions falsity arises. To return to truth is to return to a place where the plane of practices and the plane of norms are one: everything that is done must be done, everything that must be done is done. Bresson proposes an analogy with music: the performance succeeds when the right notes are played at the right moments.

In Bresson do we not have an example of what has been pejoratively termed the "metaphysics of presence"? This accusation misses the discipline, and distance, involved in Bresson's work. Cinematography involves necessity, but this necessity is controlled. The director (the cinematographer, in Bresson's terminology) precisely manipulates the real that he has exposed in his models. Presenting without representing is not a default, it is an achievement. It does not, could not, only involve stripping away. It involves rhetoric: persuading an audience to open itself to presentation. Clichés, and strongly evocative images, must be avoided, even if they are found in nature. Images that are insignificant (as Bresson parenthetically notes, "nonsignificant") must be chosen and composed in such a way that they cannot easily match the viewer's expectations. If images seem predisposed to fit together, they must be rejected, or they must be transformed by surrounding them with images which challenge that comfortable fit. The image will be in its right place not when it corresponds to the world, but when it creates the effect of presence in the viewer. The real is an effect, not a cause. Through his sensitivities and through his precision, the cinematographer makes visible something which would otherwise have remained hidden. We live in worlds of representation, and it is only through rhetoric, through manipulation of our expectations, that we can return to presentation, to the everyday itself. Or so Bresson suggests.

The filmic rhetoric that Bresson employs manipulates the viewer's desire in order to achieve the effect of the real. He writes, "Accustom the public to divining the whole of which they are given only a part. Make people diviners. Make them desire it."[2] The public's desire is amorphous, undirected. The job of the cinematographer is to seduce by means of depicting the everyday. But this is not a seduction that pulls away from the everyday and leads to something beyond: to the truth of law or the truth of love. Susan Sontag argues to the contrary.[3] She proposes that Bresson is fundamentally concerned with the internal conflicts of characters, the way they struggle against themselves. The depiction of everyday actions displays, in the characters' blankness, inner turmoil. Sontag points to the images of the priest riding his bicycle, eating, walking, and dressing in *Diary of a Country Priest* as depicting the gravest moments of struggle against oneself. Even in *Joan of Arc*, the depiction of what Sontag calls "an automaton of grace," deep inside the character, somewhere, there must still be conflict: "Conflict has been virtually suppressed; it must be inferred."[4] This is to degrade Bresson's achievement. How could there be inner conflict when the interior is quasi-hypnotic, neither conscious nor unconscious? If Bresson induces the viewer to "infer" interior conflict, it is because he falls short of his aim. The aim is to depict the real: where practice and norm are one, where conflict is impossible.

How, then, are we to understand the desire of the viewer which Bresson aims to direct? Desire, for Bresson, is complicated. It is not merely action animated by an object that is perceived to have disproportionate worth. Consider the desire depicted at the center of *Au Hasard Balthazar*: the desire of Marie. It animates, but it is fundamentally enigmatic. Her childhood affection for Jacques, professed as love, never matures into desire. To Jacques' reminders of her earlier affection, she replies "I'm not sure I love you." When pressed, "Is it that hard to know?" she can only say, "If I don't love you, I don't want to lie to you." Marie is not particularly interested in answering the question; she is not interested in the hermeneutics of love. By the end of the film, she has not become any more decisive. She tells Jacques that she has dreamed of a boy like him, a boy who accepts all that she has been through in the course of the film. Marie details these travails, and

Jacques still affirms that he wants to marry her. He would not be ashamed, nor would he blame her; he would be committed for life. After hearing all of this, Marie stands up: "You bore me." She later resolves to love him— but she resolves to first have it out with Gerard, her other love. She never makes it back to Jacques. But her desire for Gerard is equally opaque. He is a tough young man, a smuggler with a posse and a motorcycle who enjoys the suffering of others. In their first encounter, Gerard sits in Marie's car. She tells him to leave. When he doesn't, she walks away—and then turns around and sits next to him. He touches her. A tear falls down her cheek, but she does not move. Much later, when Marie's mother asks her what she sees in Gerard, Marie can only respond, "I love him. Do we know why we love someone? If he says 'come,' I come; 'do this,' I do this."

Perhaps Marie's love for Gerard is transcendent, her love for Jacques immanent. Regardless, both involve opaque desire. In these relationships, practice and norms bear no relationship to each other. Anything that is done can be right or wrong, there is no way to tell. An action is both at once, and neither. This is the opposite of the aspiration Bresson has for the real, the aspiration to depict how practice and norm are one, how everything is right: truth. Such unity is found in Balthazar, the donkey. He endures the pleasant and the unpleasant, sometimes he is well fed and sometimes he goes unfed and suffers. But he endures, doing what he does, and what is the right thing to do, however peculiar that sounds. Balthazar would seem to be the perfect Bressonian model: already emptied of personality. But he is not the perfect model, because he does not display what remains without personality: essential humanity. This is achieved in the pairing of Balthazar and Marie. Bresson is renowned for his use of reduplication: it is one of the rhetorical techniques which peels the viewer away from representation. In title cards, in narration that repeats action, and in visual displays, reduplication punctuates his films, preventing the viewer from falling into easy emotional responses. Reduplication is at the core of *Au Hasard Balthazar*. Marie and Balthazar are doubles. Carefree in childhood together, disciplined as they grow, mistreated together and finally both dying away from their homes. The miser who will not feed Balthazar also will not feed Marie. Cuts between the two propel the film forward. Balthazar perfects the passivity of Marie; Marie adds humanity to Balthazar's passivity. For

Marie, norms and practices seem to bear no relationship to each other; for Balthazar, they are identical. Marie desires absolutely opaquely, Balthazar does not desire at all. Marie loves Balthazar: he is her only "true" love (as she is looking at Balthazar, she finally decides she will love Jacques).

In the pairing of Marie and Balthazar, and the desire at once opaque and ethereal that they display together, we can understand what Bresson might mean by directing the desire of the public, and making people diviners. He aims not to provide an object that will fill the public's desire but images that will saturate the public's vision. Instead of moving from the everyday to something else, whether it be a display of law or love or inner conflict, Bresson moves from the everyday back onto itself in such a way that the everyday seems complete. Bresson transforms the everyday into the obvious, foreclosing the ordinary.

It is tempting, but too easy, to track a movement of the representation of the everyday from Bresson, in the 1960s, fascinated with transforming the everyday to the obvious, to *Seinfeld* and *Friends* in the 1990s, offering a hermeneutics that transforms the everyday into Law or Grace, and culminates in the microbudget filmmaking of the beginning of the new millennium, the supersessionist logic having been shed along with other cultural excesses of the 1960s and 1990s. In the emerging subgenre of microbudget films that is sometimes referred to as mumblecore, the everyday is again on display. Like Bresson's films, mumblecore projects often use nonprofessional actors. But unlike Bresson's work, they employ an ultrarealistic, quasi-documentary style, and they often employ traditional narrative tropes revolving around romantic relationships. At their least interesting, these films create a representation homogeneous with the lives and personalities of their actors. Joe Swanberg's *LOL* (2006) mixes actual audio and video created by the actors out of character with improvised performances. *Hannah Takes the Stairs* (2007), featuring many of the directors and actors associated with mumblecore, was crafted collaboratively, again relying largely on improvisation. While these works are not exclusively theatrical, they display the world smoothed over by enchantment. Cultural self-representation is reproduced in filmic representation.

In contrast, Andrew Bujalski brings to his filmmaking a discipline, rigor, and aesthetic sensibility of the highest caliber. Although he is associated with mumblecore, he has distanced himself from the label, suggesting that it unhelpfully unifies a group of very distinctive filmmakers. Bujalski, who studied with Chantal Akerman at Harvard, is attentive to the rhetoric of film in a way that others associated with mumblecore are not. His first two films, *Funny Ha Ha* (2002) and *Mutual Appreciation* (2005), were shot in black-and-white with a handheld camera. While it is fair to call his films documentary style, they are attentive to framing, light, and composition without an overwhelming aestheticism. Dialogue follows a natural rhythm, but includes a density of wit that has an almost hyperrealistic effect. Characters make the sorts of clever quips that are natural, but do so with such a frequency that the appearance of improvisation is destabilized.

What is immediately striking about Bujalski's films is that there is a lot of mumbling. Actors do not enunciate. While in other films associated with mumblecore, the effect of mumbling is to confirm the films' documentary-style credentials, and ultimately all of the dialogue is audible, Bujalski takes his mumbling much more seriously. There is no attempt to help the viewer by maintaining a baseline of audibility in the actors' voices or by technical means. This is because what the actors are saying *does not matter*. Where Bresson was concerned with clearing his models of thoughts, of personality, Bujalski is concerned with clearing his actors of words, of the ability to express themselves. They speak but they do not say anything; or, more precisely, their words are not efficacious. In this he is entirely at odds with others associated with mumblecore, who see microbudget filmmaking as a means to all the more transparently express what a character would think and feel. For directors like Swanberg, improvisation does not just capture spontaneity; it exposes the truth of the situation. This is a notion that Bujalski clearly rejects.

By ostentatiously devaluing the words of his actors, Bujalski draws attention to what might be called, in a cliché manner, the failure to communicate among his characters. They are constantly talking, almost all they do is talk, but nothing is said. In *Mutual Appreciation*, Alan, the musician protagonist who has just moved to New York, is asked (significantly, by a woman) about what happened to his old band. He says that it does not make for an interesting story, there were "creative differences," it is "hard to explain," it would be hard to say "without making it sound petty." We have an effect without a cause: Alan's band having broken up, Alan being in New York, this is just how it is. The cause does not even come after the effect is displayed; the cause does not matter at all. It is not that the cause could not be spoken, that there is some libidinal desire attached to it that represses. Nor was it easier, in the conversation, to pass over the cause. Alan was asked directly about it. It would be *too easy* to respond with a cause; it would be to *say something*, which is precisely what Alan, and the other characters, at least the other male characters, do not do. Their supersaturated wit helps in this: everything is a half-joke; if it were serious, or if it were an intended joke, it would not be said. This is how the everyday is represented here without moving beyond itself. The everyday consists in talking, and talking does not matter.

This verbal muck is reflected in the physical positioning of the actors. More often than not, they are lethargically sitting or lying on beds. The camera does not pay particular attention to this; it gives the actors a comfortable distance. The verbal muck is also reflected in the first lines that Alan sings in his musical performance: "Whenever light shines down on misery / It can only make things worse" (two full songs are filmed; Alan is played by Justin Rice of the band Bishop Allen). Language without reference, language that does not matter; that is simply the most practical option. Why not ascend from the everyday to something else—to inner conflict or to law or to love? Because that "can only make things worse." What remains of the everyday is not luminescent; it is gray.

But sometimes things do need to be said. Speaking without saying becomes frustrating—especially to the woman, to Ellie. *Mutual Appreciation* is a love triangle, and she is the apex, the girlfriend of Alan's friend Lawrence. When Alan is feeling ambivalent about the advances of an enthusiastic radio host who has taken a romantic interest in him (of course he is always feeling ambivalent), Ellie tells more than asks him, "Why don't you have the courtesy to tell her what's going on?" Ellie does not want ambiguity. Alan begins to reply, "If, like, I'm not giving her anything . . ." If there are no expectations, there are no obligations. Why write a contract if you are not doing business? But, of course, they are doing business. The girl has kissed him, and when asked if he "kissed back" he, typically, equivocates. Ellie persists in her advice, in her desire to clarify: "Take the moral high ground and be an honest person." Later, when she is alone for the first time with Alan, she tells him, "I'd like to talk about real things with you . . ."—Alan interjects, half-sarcastically, ". . . reality . . ."—". . . yeah, reality would be nice to talk about, I just . . . it's like we never get to that point, really, you know what I mean?"

It seems as though the male characters thrive in ambiguity and ambivalence, the females strive for clarity. Moreover, the women in Bujalski's films, particularly the two women in *Mutual Appreciation*, are capable of desire; the men are not. The radio host repeatedly corners Alan (on a chair, on a bed) and begins to make out with him. Ellie desires both Lawrence and Alan, that is the crux of the film. But Ellie's desire for "honesty" is misleading. She wants Alan to be honest so that she can have a sense of where she stands with him. Moreover, Ellie is not interested in finding the truth of her desire; she does not feel compelled to discern which of the two men she truly loves. She does not really desire clarity, she is just dissatisfied with ambiguity. She desires something; the men, it seems, desire nothing. They are emasculated. Lawrence is volunteered by one of his female students to read a monologue written by a woman describing her experiences of womanhood. Alan stumbles into the tail end of a party; as he enters, the three girls that remain at the party are talking about circumcision. It does not take long for Alan to find himself in a wig, makeup, and a dress. When asked if he has a girlfriend, he says he is neither gay nor does he want a girlfriend (a few minutes before he had called is ex-girlfriend; again, the verbal muck is without limit).

The climax of the film—there does not feel as though there is a narrative arc, but there is one—is a moment of elision. Lawrence is out of town; Ellie is at Alan's apartment. They are sitting on his bed. The scene unfolds painfully slowly and awkwardly, not at all romantically. Alan takes Ellie's hand. She cautiously responds, "OK, Alan . . ." He touches her arm, saying "I can stop at any . . ." She responds, in a clinical tone, "Yeah. That feels nice." She leans back on the bed, lays down. He does the same. "This cannot happen." "No." "This is not going to happen." "No, it's not." They talk, but they do not move; they are still lying, holding hands. Ellie says she should go. Alan counters: just stay for ten or twenty minutes. Ellie agrees to ten.

The film cuts to the next morning. Alan's roommate offers coffee to Ellie as she leaves. The elision is peculiar. It suggests an earlier era when the activities of the bedroom were necessarily elided on film, censored. In our era, of course, quite the opposite is the case—so to do so suggests that such activities did not happen. The film does not provide any clarification. When Ellie confesses her transgression to Lawrence, she says, "We just acknowledged that we were attracted to each other a little bit. Nothing happened, we didn't kiss each other, we just stated it out loud." Lawrence responds, "Wouldn't it have been more fun if you'd just always had an unspoken thing, you know? Why not keep it to yourselves?" This is, of course, precisely what the film has done. But what is peculiar about this secret at the center of the film is that it does not attract. The secret does not animate the film; indeed, it does not attract any particular attention. The pace and tone of the film do not change. The film, like its characters, continually undercuts its own seriousness. At what would seem like the moment of greatest tension, when Lawrence is questioning Ellie, his question is interrupted by water boiling for tea. Instead of underscoring the tension with a whistle, the boiling tea kettle is silent, just mentioned. It cuts off the conversation, forcing a quick shift in topics: "Are you sure you don't want any tea?" "Well, what flavors do we have?" "Green, mint that your mother gave us . . ." They drink tea. Ellie insists, "I don't understand why you are so calm?" This is the story of the film, a disturbing calmness, the seemingly significant intermingled with the everyday. The everyday does not lead somewhere else; it stays where it is. The viewer must confront it because it is not stylized. Its clichés are thwarted. It forces the viewer to take its pace, to confront the everyday on its terms, which are the terms of the everyday itself.

Yet this is not quite right. Bujalski does not collapse the planes of practices and norms as Bresson does. It is not that what is done is always what is to be done. But in the mumbling, in that linguistic muck, it seems as though there are neither norms nor practices. If anything like normativity makes an appearance, it is when Ellie tells Alan to be "an honest person." At another point, the first time that Ellie and Alan are alone, after she confesses her desire and Alan does not seem to reciprocate, she tells him, "You are a good man, Alan." He responds, "Now that's something I can firmly disagree with." Despite these words—perhaps because of them—Bujalski's characters, or at least his male characters, most often do what they are supposed to do. Finally, Alan does have a "relationship talk" with the radio host and, despite sleeping with (in some sense) his best friend's girlfriend, Alan is conflicted about it, more conflicted than usual. Perhaps it is through the mumbling, through the bracketing of their language, that Bujalski draws our attention to what characters do, and what they ought to do (indeed, *Mutual Appreciation* would retain much of its poignancy if it was silent, such is the importance of body language). The audience knows what the characters ought to do: the love triangle narrative is a cliché if ever there was one. Bujalski displays the everyday by eliciting and so exploiting the audience's sense of the normative, neither showing nor collapsing a sense of the normative within his films, any possibility for such a sense having been rendered null by all the mumbling.

The only problem is that the female role, in Bujalski's first two films, distracts.[5] Animated by desire which they do not understand, Marnie in *Funny Ha Ha* and Ellie in *Mutual Appreciation* cause men to misbehave. They try to shine light on misery, and they makes things worse. Light does not illuminate the everyday, it distorts. It is the cause of the withdrawal into language, into mumbling. Alan is in New York because of his ex-girlfriend; Lawrence leaves Alan and Ellie alone for the weekend because he was invited to the wedding of his ex-girlfriend (Ellie is sure they will "flirt"). And, of course, it is Ellie, trying to figure out what she wants, and thinking that she can succeed, that leads to the ambiguity and anxiety of each side of the love triangle. Are these not all extensions of the moments of emasculation? The lyrics of Alan's song follow the first person seduction of boy by girl. The girl was pretty and blushing, shining, smiling. But she is a "gypsy curse," leaving, and leaving the boy's hopes "drowned out and dead." While the story is that of a typical love song, here it is as if the boy has no agency. The girl desires (blushing when they meet, taking his hand), when they were together the boy's days "were hers"—and then she left. The boy did not feel his hopes crushed at the time, only in retrospect, as he sees his misery, as light shines down. If Bresson dazzles, Bujalski darkens.

Mutual Appreciation is about seduction, and it is animated by desire. But the effect of desire is not to purify but to muzzle, to castrate. The everyday is represented as ordinary, but the ordinary is left speechless. This is a depiction of quietism. The quietist is a seductress. She speaks sweet words which say nothing. She speaks about philosophy, about politics, about social issues, but she does not commit herself—either to affirming or to denying. Her sweet words identify conceptual unclarities and metaphysical mysteries. She says nothing because to say something is to commit herself. To say something is to speak about individuated norms: in circumstances such as *this*, *that* is what should be done. But to make this statement is to offer a representation of the world which the quietist refuses to do because of its inevitable error. Her smooth talking is not just smooth but slippery and slick. It lacks the traction that a commitment to practices and norms provides, traction which is the ability to speak about and be held accountable to the world. The quietist does not say anything to which anyone does, or could, legitimately object. She does not dirty her hands in the world for fear of contamination with its ubiquitous error. She does not retreat from the ordinary, but neither does she commit in her engagement. The ordinary becomes a realm of mumbling into which we were lured by a flashy promise.

A quietist politics of the ordinary acknowledges the richness of the social world, the gap between the plane of practices and the plane of norms, and even may seem committed to change. It acknowledges ambiguity and tragedy, renounces the quest to become "scientists of justice." It turn to poetry as "an engine of difference, a way of sorting the truths that come into being, placing them into words for us to consider ... the struggle of the democratic poet must be to move from annotation to the undefinable moment of new thought, new movement, when what is exposed is not a fixed point but the fleetingness of desire."[6] The quietist recognizes that it is just "as if" there are practices and norms. This makes poetry possible: language and thought can be reconfigured in new, previously unimagined ways. Evolution and revolution are thought to coincide. But what gives this novelty traction? It must persuade, and its persuasive force comes about through its ability to harness desire. What is novel is a reconfiguration of the ordinary that lures further reconfiguration. New truths come about, but new truths are not adjudicated. Poetry works only if it persuades, only if it fuels desire. This is the desire of *what will be*, not an object but pure possibility. It is flirtation, it is, as Levinas puts it, the "eternal virgin" which shines from beyond interiority and exteriority, beyond immanence and transcendence.[7] It is desire that entices and castrates, for it leaves nothing to be said, except for mumbles. The promise of politics ends in a vain struggle because it lacks commitment; it lacks the virtues of faith and love.[8] It is just "as if" there is a plane of norms and a plane of practices, a fictionalism which is a luxury of those who do not suffer.

The quietist feminism of Linda Zerilli refuses the question of whether or not the category of "woman" is useful for political practice.[9] Zerilli refuses "theory," refuses the "craving for generality" that turns politics into a technique, a means of achieving goals formulated in theory. She refuses "to reach beyond the common to transfigure the commonplace"; she refuses "a place outside our practices from which to form universal concepts under which to subsume particulars in the name of predicting and achieving social change."[10] Politics must not be split into "theory" and "practice." Instead, politics is redescription: seen differently, new possibilities become visible. And, politics is action: gender is a practice constantly repeated differently, a practice without a norm (Zerilli is explicitly critical of Judith Butler for positing a difference between practices and norms). These two are the same: redescription is political action. Women wearing men's clothes is a practice which can "dramatize a figure of the newly thinkable that allows us to envision bodies anew" (61). Imagination, practice, and politics all fold together, along with norms, values, and language. Here again, the everyday is left in place. It is understood as dynamic. But it does not involve any gap between practices and norms. To make such a divide would be a tempting, problematic fiction. It would be to introduce just the sort of "epistemological" debates that distract from the practice of (in this case feminist) politics. Yet it is this refusal which castrates. It subjects to the hegemony of the visible. The professions of novelty are the professions of the sophist, reconfiguring the language and imagery of the everyday in order to persuade that his cause is just. By eliding the difference between practices and norms, he makes it seem as if his cause is everyone's cause. He prevents the adjudication of his claims against social norms, replacing it with phantasmal, libidinal judgment.

This is how Ellie castrates: she allows desire to trump the authority of norms. She acknowledges the existence of norms, allowing her desire to overshadow them. When she is first alone with Alan, she complains about her boyfriend, then catches herself. She tells Alan that she wants to kiss him and she knows it is wrong. She even explains the provenance of her desire: in a long-term relationship with her boyfriend, she begins to be attracted to men "on the periphery" of her social world. This is the lure of the quietist: she acknowledges ordinary norms and practices but does not acknowledge their ultimate authority. The result, in *Mutual Appreciation*, is that the men remain emasculated, incapable of action. At the end of the film, Alan is still talking about forming the band he has been planning on forming from the very start of the film; now he is talking about asking a six-foot-tall female bass player to join. Lawrence continues practicing his feminist monologue and making tea.

The quietist ignores the difference between practices and norms; her opposite finds it everywhere. All of life takes on the intensity of love, all of life is difficult, is struggle. Here we find the limits of Gillian Rose's work. Her texts, up to *Judaism and Modernity* and especially *The Broken Middle*, became increasingly difficult, inaccessible. Her goal was to fold style and substance into each other, to write about difficulty difficultly. A tangled web of conflict between practices and norms was everywhere in the same way that the quietist finds it nowhere, but with the same result. An astounding number of readers come away from Rose's work with the belief that she writes as a Christian, that the "broken middle" she describes is mended by Christ.[11] Others conclude that her opposition to deconstruction is superficial. In short, the impotent text becomes an instrument of sophistry, its readers finding in it that to which they are already committed, and using it to further those commitments.

Desire fueled, and suffused, Rose's philosophical texts as well as her autobiographical narratives. She recalls explaining to her friend, Yvette, that she understood romantic relationships in terms of "creative closeness." By this she seems to mean a blurring of the line between love and friendship, an understanding of the two as a difference of intensity, a quantitative difference, not a qualitative difference. Yvette, an energetic elderly voluptuary, dismisses Rose's "creative closeness" as a "totalitarian attitude."[12] Why would this be? Because here we find desire playing the same role as it did for the quietist: it trumps norms. To find difficulty nowhere and to find it everywhere are both outcomes sustained by allowing desire to trump norms. (Yvette, in contrast, was careful to distinguish the few times that she had been "in love" from her lovers and those from her friends; this did not diminish the intensity of her "lustful love" in the least.) In the final pages of *Love's Work*, Rose reflects on the effects of her attitude toward "creative closeness." She describes the mutuality of love, and of the love she had toward her younger lovers. Then she describes how she, unilaterally, has ended these erotic loves, continuing them as friendships. Her reasoning, as she describes it, was that she felt she was holding back these younger men. But the result, in retrospect, was to make them even more unhappy. It is hard not to read these reflections in the same way as we read *Mutual Appreciation*: the female with the false consciousness of mutuality who is, in fact, the one who desires—and who leaves ruins in her wake.[13]

What is the alternative to the quietist and her opposite? The alternative is to represent the ordinary rhetorically. It is to be aware of one's audience and, as Bresson urged, to speak to that public. Unlike what we find in Bresson's work, a rhetoric of the ordinary need not—must not—strive to manipulate, and saturate, the desire of the public. Instead, it must know when to speak and when to remain silent. It must be willing to employ a variety of techniques. There are times for difficulty and times for ease. There are times for persuasion and times for passivity. The ordinary is an exceptional space, a phantasmal space. It cannot be accessed directly. It can only be represented. To represent the everyday as the ordinary is to display the distinct planes of norms and of practices that were always there, just obscured.[14] Such representation must occur in a space of exception, insulated from enchantment. This deliberative, Socratic moment must be separated from the political moment, the moment when politics is packaged in the language of enchantment in order to persuade.[15] This exceptional moment of the ordinary within the everyday must not be forgotten or expanded. It is sustained by the virtues of love and faith.

APPENDIX

Political Theology as a Rigorous Science

WE ARE INTERESTED IN PRACTICE, BUT WE CANNOT JUST LOOK AT practice. The ordinary is enchanted. It is always already stylized. The ordinary is jagged, chaotic, unsystematic. It presents itself to us as smooth, flowing, continuous—albeit sometimes surprising. Turning to the ordinary is not as easy as the pragmatist makes it out to seem. In fact, it is impossible. The image of the ordinary as jagged, chaotic, and unsystematic is a representation of what cannot be represented. It projects the impasses of the enchanted ordinary onto an imagined disenchanted plane, a plane from which enchantment is to be condemned. Yet it is precisely this maneuver, this commitment to the impossible, which is necessary for efficacious political critique and action. This is the proper root of political theology.

Before we can see this commitment to the impossible as political theology, we must see it as political philosophy. How can we access the ordinary? By conceiving of political philosophy as a rigorous science.[1] To become a rigorous science has been a longstanding ambition of philosophy, but this ambition has come into disrepute of late in some circles. Empiricism purports to offer a rigorously scientific foundation, but takes as given its analytical concepts. The conclusions reached based on these concepts have the appearance of authority, and so have the effect of retrospectively legitimating the concepts with which it began. A poll asks voters in a region whether they would prefer to vote for a "conservative" or a "liberal" candidate. About 60 percent say conservative, 40 percent say liberal. More candidates call themselves conservative to match voter preferences. Commentators discuss how conservative the region is, how few liberals there are. Further research tests whether conservatives prefer sales taxes or income taxes, how much they value the right to bear arms, how religious they are. Words have been plucked from everyday language use and become the basis for empirical study; data is accumulated; and soon the words' provenance in everyday conversation is forgotten, hidden in the shadow of the authorizing scientific apparatus. Scientific results spiral away from the ordinary—and, from their privileged position, drag the ordinary along with them. They are persuasive. When they are reported on the evening news, or to the campaign manager, they convince ordinary folks to see themselves differently, and so they change how ordinary folks speak and act. Such is the rigor of the political scientist.

Those who complain loudest about empiricism—let us call them political theorists—achieve their purported rigor in much the same way as their political-scientist cousins. Words are plucked from everyday language usage, but they are quickly stripped of their everyday meanings. This meaning is filled in again through some authorizing apparatus: through a canon of texts or through logical analysis (which, more often than not, boils down to just a different canon of texts). It is the concept that is supposed to be in question: the concept of justice, or equality, or liberalism, or tolerance, or violence. What have Hobbes, Locke, Rousseau, and Mill (or, for the edgier political theorists, Nietzsche, Strauss, and Arendt) said about equality? What necessary and sufficient conditions can we set to capture the statements about tolerance that most would deem true? Again, the authorizing apparatus certainly provides the appearance of rigor. Yet the results of the political theorist, like those of the political scientist, spiral away from the ordinary. Unlike the results of the political scientist, the results of the political theorist do not drag the ordinary along with them. Ordinary folks are baffled when they hear that what justice really means involves the minimax principle, or that the figure of the foreigner is central to the concept of justice.

It seems as though we are pulled in two conflicting directions: the demands of rigor pull away from the ordinary while the demands of rhetoric are rooted in the ordinary. To envisage political philosophy as a rigorous science would seem to require both. As a science, it is necessary to describe politics as it is, in such a way as to open new possibilities for political action. In short, its results must work. However, as rigor is added, as concepts are refined, as the enterprise is sharpened, its political efficacy slips away. What remains are pompous, grandiloquent theorists who are certain that they are making the world a better place while in fact all they are doing is entrenching an esoteric, elite discourse, guarding the canon. Yet the political figures who stick closest to the ordinary—editorial writers and political pundits—simply reformulate and regurgitate. At most, they reinforce political commitments. The most persuasive figure is one who is rooted in the ordinary and who appeals to an authorizing mechanism accepted from within the ordinary, for example, tradition. Citing the words of past leaders and the deeds of past patriots, this orator persuades her listener to see things, and act, in ways the listener would not have expected before hearing her speech. Such an orator does not spin away from the ordinary; she spins the ordinary. She brings to prominence some of its less prominent features. But this could hardly be called scientific rigor.

Perhaps we are approaching the problem backward. Perhaps a rigorous science need not be defined by the size of its authorizing apparatus. Instead of searching for *first* principles, might we look for *last* principles? Instead of an apparatus that comes before the phenomenon in question, an apparatus based on last principles yields priority to the phenomenon. As Jean-Luc Marion writes, "The last principle takes the initiative of offering the initiative to the phenomenon. It comments on the act by which what shows itself gives itself and what gives itself always shows itself on the basis of the irreducible and first *self* of appearing."[2] On this view, apparatus and phenomenon are dancing partners, always in lockstep, but the phenomenon leads. We must allow the phenomenon to show itself; our job is simply to comment on the display. Constructing an apparatus to do this is much less simple than it might, at first, appear. Any description at all would seem to mismatch the phenomenon. It is our word that we are applying to that phenomenon, not that phenomenon generating words. Moreover, aren't we always encountering mirages? What seems like a phenomenon turns out not to be one at all. How do we know that what we are seeing is showing itself? Answering that question was the reason first principles were proposed to start with.

What if there was a phenomenon which just consisted in its showing? In such a case, there would be no need to process the appearance of the phenomenon because the appearance would be identical with the phenomenon. In fact, any attempt to process the appearance—with philosophical machinery—would distort. In such a case as this, the job of philosophy would be the work, not of constructing machinery, or reconfiguring (deconstructing) machinery, but of demolishing machinery—even the machinery which seems natural, which even conventional wisdom accepts. Such a phenomenon would be like light. Because it appears just in its appearing and not beyond its appearing, to "see" it, all of the particular phenomena that it illuminates must be bracketed. They must not be ignored, because then the phenomenon itself would vanish. Light itself is not such a phenomenon because, of course, it does not show itself. It must be seen: the blind know not what light is.

Michel Henry proposes that there is such a phenomenon: life. He writes, "Life is nothing other than that which reveals itself—not something that might have an added property of self-revealing, but the very fact of self-revealing, self-revelation as such."[3] This has been forgotten by philosophers, by scientists, and by ordinary people. Living is ignored while the activities of life are privileged (just as light is so often ignored). The biologist brings scientific abstraction and the philosopher brings conceptual abstraction to life, dismissing living itself as mere appearance. Life becomes electric currents, chains of neurons, chemical compositions; it becomes objects of thought, objects of desire, discrete concepts and perceptions. Even Heidegger subordinates life to a status among worldly truths. Ignored by scientists and philosophers are the ordinary experiences of life that all share: "They, too, live and love life, wine, and the opposite sex; they get jobs, have careers, and themselves experience the joy of new departures, chance encounters, the boredom of administrative tasks, the anguish of death."[4] Yet nonscientists, ordinary folks, also overlook life, focused instead on living beings and their properties, Mr. Jones who owns a red car and Miss Smith who is a hairdresser. We see even ourselves as just a living being with a set of properties. Life is elided.

Life is like light: it is present in all of its activities, but it is not discernible from any one in particular, nor is it discernible when they all are set aside. Unlike light, the domain of life is without bounds. Consciousness and unconsciousness, concepts and perceptions, needs and desires are all secondary—indeed, we might say hypostases—of life itself. The study of life is the work of critique. It is the work of mobilizing philosophical machinery, but this is machinery of demolition, machinery to destroy the obscuring apparatuses of science, of the history of philosophy, and of everyday enchantments. It is also the work of cultural critique, shaking off (or at least shaking up) the ideological apparatuses that support the elision of life. Henry argues that this work of cultural critique is extremely pressing, as the elision of life is pushing new extremes with the growth of virtual reality, genetic technology, and the practices associated with what the papacy has called the "culture of death."[5]

The answer to the question of how philosophy could become a rigorous science, then, is for philosophy to return to life. Is this a solely critical project, a project of pure demolition? Michel Henry names what remains after this work of demolition as "autoaffection." By this he means pure affect, affect that is undifferentiated, not directed at objects, neither conscious feeling nor unconscious desire. If anything, it is closer to hypnosis, wakefulness without the ability to direct one's own thoughts or feelings, though in autoaffection there is no hypnotist directing one's thoughts.[6] There can be no external cause of this affect; otherwise life would not qualify as a phenomenon consisting wholly in its appearing. What is left is "a monolithic affective body whose phenomenality is affectivity itself."[7] The individual is not one who feels, who experiences affection; the subject is a byproduct, a hypostasis, of affection.

Perhaps there is a way to accept life as the privileged phenomenon without accepting affectivity as a proper characterization of life. Indeed, the move from the ordinary experiences of living—enjoying wine, working at a job, the joys of chance encounters, the boredom of administrative tasks—to pure affection seems more like the employment of philosophical machinery than its destruction. It makes more sense to characterize these activities as practices, their generic form as pure *doing*, not pure *feeling*. What does life consist in if not what one does? The forms that this doing takes are not determined by oneself: they are practices, impersonally existing. Brushing one's teeth, enjoyment a glass of wine, bureaucratic paperwork: these are all practices which one does, but not the pure doing. Just as affection, understood as auto-affection, comes before the subject, doing, as pure doing, comes before the subject. Understood as doing rather than as affection, life still retains its status as privileged phenomenon which consists entirely in its appearing. There is nothing concealed beneath the appearance: what one does is simply what one does. Causes, effects, and reasons come afterward, not before: they are conceptual machinery that philosophy as a rigorous science must demolish.

This approach to understanding philosophy as a rigorous science seems useless. Whatever one is left with—whether it is autoaffection, as Michel Henry proposes, or givenness, as Jean-Luc Marion proposes, or pure doing, as I propose—seems to run into the same problem as first philosophy. They don't matter. Whether or not autoaffection is a correct description of a special phenomenon, it is our everyday ways of talking and acting that have the possibility to impact our lives. These are dismissed as corrupted by the philosopher who understands himself as a rigorous scientist. But, so what if they are corrupted if they are what matters? At least the philosopher bringing in heavy machinery accepts the importance of the ordinary. The philosophy destroying machinery appears to be naming his refusal to en-gage—and then elevating that name above the ordinary world itself. The only thing that can be said about the exulted name is that it is always right, never wrong.[8] Is this not but a subtler form of supersessionism?

This certainly does seem to be the case for Marion's and Henry's pro-posals, but there is something different about taking the privileged name to be "doing." Take a piece of conventional wisdom: a thing is what it is if it does what it does. Or, more precisely, it is what it seems to be if it does what it is supposed to do. This is not some highfalutin philosophical theory; this is what we do in everyday life, it is how we live. We see things one way, but are forced to change our minds if what happens does not match with what we expected. In other words, there is some way in which the exulted term *doing*, what remains after all theoretical machinery has been cleared away, does influence our everyday lives. Moreover, this does not diminish its exulted status as always right, never wrong. What doing as such names is always right because what is done is what is always supposed to be done. In other words, doing as such is the ideal that we aspire to in our everyday lives, the ideal of getting things right, of seeing things as they are. This is why it is a privileged phenomenon: the appearing of the phenomenon and the phenomenon itself are always identical.

Understood in this way, doing as such is not a name for life, life is a name for doing as such. The two are not identical. Marion and Henry are right that we live in a fallen world. But the world is fallen because things do not do what they are supposed to do. Life is split between practices and norms, between what is done and what ought to be done; more precisely, life is the dynamic tension between the two. The world is fallen, so we cannot gaze directly at doing as such. Practices and norms are our best approximations. They are always ultimately wrong, but they are useful fictions. Norms attempt to represent practice, practice attempts to follow norms; both attempts are necessary failures.

A norm says: in *those* circumstances, *these* are the things that ought to be done. If they are not done, there will be a reprimand; if they are done, there will be praise. Reprimand and praise need not be explicit. They need not be a speeding ticket or a pat on the back. One *could* be caught any time one is speeding, one *could* be praised as a careful driver every time one is not. Norms need not be institutionalized: anyone can reprimand, and reprimand may take many forms. If one tells an off-color joke in polite company, a norm may be broken but the reprimand may only be slightly pained looks. Afterward, listeners will say to each other: "She should not have told that joke!" When asked (by a reality television interviewer) why not, the offended auditor will respond: "Because that is not what one does!" "What one does" slips into "the thing one ought to do." However fashionable it may be to say that one lives in a world without norms, they are always there—whether on the nude beach or in the consensus meeting or in the "free society." Practices, "what one does," are pulled toward norms, "the thing to do." Even the slightest reprimand and praise, or the perception that they are deserved, brings practice toward norms. Like well-trained horses, just the slightest movement of the reins rights us (like horses, we were broken as children). This is what it means to be acculturated: not only to have acquired the practices of a community but to have acquired an acute sensitivity to reprimand and praise.

Even in the well-acculturated, norms and practices never converge. Sometimes they seem to; sometimes we seem to access that exulted realm where living becomes doing as such. These are times when we are so accustomed to doing something that it seems like we can never get it wrong: when we fill out the same form we fill out every morning, when we put on our pajamas, when we drive to work. They seem as if they can never go wrong, but they can. Car accidents happen, forms change, we make mistakes, clothes age and tear. The world is fallen; as soon as we begin to forget, we are reminded with a jolt. Just when it seems as though ordinary life flows smoothly, we are reminded of its rough, jagged texture that we smooth over. Smoothness is an illusion, not an aspiration.

To put the point another way: the tragic is a failure, an inevitable failure, of norms to do their job right. To do their job right, they would perfectly represent what happens. When something goes dramatically wrong, we are reminded that norms do not yet do their job right. Recently, the inverse picture has been advanced by, among others, Slavoj Žižek. On this picture, all we have access to is the plane of norms (the symbolic). Dramatic failures remind us of this (they expose the real). On one picture, we have access to practices, on the other, to norms, but on both pictures we are humbled by failures; access is imperfect.

What I am suggesting is a picture of the plane of norms parallel to the plane of practice. Each plane is textured with ridges and grooves. The two planes are suspended at a distance from each other. The ridges and grooves on each are aligned, though not perfectly. Practices give rise to norms, norms give rise to practices: the two planes are held together. But norms always misrepresent practices, and practices always fail to match norms: the two planes are held apart. At some moments, it seems like the gap narrows: it appears that what one does is just the thing to do. At other moments, it seems like the gap widens: failures make it seem as though practices and norms could never match. Both are illusions; both obscure the space in between, the middle: this is the constitutive gap, the place where ordinary life is lived.

Note how dramatically this picture differs from the picture offered by Marion and Henry. In their work, and in the supersessionist imagination more generally, there is some source of normativity outside the world. Only traces of it are present in our world. Our job then must—*must!*—be to gather up those traces. In the case of Henry, autoaffection is the source of normativity and our job is to cut through our messy world to preserve and gather the traces of autoaffection. In the case of a Kantian, we find ourselves in a messy world, and our task is to identify and gather the traces of reason. And so on. There are things we ought and ought not to do in the world, but the force of these oughts is borrowed from above, as it were. The project of philosophy is to gaze upward, toward the starry skies (or toward the moral law within). A line of transcendence cuts through the plane of immanence: this is the geometry of supersessionism.

I have been calling "enchantment" the transformation that turns the geometry of practices and norms into the geometry of supersessionism. One way this happens: the source of what one ought to do is condensed into a God, or a book, or an algorithm—a line of transcendence perpendicular to the plane of immanence. The world is enchanted from above. Or, the world could be enchanted from within. In this case, the planes of practices and norms collapse into each other; everything that one does ought to be done. The gods and spirits live within our world, not outside of it. In both cases, ordinary life, that daily work of navigating between norms and practices, disappears. In both cases, "because it is the thing to do" is not deemed an adequate answer to the question, "Why do I do this?" That answer either says too little or too much. When it says too little, a story must be told to authorize the ought. Only if the ought has a proper provenance is it legitimate, only if it comes from God or His representatives, only if it comes from the undistorted use of reason, only if it comes from tradition. When it says too much, the question is refused as illegitimate. One just *does*, an ought is only introduced through conceptual confusion. The two answers are the same: the authority projected outside the world authorizes norms that look suspiciously like, or equally suspiciously unlike, current practices.

This is the language of enchantment. It smoothes. The failure of every practice to match a norm is hidden. Everything makes sense: everything happens because it was supposed to happen. There is an authority ensuring that the world makes sense. Enchantment succeeds when it makes what is done seem entirely natural. It makes us feel as though the question of whether what we are doing is what we ought to be doing is irrelevant, as irrelevant as it is when we follow any routine. In other words, enchantment fills the gap between practices and norms. The effect is that critique becomes impotent. We do not complain about norms, we complain about enchantment. We grumble about the authority, we do not examine the norms. Enchantment mystifies authority, drawing our attention in a peculiar way, through saturation. It seems to display to us everything there is. Our field of vision is filled. There is no reason to look for anything else; everything is there. Everything works smoothly. Everything has an explanation. It is beautiful. What more could there be?

Everyday language enchants. It makes us feel comfortable in our world. It makes us feel as if everything fits together nicely, as if we will always do the right thing, or have an explanation for why we did not. Its authority is invisible because it saturates. If it is not the mirror of nature, than it constitutes our world. It turns the ordinary into the obvious. And this is idolatrous. An idol captures and fills the gaze. It dazzles. But it ultimately mirrors rather than reveals. It mirrors the desires of the viewer, mirrors with an "invisible mirror."[9] The mirror is invisible because sight has been saturated with the idolatrous reflection. Everything is seen, there is no need to see more. Enchantment is the hegemony of the visible. This is what the pragmatist misses. She is interested in practices and norms, but she just looks for them and thinks she will see them. What she sees is not the ordinary but the obvious. She sees the enchanted world, saturated with the tools of enchantment: everyday language and concepts. Practices and norms as they are discussed in everyday language are not practices and norms in fact. They are the idolatrous simulacra of practices and norms. It is only through returning to the ordinary that practices and norms themselves are exposed.

How does one cut through the obvious to return to the ordinary? By employing philosophy as a rigorous science. By employing philosophical tools to demolish the machinery that would interpret the ordinary. The most insidious machinery is the invisible mirror of enchantment. Philosophy as a rigorous science rejects the hegemony of the visible. That is how it can return to practices and norms. And that is why, paradoxically, disenchantment is theological. By rejecting the hegemony of the visible, the invisible matters. When Marion and Henry conceive of philosophy as a rigorous science, they take its work to be purely critical—and then they wallow in what remains, in autoaffection or in pure givenness. Philosophy conceived of as a rigorous science in the way that I am suggesting does not enjoy a beach party after its critical work is done. Its critical work is to return from the obvious to the ordinary, but because the ordinary involves practices and norms, the critical work is simply an opening. It becomes possible to examine practices and norms, generically, and their relation to each other. These questions are foreclosed by the obvious, are opened by the ordinary.

All of this talk about the geometry of practices and norms might have something to do with ethics, with how to live, but what does it have to do with politics? Moreover, why must *political* philosophy be a rigorous science? Norms are always social. They are constituted socially, through reprimand and praise. Put rather crudely, practices try to live up to social expectations: people try to do what they are supposed to do. Life, navigating practices and norms, is always already life together. Enchantment is also social. Indeed, it is supremely social because it collapses the distinction between practices and norms. Everything becomes social.

Still, what is wrong with wallowing in the obvious? What could possibly motivate an investigation into the ordinary? The answer is politics, in the practical sense. Say that we want to advance a political goal. What is the best way to do so? A popular view has it that we should lay out the situation: who is involved, what their motivations are, what would cause them to change their minds, and so forth. Then, we apply political judgment, a special form of practical wisdom, to all of these facts that are laid out in front of us.[10] This is how elections are won, how public opinion is swayed, how politicians gain support. But this mode of analysis is subject to the hegemony of the visible. It saturates the vision with facts on which judgment will be based. But what if there are more options that are not on the table, options which could be brought to the table? This possibility is precluded by accepting the hegemony of the visible. It is made possibly by considering political philosophy as a rigorous science. By cutting through the obvious to the ordinary, new, unexpected, unthought options appear.

The point seems abstract, but it becomes very concrete when we consider historical examples. In apartheid South Africa, the options on the table, to the most astute political observer, were different forms of racial segregation. The talented politician would then apply political judgment to those options and decide which of several plausible forms of institutional segregation for, say, maternity wards to adopt. To refuse the options presented would be considered irrational. It would be a mark of one with a poor capacity for practical wisdom, poor political judgment. Political philosophy, understood as a rigorous science, provides a tool to refuse the available options—governed by the hegemony of the visible—without a slide into the irrational and absurd. It provides a tool for making new options available, for beckoning forth from the invisible unpredictable possibilities. It is political theology.

This tool is risky. No one knows what could emerge from the invisible. Yet, in some circumstances, it is a perfectly reasonable risk. Particularly in impasses, where it feels as if the obvious is straining, political philosophy as a rigorous science proves invaluable. These are exceptional moments. There is a danger that this will be forgotten, that political philosophy will come to be contaminated with the obvious. More than a danger: this is broadly the case, it is how political science and political theory come to displace political philosophy. Political science and political theory are subject to the hegemony of the visible, the former admittedly so, the latter implicitly so. Political science supposes a world saturated with the empirical; political theory presumes to pass beyond what can already be seen but without employing any machinery capable of doing so. The political scientist employs a visible mirror; the political theorist employs an invisible mirror. If these are taken as the only options for political philosophy, calls to abandon the enterprise and return politics to the realm of practical wisdom make sense.

Political philosophy as a rigorous science employs the machinery of demolition, not construction. But when it is contaminated by enchantment, machinery that would seem to demolish actually constructs, resulting in the facade of the ordinary with the substance of the obvious. The quest to disaggregate practices and norms is tainted such that it is not what people do that ultimately matters. Indeed, just naming the ordinary transforms it into the obvious. To be named is to be brought under the sway of the hegemony of the visible. Of course, this is not to suggest a fetishization of the ordinary as unnameable. That would be but a different form of idolatry, a different form of supersessionism. If the ordinary, the subject of political philosophy, is neither nameable nor unnameable, how are we to proceed?

Political philosophy must proceed in the guise of the obvious, in the guise of enchantment. It must seem to accept the prevailing way of seeing and of talking, even though it does not. Political philosophy as a rigorous science views enchantment as rhetoric, language intended to persuade. Normally, rhetoric sings the praises of the obvious. Language provides the tentacles of enchantment by saturating, by dazzling—and this is the work of persuasion. Rhetoric saturates a field so that it seems as though what one does and what one ought to do are one and the same. Political philosophy must advance in the guise of rhetoric because otherwise it would be quashed. It would have no relevance to the ordinary because the ordinary is only accessible through the obvious. In order to do the work of political philosophy, to destroy theoretical machinery that is explicit and implicit, an audience must be persuaded.

This is the difference between Socrates and the Sophists. Socrates was just as much a rhetorician as the Sophists. Like them, he started with the obvious, with the everyday language of the enchanted world. And, like them, he sought to persuade. But, unlike them, Socrates did not seek to persuade his interlocutors of a position he already held. The art of sophistry is the art of taking a position which one has been given and making it compelling. Sophistry is the manufacture of idols, dazzling arrays of words that will make the listener realize that she agreed all along. Language saturates, smoothes, seemingly taking account of all of the possibilities. That is how it persuades, and that is how it enchants. In contrast, Socrates begins with the obvious, but not with a particular goal in mind. In his relentless inquiry, he refuses to be dazzled by the obvious. He refuses to be enchanted. He uses examples from the obvious to move beyond the obvious.

The Socratic moment is exemplary, but in Socrates it is only a moment. When political philosophy is understood as a rigorous science, as the examination of what is done, of practices and norms, the critical moment gains traction. It shakes off enchantment in order to see clearly what is done. Some means of persuasion is necessary in order to expose the ordinary, and some means of persuasion is necessary to bring back what is found in the ordinary to the enchanted world. To do this, the skills of the Sophist are necessary. Rhetoric must be mobilized. In this case, rhetoric does not further enchantment, does not persuade of a pregiven, already visible perspective. Rather, rhetoric uses the tools of the obvious to bring to light something which was not obvious from within the obvious. The invisible does not simply reveal itself; it manifests itself through rhetoric.

There is a tendency to ignore rhetoric. There is a popular view that saying is a kind of doing, just another practice, interwoven in "habitus." This is a full embrace of enchantment. It explicitly affirms that enchantment saturates, that there is no way of distinguishing the plane of practices from the plane of norms. All rhetoric does is reconfigure the obvious to advance the interests of one party or another. Philosophy is impotent. Such a view presents a sharp contrast with philosophy understood as a rigorous science. When the difference between the plane of norms and the plane of practices is not acknowledged, the picture that results is of a gradual, harmonious, aesthetic growth—a sort of dance. And it is precisely this picture which limits the possibilities of politics.

It is also a picture which ignores ordinary life. What people do, everywhere, is navigate the middle, between the planes of practices and norms. People talk about what they ought to do, what they wish they had done, what a situation calls for, how a situation was misread. This is not a simulacrum of the philosophical, this is the philosophical. It is the stories that try to make sense of daily activity, and the storytellers who take themselves all too seriously, that enchant. It is they who dazzle, they who are guardians of the hegemony of the visible. They speak loudly and write prolifically. But no one is fooled, not even they themselves. Michel Henry writes of the biologist who dedicates his career to studying life but ignores his own life. The same is true for theorists writ large: in their quest to speak about life they ignore ordinary life, they ignore the daily work of navigating practices and norms (it is tempting to attribute this to the false consciousness of the bourgeois lifestyle).

Political philosophy is the root of political theology. Done rightly, political philosophy makes visible the invisible, and it does so through rhetoric. A particularly efficacious rhetorical technique is to use the language of religion, a language that has wide cultural resonance in the contemporary context. It is, after all, the quintessential language of enchantment. The language of theology can be used sophistically or philosophically; almost always it is used sophistically. It is most often used to enchant, to dazzle. It seems to offer an answer for everything. Theologians say what is supposed to be said, and in doing so they persuade. The language they use does not refer to practices or norms; it is used because it is expected, because it will dazzle—because it will persuade. The language of love, faith, and hope, of tradition, liturgy, sanctity, revelation, and prophecy: this is the familiar language of enchantment, but it can also be the rhetoric of political philosophy. It can be the cloak of the obvious which political philosophy must take on when it walks in the open. This is language that evokes the invisible, but it can be employed to invoke the invisible.

Notes

Introduction: Beyond Supersessionism

Some of the material in this introduction was previously published as "Law, Grace, and Race: The Political Theology of *Manderlay*," *Theory and Event* 11:3 (2008).

1. Nietzsche, *Will to Power*, 250, 251.

2. Wolin, *Politics and Vision*, 490. Cf. Nietzsche, *Ecce Homo*, 144: "The concept of politics will have then merged entirely into a war of spirits, all power structures from the old society will have exploded—they are all based on lies."

3. Schmitt, *Political Theology*, chap. 3.

4. Lilla, *Stillborn God*.

5. Gauchet, *Disenchantment of the World*; Taylor, *Secular Age*.

6. This point is made by Stout, "Modernity Without Essence."

7. Strauss, "Progress or Return?" 123.

8. Brown, *Politics Out of History*, 173.

9. See, for example, Glaude, *In a Shade of Blue*.

10. Brown, *Politics Out of History*, 17.

11. The archbishop of Canterbury mentions this in a sermon available online, at the Anglican Communion Web site, www.anglicancommunion.org/acns/news.cfm /1996/12/25/ACNS1064 (accessed October 17, 2010).

12. My usage of practices and norms, however, is somewhat idiosyncratic, perhaps closer to that of anthropologists than that of philosophers (compare Wallace, *Norms and Practices*). Because practices, on my account, are not individuated, I use the singular and plural interchangeably.

13. Rose writes of "law"; I argue that this should be read as social norms in my *Law and Transcendence*, chap. 1.

14. Rose, *Mourning Becomes the Law*, 2.

15. Ibid., 36.

16. Lloyd, "On the Use of Gillian Rose." Milbank writes, in his obituary of Rose, "At the threshold of her own, eternal consummation, Gillian Rose leaves us to reflect further on the conditions, both political and metaphysical, under which healing may at last supersede rupture."

17. The percolation imagery is actually Rose's, but she uses it to mean something rather different.

18. See Boyarin, "A Broken Olive Branch."

19. Mathewes, *A Theology of Public Life*.

20. Butler, *Gender Trouble*.

Chapter 1: Love

Some of the material in this chapter was previously published as "On Gillian Rose and Love," *Telos* 143 (Summer 2008): 47–62.

1. Rose, *Love's Work*, chap. 8. All parenthetical page number references to Rose in this chapter are from *Love's Work*.

2. Rose, *Dialectic of Nihilism*; Rose, *Hegel Contra Sociology*; Rose's views on this are discussed and developed in Lloyd, *Law and Transcendence*.

3. Rose, *Hegel Contra Sociology*. Compare Butler, *Subjects of Desire*, who offers a similar reading of Hegel. Rose and Butler's accounts of Hegel are discussed in more detail in Chapter 2. Jean-Luc Marion develops "first philosophy" in "The Other First Philosophy."

4. For example, Milbank, "Living with Anxiety."

5. Cf. Derrida, "Force of Law."

6. Cf. Žižek, *Sublime Object of Ideology*.

7. The following discussion draws on Benveniste, *Indo-European Language and Society*; and Staten, *Eros in Mourning*, chap. 2.

8. Staten, *Eros in Mourning*, 28, citing J. T. Kakridis, *Homeric Researches* (Lund: C. W. K. Gleerup, 1949), 20.

9. Plato, *Lysis* 219d. The discussion here draws on Vlastos, "The Individual as an Object of Love in Plato."

10. Compare this to Slavoj Žižek's illustration of what might be called the supersessionist understanding of sexual intercourse:

> In the well-known vulgar joke about a fool having intercourse for the first time, the girl has to tell him exactly what to do: "See this hole between my legs? Put it in here. Now push it deep. Now pull it out. Push it in, pull it out, push it in, pull it out . . ." "Now wait a minute," the fool interrupts her, "make up your mind! In or out?" What the fool misses is precisely the structure of a drive which gets its satisfaction from the indecision itself, from repeated oscillation. (Žižek, *Parallax View*, 64)

11. Murdoch, *Sovereignty of Good*, 65.

12. Murdoch, quoted in Hall, "Limits of the Story," 5.

Chapter 2: Faith

Some of the material in this chapter was previously published as "The Secular Faith of Gillian Rose," *Journal of Religious Ethics* 36:4 (2008): 683–705.

1. See the incisive discussion of these issues in Dubler, "Secular Bad Faith."

2. Quoted in Rorty, *Achieving Our Country*, 10.

3. I mean to evoke the discussion of presentation and representation in Badiou, *Being and Event*.

4. Cf. Haugeland, "Heidegger on Being a Person"; Brandom, "Freedom and Constraint by Norms"; Hart, *The Concept of Law*, chap. 5.

5. This point is made persuasively in the work of Judith Butler. See especially Butler, *Gender Trouble*.

6. Brandom, "Freedom and Constraint by Norms." Brandom expands on these views, although in a direction less relevant to this discussion, in his *Making It Explicit*. For a powerful critique of Brandom's work, see Rosen, "Who Makes the Rules Around Here?"

7. Rose, *Paradiso*, 63.

8. Rose, *Love's Work*, 35.

9. Stout, *Democracy and Tradition*.

10. Rose, *Love's Work*, 54.

11. Ibid., 35.

12. Butler, *Subjects of Desire*; Rose, *Hegel Contra Sociology*. Catherine Malabou's more recent work on Hegel has strong affinities with the work of Butler and Rose. See Malabou, *Future of Hegel*.

13. Butler, *Subjects of Desire*, 20. Page numbers in parentheses in the following passage refer to this source.

14. Ibid., 62, 68; Butler, *Undoing Gender*.

15. Rose, *Hegel Contra Sociology*, 159.

16. Rose, *Love's Work*, 20.

17. Rose, *Paradiso*, 31–32.

18. Rose, *Broken Middle*, 148.

19. Ibid.

20. Rose, *Love's Work*, 98.

21. Rose, *Broken Middle*, 148.

22. Ibid.

23. Ibid., 151.

24. Ibid., 293.

25. Rose, *Love's Work*, 135.

26. Rose, *Broken Middle*, 307.

27. Ibid., 87.

28. Rose, *Love's Work*, 9.

29. Lynn Rose, in conversation with the author, suggested that her daughter's memoir is heavily fictionalized.

30. This paragraph and those that follow draw on Adams, "Moral Faith."

31. Dewey, *A Common Faith*; Dewey, "Creative Democracy." There was a fascinating, nearly contemporaneous interest in a similar conception of faith among American liberal Protestants. Modernists used "'belief' to stipulate a hypothesis or idea, whereas 'faith' is a constancy built from the persistent weighing of asserted beliefs." Lofton, "Methodology of the Modernists," 389n48.

Chapter 3: Hope

1. Compare Mathewes, *Theology of Public Life*, to Rorty, *Philosophy and Social Hope*. Akiba Lerner has recently offered a Jewish account of the virtue of hope; I find it unpersuasive. Lerner, "Rorty, Buber, and the Revival of Social Hope."

2. Augustine, *Enchiridion*.

3. Rose focuses particularly on the work of Mark C. Taylor and John Milbank, associating them both with this longing for a "New Jerusalem." Rose, *Broken Middle*, chap. 6.

4. Rose, "Interview," 217.

5. Rose, *Mourning Becomes the Law*, 146.

6. Freud, "Mourning and Melancholia"; cf. Rose, *Mourning Becomes the Law*.

7. Butler, *Gender Trouble*.

8. Brown, *States of Injury*; cf. Butler, *Psychic Life of Power*, introduction.

9. Edelman, *No Future*.

10. This is a common view in the analytic philosophy literature on hope. For an overview of that literature and a proposal to focus on what I would call the rhetorical power of hope, see Martin, "Hopes and Dreams."

11. Rorty, *Philosophy and Social Hope*.

12. Rorty, *Achieving Our Country*, 3.

13. Ibid., 7.

14. Ibid.

15. Lasch, *True and Only Heaven*.

16. Walzer, *Exodus and Revolution*.

17. Ibid., 102.

18. Deneen, *Democratic Faith*, xvii.

19. Bercovitch, *American Jeremiad*, xi. See also Guyatt, *Providence and the Invention of the United States*.

20. Rose, *Paradiso*, 21. Clément Rosset makes a similar point in the first chapter of his *Joyful Cruelty*.

Chapter 4: Tradition

1. For example, Stout, *Democracy and Tradition*; West, *Democracy Matters*.

2. Benjamin, *Illuminations*, 144–45.

3. Ibid., 117.

4. Gauchet, *Disenchantment of the World*.

5. Kafka, *Amerika*, 3.

6. See, for example, Cornel West's discussion of *Moby-Dick* in *Democracy Matters* and, with a focus more on social imagination than on virtue, John Lardas [Modern], "Specters of *Moby-Dick*."

7. Quoted in Benjamin, *Illuminations*, 116.

8. For an example of a political reading of Kafka that focuses on the Kafkaesque, see Bennett, "Deceptive Comfort."

9. Kafka, *The Trial*, 213–15.

10. Butler, *Gender Trouble*, xiv. See also Derrida, "Before the Law," on which Butler draws.

11. Agamben, *Homo Sacer*, 50.

Chapter 5: Liturgy

1. Carlsson, *Critical Mass*; Ferrell, *Tearing Down the Streets*, chap. 3 (quote from 116); McGrath, "Holy Rollers."

2. Cavanaugh, *Torture and Eucharist*, 275 (call and response abridged from 274–75).

3. Ibid., 277.

4. Durkheim, *Elementary Forms of Religious Life*.

5. Turner, *Ritual Process*.

6. This and following paragraphs draw on Buc, *Dangers of Ritual*. See also Milbank, *Theology and Social Theory*. For a response to Buc, see Koziol, "Dangers of Polemic."

7. Quoted in Buc, *Dangers of Ritual*, 144–46.

8. See, for example, Bell, *Ritual Theory, Ritual Practice*.

9. Pickstock, *After Writing*; Mathewes, *Theology of Public Life*; Schwartz, *Sacramental Poetics*. I expand on the ideas discussed below in Lloyd, "Liturgy in the Broadest Sense."

10. Kepnes, *Jewish Liturgical Reasoning*.

11. See Pickstock, "Liturgy, Art, and Politics," 178.

12. Ibid. 160. I draw on this article, as well as Cavanaugh, *Theopolitical Imagination*, throughout the discussion that follows.

13. Pickstock, "Liturgy, Art, and Politics," 167. See also the chapter of Pickstock's *After Writing* titled "The Decline of the Liturgical Order."

14. See especially Milbank, "On Complex Space," as well as Milbank, "'Postmodern Critical Augustinianism,'" and Pickstock, "Music."

15. Cavanaugh, *Torture and Eucharist*.

16. This focus on aesthetic judgment has recently gained traction in quite a different quarter: among political theorists working in the wake of Hannah Arendt's *Lectures on Kant's Political Philosophy*. For example, see Zerilli, "Toward a Feminist Theory of Judgment."

17. Schmemann, *Liturgy and Tradition*, 12. See also Schmemann's *Introduction to Liturgical Theology*, which advocates a shift from asking "how" worship is done to asking "what" is done in worship.

18. Kavanagh, *On Liturgical Theology*. Wainwright contests Kavanagh's understanding of this phrase. Wainwright, *Doxology*, 219–25. This was also a focus of interest amongst the late nineteenth- and early twentieth-century modernists. See, for example, Tyrrell, "*Lex Orandi, Lex Credendi*."

19. Kavanagh, *On Liturgical Theology*, 75.

20. Ibid., 100.

21. Ibid., 125.

22. My colleague Kathryn McClymond is currently preparing a book on ritual gone wrong that focuses on the proliferation of rules for when ritual rules are not followed. The instinct, in ritual, or at least in what is studied as ritual, is to cover every possible practice with a norm.

23. Lacoste, *Experience and the Absolute*, 37, 24.

24. See Lacoste, "La connaissance silencieuse."

25. Lacoste, *Experience and the Absolute*, 152.

26. Carlsson, *Critical Mass*, 6.

27. Ibid., 7, 8 (capitalization altered). See also Ferrell, *Tearing Down the Streets*, 112: "At its most basic, the simple, direct act of bicycle riding en masse alters the meaning of

riding for those involved; rolling along together, cyclists invent new experiences from the immediacy of their own collective activity."

28. Chris Carlsson, quoted in Ferrell, *Tearing Down the Streets*, 107.

29. Ferrell, *Tearing Down the Streets*, 114.

30. Weil, *Letter to a Priest*, 78.

31. Weil, *Waiting for God*, 35.

32. Ibid., 8.

33. Althusser, "Ideology and Ideological State Apparatuses," 157.

34. Weil, *Gravity and Grace*, 105.

35. Weil, *Letter to a Priest*, 62.

36. Ibid., 61.

Chapter 6: Sanctity

Some of the material in this chapter was previously published as "On Saying Yes: Perversion and the Sacred," *Symptom* 8 (Winter 2007), at *The Symptom* Web site, www.lacan.com/symptom8_articles/lloyd8.html (accessed August 30, 2010).

1. Andrew Shanks develops the useful distinction between a "desire for justice" and a "desire for innocence," associating the former with the work of Gillian Rose, in his *Against Innocence*.

2. The account here and below expands on Lloyd, "On Saying Yes." I make no claim to Lacanian "orthodoxy." I take what seems useful from Lacanian theory, drawing especially on Fink, *Clinical Introduction to Lacanian Psychoanalysis*; Miller, "A Discussion"; Miller, "On Perversion"; and Lacan, "Kant with Sade." For a more "orthodox" Lacanian perspective on sanctity, see Regnault, "Saintliness and Sainthood."

3. "Osama bin Laden and President Bush, although politically opponents, share a pervert structure: they both act upon the presupposition that their acts are directly ordered and guided by the divine will." Žižek, "Fundamental Perversion," 127.

4. Weil, *Waiting for God*, 23.

5. Weil, *Gravity and Grace*, 144. The parenthetical quotations that follow are from this text.

6. Ibid., 58. The page numbers in parentheses in the following passage also refer to *Gravity and Grace*.

7. See "Angry Angels," in Rose, *Judaism and Modernity*.

8. Weil, *Waiting for God*, 49.

9. Weil, *Gravity and Grace*, 12.

10. Ibid., 19.

11. Ibid., 18.

Chapter 7: Revelation

1. The phrase comes from Rorty, "Religion as a Conversation-Stopper"; Rorty later moderated his position.

2. For a discussion of authority along these lines, see Raz, "Authority, Law, and Morality."

3. This account of the event follows Romano, *Event and World*.

4. The incident he discusses takes place in William Faulkner's novel *The Reivers.* Romano, *Event and World*, 34.

5. For an accessible entry point to Badiou's work, see his *Ethics* or his *Saint Paul.* For a more comprehensive statement, see his *Being and Event.*

6. Birth is a privileged topic in Romano's account of the event. See his *Event and World.*

7. Discussion with George Shulman has helped me think through these issues. See Shulman, *American Prophecy.*

8. See, for example, Balfour, *Evidence of Things Not Said.*

9. Baldwin, "The Rockpile," 16.

10. Baldwin, "Autobiographical Notes," in *Notes of a Native Son*, 4.

11. Baldwin, "Many Thousands Gone," in *Notes of a Native Son*, 27.

12. Marion, "Reason of the Gift."

13. Ibid., 122.

14. Baldwin, "Everybody's Protest Novel," in *Notes of a Native Son*, 17.

15. Baldwin, "Autobiographical Notes," 3.

16. Baldwin, "Everybody's Protest Novel," 14.

Chapter 8: Prophecy

1. Asad, *Formations of the Secular*, 44.

2. Marcus, *Shape of Things to Come*, 11.

3. Levinas, "Being-for-the-Other," 116.

4. Walzer, *Thick and Thin*, 42.

5. Walzer, *Exodus and Revolution*, 91; Walzer, *Interpretation and Social Criticism.*

6. West, *Prophetic Thought in Postmodern Times*, 3.

7. Sharlet, "Supreme Love and Revolutionary Funk," 59.

8. West, *Prophetic Reflections*, 58.

9. Ibid., 67.

10. Ibid.

11. Ibid., 74.

12. West, *Democracy Matters.*

13. West, *American Evasion of Philosophy*, 226.

14. Ibid., 225.

15. Foucault, *History of Sexuality*, 95.

16. Baldwin, "Notes of a Native Son," in *Notes of a Native Son*, 71.

17. See McDowell, "Virtue and Reason," for a development of this account of virtue.

18. For example, Stout, *Democracy and Tradition*, chap. 2.

Conclusion: Politics of the Middle

1. Bresson, *Notes on the Cinematographer*, 43.

2. Ibid., 107.

3. Sontag, "Spiritual Style in the Films of Robert Bresson." See also Schrader, *Transcendental Style in Film.*

4. Sontag, "Spiritual Style in the Films of Robert Bresson," 187.

5. Bujalski's third film, *Beeswax* (2009), centers on twin sisters.

6. Dumm, *Politics of the Ordinary*, 48.

7. Levinas, *Totality and Infinity*, pt. 4.

8. Cf. Mansfield, *Manliness*.

9. Zerilli, *Feminism and the Abyss of Freedom*; see also Zerilli, "Toward a Feminist Theory."

10. Zerilli, *Feminism and the Abyss of Freedom*, 34.

11. For a discussion of some examples, see Lloyd, "On the Use of Gillian Rose."

12. Rose, *Love's Work*, 25. See also Rose, "Interview," 218.

13. Rose concludes, "The Lovers must leave a distance, a boundary, for love: then they approach and retire so that love may suspire. This may be heard as the economics of eros; but it may also be taken as the infinite passion of faith." *Love's Work*, 142.

14. Giorgio Agamben describes the enchantment which obscures:

The very possibility of distinguishing life and law, anomie and *nomos*, coincides with their articulation in the biopolitical machine. Bare life is a product of the machine and not something that preexists it, just as law has no court in nature or in the divine mind. Life and law, anomie and *nomos*, *auctoritas* and *potestas*, result from the fracture of something to which we have no other access than through the fiction of their articulation and the patient work that, by unmasking this fiction, separates what it had claimed to unite. . . . To show law in its nonrelation to life and life in its nonrelation to law means to open a space between them for human action, which once claimed for itself the name of "politics." (Agamben, *State of Exception*, 87–88)

15. While I am largely sympathetic to Villa's *Socratic Citizenship*, I am not convinced that Villa sufficiently appreciates the exceptionality of the Socratic moment.

Appendix: Political Theology as a Rigorous Science

1. Of course I have in mind Husserl, "Philosophy as a Rigorous Science."

2. Marion, "The Other First Philosophy," 793.

3. Henry, *I Am the Truth*, 27. See also Henry, *Material Phenomenology*. A similar point has recently been made from quite a different perspective by Michael Thompson in his *Life and Action*.

4. Henry, *I Am the Truth*, 38.

5. See ibid., conclusion; Henry, *La barbarie*.

6. See Henry, *Material Phenomenology*, 128; cf. Henry, *Genealogy of Psychoanalysis*.

7. Henry, *I Am the Truth*, 31.

8. For example, Marion, "Reason of the Gift," 133: "The gift is never wrong, because it never does wrong. Never being wrong, it is always right (literally, has reason)."

9. See Marion, *God Without Being*, chap. 1.

10. For example, Geuss, *Philosophy and Real Politics*.

Bibliography

Adams, Robert Merrihew. "Moral Faith." In *Finite and Infinite Goods: A Framework for Ethics*, 373–89. Oxford: Oxford University Press, 1999.

Agamben, Giorgio. *Homo Sacer: Sovereign Power and Bare Life*. Trans. Daniel Heller-Roazen. Stanford, CA: Stanford University Press, 1998.

———. *State of Exception*. Trans. Kevin Attell. Chicago: University of Chicago Press, 2005.

Althusser, Louis. "Ideology and Ideological State Apparatuses." In *Lenin and Philosophy, and Other Essays*, trans. Ben Brewster, 127–89. New York: Monthly Review Press, 1972.

Arendt, Hannah. *Lectures on Kant's Political Philosophy*. Chicago: University of Chicago Press, 1992.

Asad, Talal. *Formations of the Secular: Christianity, Islam, Modernity*. Stanford, CA: Stanford University Press, 2003.

Augustine. *The Enchiridion on Faith, Hope, and Love*. Washington, DC: Regnery, 1996.

Badiou, Alain. *Being and Event*. Trans. Oliver Feltham. London: Continuum, 2005.

———. *Ethics: An Essay on the Understanding of Evil*. Trans. Peter Hallward. London: Verso, 2002.

———. *Saint Paul: The Foundation of Universalism*. Trans. Ray Brassier. Stanford, CA: Stanford University Press, 2003.

Baldwin, James. *The Fire Next Time*. New York: Vintage Books, 1992.

———. *Notes of a Native Son*. New York: Bantam Books, 1964.

———. "The Rockpile." In *Going to Meet the Man: Stories*, 13–25. New York: Vintage Books, 1995.

Balfour, Lawrie. *The Evidence of Things Not Said: James Baldwin and the Promise of American Democracy*. Ithaca, NY: Cornell University Press, 2001.

Bell, Catherine. *Ritual Theory, Ritual Practice*. Oxford: Oxford University Press, 1992.

Benjamin, Walter. *Illuminations*. Ed. Hannah Arendt. Trans. Harry Zohn. New York: Schocken Books, 1969.

Bennett, Jane. "Deceptive Comfort: The Power of Kafka's Stories." *Political Theory* 19:1 (February 1991): 73–95.

Benveniste, Émile. *Indo-European Language and Society*. Trans. Elizabeth Palmer. Coral Gables, FL: University of Miami Press, 1973.

Bercovitch, Sacvan. *The American Jeremiad*. Madison: University of Wisconsin Press, 1978.

Boyarin, Daniel. "A Broken Olive Branch." In *Symposium on John Milbank's Theology and Social Theory*, special issue, *Arachne* 2:1 (1995): 124–30.

Brandom, Robert. "Freedom and Constraint by Norms." *American Philosophical Quarterly* 16 (1979): 187–96.

———. *Making It Explicit: Reasoning, Representing, and Discursive Commitment*. Cambridge, MA: Harvard University Press, 1994.

Bresson, Robert. *Notes on the Cinematographer*. Trans. Jonathan Griffin. Copenhagen: Green Integer, 1997.

Brown, Wendy. *Politics Out of History*. Princeton, NJ: Princeton University Press, 2001.

———. *States of Injury: Power and Freedom in Late Modernity*. Princeton, NJ: Princeton University Press, 1995.

Buc, Philippe. *The Dangers of Ritual: Between Early Medieval Texts and Social Scientific Theory*. Princeton, NJ: Princeton University Press, 2001.

Butler, Judith. *Gender Trouble: Feminism and the Subversion of Identity*. 10th anniversary ed. New York: Routledge, 1999.

———. *The Psychic Life of Power: Theories in Subjection*. Stanford, CA: Stanford University Press, 1997.

———. *Subjects of Desire: Hegelian Reflections in Twentieth-Century France*. New York: Columbia University Press, 1987.

———. *Undoing Gender*. New York: Routledge, 2004.

Carlsson, Chris, ed. *Critical Mass: Bicycling's Defiant Celebration*. Edinburgh: AK Press, 2002.

Carter, J. Kameron. *Race: A Theological Account*. Oxford: Oxford University Press, 2008.

Cavanaugh, William T. *Theopolitical Imagination*. London: T. and T. Clark, 2002.

———. *Torture and Eucharist: Theology, Politics, and the Body of Christ*. Oxford: Blackwell, 1998.

Deneen, Patrick J. *Democratic Faith*. Princeton, NJ: Princeton University Press, 2005.

Derrida, Jacques. "Before the Law." In *Acts of Literature*, ed. Derek Attridge, 181–220. New York: Routledge, 1992.

———. "Force of Law: The 'Mystical Foundation of Authority.'" In *Deconstruction and the Possibility of Justice*, ed. Drucilla Cornell, Michel Rosenfeld, and David Gray Carlson, 3–67. New York: Routledge, 1992.

Dewey, John. *A Common Faith*. New Haven, CT: Yale University Press, 1934.

———. "Creative Democracy: The Task Before Us." In *John Dewey: The Later Works, 1925–1953*, ed. Jo Ann Boydston, 14 (1939–1941), 224–30. Carbondale, IL: Southern Illinois University Press, 1988.

Dubler, Joshua. "The Secular Bad Faith of Harry Theriault, The Bishop of Tellus." In *Secular Faith*, ed. Vincent Lloyd and Elliot Ratzman, 44–75. Eugene, OR: Cascade Books, 2010.

Dumm, Thomas L. *A Politics of the Ordinary*. New York: New York University Press, 1999.

Durkheim, Émile. *The Elementary Forms of the Religious Life*. Trans. Joseph Ward. New York: Free Press, 1965.

Edelman, Lee. *No Future: Queer Theory and the Death Drive.* Durham, NC: Duke University Press, 2004.

Ferrell, Jeff. *Tearing Down the Streets: Adventures in Urban Anarchy.* New York: Palgrave, 2001.

Fink, Bruce. *A Clinical Introduction to Lacanian Psychoanalysis.* Cambridge, MA: Harvard University Press, 1999.

Foucault, Michel. *The History of Sexuality, Volume 1: An Introduction.* Trans. Robert Hurley. New York: Vintage Books, 1990.

Freud, Sigmund. "Mourning and Melancholia." In *The Standard Edition of the Complete Psychological Works of Sigmund Freud,* 24 vols., ed. James Strachey, 14: 243–58. London: Hogarth Press, 1953–74.

Gauchet, Marcel. *The Disenchantment of the World: A Political History of Religion.* Trans. Oscar Burge. Princeton, NJ: Princeton University Press, 1997.

Geuss, Raymond. *Philosophy and Real Politics.* Princeton, NJ: Princeton University Press, 2008.

Glaude, Eddie S. *In a Shade of Blue: Pragmatism and the Politics of Black America.* Chicago: University of Chicago Press, 2007.

Guyatt, Nicholas. *Providence and the Invention of the United States, 1607–1876.* New York: Cambridge University Press, 2007.

Hall, Pamela M. "Limits of the Story: Tragedy in Recent Virtue Ethics." *Studies in Christian Ethics* 17:1 (2004): 1–10.

Hart, H. L. A. *The Concept of Law.* 2nd ed. Oxford: Clarendon Press, 1994.

Haugeland, John. "Heidegger on Being a Person." *Nous* 16:1 (March 1982): 15–28.

Henry, Michel. *La barbarie.* Paris: Presses Universitaires de France, 2004.

———. *The Genealogy of Psychoanalysis.* Trans. Douglas Brick. Stanford, CA: Stanford University Press, 1993.

———. *I Am the Truth: Toward a Philosophy of Christianity.* Trans. Susan Emanuel. Stanford, CA: Stanford University Press, 2003.

———. *Material Phenomenology.* Trans. Scott Davidson. New York: Fordham University Press, 2008.

Husserl, Edmund. "Philosophy as a Rigorous Science." In *Phenomenology and the Crisis of Philosophy,* trans. Quentin Lauer, 71–147. New York: Harper Torchbooks, 1965.

Kafka, Franz. *Amerika.* Trans. Willa Muir and Edwin Muir. New York: Schocken Books, 1996.

———. "Before the Law." In *The Complete Stories,* ed. Nahum N. Glatzer, 3–4. New York: Schocken Books, 1971.

———. *The Castle: A New Translation.* Trans. Mark Harman. New York: Schocken Books, 1998.

———. *The Trial.* Trans. Breon Mitchell. New York: Schocken Books, 1998.

Kavanagh, Aidan. *On Liturgical Theology.* Collegeville, MN: Liturgical Press, 1992.

Kepnes, Steven. *Jewish Liturgical Reasoning.* Oxford: Oxford University Press, 2007.

Koziol, Geoffrey. "The Dangers of Polemic: Is Ritual Still an Interesting Topic of Historical Study?" *Early Medieval Europe* 11:4 (2002): 267–88.

Lacoste, Jean-Yves. "La connaissance silencieuse." In *Présence et parousie*. Geneva: Ad Solem, 2006.

————. *Experience and the Absolute: Disputed Questions on the Humanity of Man*. Trans. Mark Raftery-Skehan. New York: Fordham University Press, 2004.

Lacan, Jacques. "Kant with Sade." In *Écrits*, trans. Bruce Fink, 645–668. New York: W. W. Norton, 2006.

Lardas [Modern], John H. "Specters of *Moby-Dick*: A Particular History of Cultural Metaphysics in America." Ph.D. diss., University of California, Santa Barbara, 2003.

Lasch, Christopher. *The True and Only Heaven: Progress and Its Critics*. New York: W. W. Norton, 1991.

Lerner, Akiba. "Rorty, Buber, and the Revival of Social Hope." Ph.D. diss., Stanford University, 2007.

Levinas, Emmanuel. "Being-for-the-Other." In *Is It Righteous to Be? Interviews with Emmanuel Levinas*, ed. Jill Robbins, 114–20. Stanford, CA: Stanford University Press, 2001.

————. *Totality and Infinity: An Essay on Exteriority*. Trans. Alphonso Lingis. Dordrecht: Kluwer Academic Publishers, 1991.

Lilla, Mark. *The Stillborn God*. New York: Alfred A. Knopf, 2007.

Lloyd, Vincent W. *Law and Transcendence: On the Unfinished Project of Gillian Rose*. Basingstoke: Palgrave Macmillan, 2009.

————. "Liturgy in the Broadest Sense." *New Blackfriars* (forthcoming).

————. "On Saying Yes: Perversion and the Sacred." *Symptom* 8 (Winter 2007). See *The Symptom* Web site, www.lacan.com/symptom8_articles/lloyd8.html (accessed August 30, 2010).

————. "On the Use of Gillian Rose." *Heythrop Journal* 48 (September 2007): 697–706.

Lofton, Kathryn. "The Methodology of the Modernists: Process in American Protestantism." *Church History* 75:2 (June 2006): 374–402.

Malabou, Catherine. *The Future of Hegel: Plasticity, Temporality and Dialectic*. Trans. Lisabeth During. London: Routledge, 2005.

Mansfield, Harvey. *Manliness*. New Haven, CT: Yale University Press, 2006.

Marcus, Greil. *The Shape of Things to Come: Prophecy and the American Voice*. New York: Farrar, Straus and Giroux, 2006.

Marion, Jean-Luc. *God Without Being: Hors-Texte*. Trans. Thomas A. Carlson. Chicago: University of Chicago Press, 1991.

————. "The Other First Philosophy and the Question of Givenness." Trans. Jeffrey L. Kosky. *Critical Inquiry* 25:4 (Summer 1999): 784–800.

————. "The Reason of the Gift." In *Givenness and God: Questions of Jean-Luc Marion*, ed. Ian Leask and Eoin Cassidy, 101–34. New York: Fordham University Press, 2005.

Martin, Adrienne M. "Hopes and Dreams." *Philosophy and Phenomenological Research* (forthcoming).

Mathewes, Charles T. *A Theology of Public Life*. Cambridge: Cambridge University Press, 2007.

McDowell, John. "Virtue and Reason." *Monist* 62 (1979): 331–50.

McGrath, Ben. "Holy Rollers: The City's Bicycle Zealots." *New Yorker*, November 13, 2006.

Milbank, John. "Living with Anxiety." Review of *The Broken Middle*, by Gillian Rose. *Times Higher Education Supplement*, June 26, 1992.

———. Obituary of Gillian Rose. *The Independent*. December 13, 1995. Available at www.independent.co.uk/news/people/obituaries-professor-gillian-rose-1525497. html (accessed August 30, 2010).

———. "On Complex Space." In *The Word Made Strange: Theology, Language, Culture*, 268–92. Oxford: Blackwell, 1997.

———. "'Postmodern Critical Augustinianism': A Short Summa in Forty-Two Responses to Unasked Questions." *Modern Theology* 7:3 (April 1991): 225–37.

———. *Theology and Social Theory: Beyond Secular Reason*. 2nd ed. Oxford: Blackwell, 2006.

Miller, Jacques-Alain. "A Discussion of Lacan's 'Kant with Sade.'" In *Reading Seminars I and II: Lacan's Return to Freud*, ed. Richard Feldstein, Bruce Fink, and Maire Jaanus, 212–37. Albany: State University of New York Press, 1996.

———. "On Perversion." In *Reading Seminars I and II: Lacan's Return to Freud*, ed. Richard Feldstein, Bruce Fink, and Maire Jaanus, 306–20. Albany: State University of New York Press, 1996.

Murdoch, Iris. *The Sovereignty of Good*. London: Routledge and Kegan Paul, 1970.

Nietzsche, Friedrich. *Ecce Homo*. In *The Anti-Christ, Ecce Homo, Twilight of the Idols, and Other Writings*, trans. Judith Norman. Cambridge: Cambridge University Press, 2004.

———. *Will to Power*. Vol. 14 of *Complete Works*, ed. Oscar Levy, various translators. New York: Russell and Russell, 1964.

Pickstock, Catherine. *After Writing: On the Liturgical Consummation of Philosophy*. Oxford: Blackwell, 1999.

———. "Music: Soul, City, and Cosmos After Augustine." In *Radical Orthodoxy: A New Theology*, ed. John Milbank, Catherine Pickstock, and Graham Ward, 243–77. London: Routledge, 1999.

———. "Liturgy, Art, and Politics." *Modern Theology* 16:2 (April 2000): 159–80.

Raz, Joseph. "Authority, Law, and Morality." In *Ethics in the Public Domain: Essays in the Morality of Law and Politics*, 194–221. Oxford: Clarendon Press, 1994.

Regnault, François. "Saintliness and Sainthood." Trans. Peter Bradley. *lacanian ink* 33 (2009): 115–25.

Romano, Claude. *Event and World*. Trans. Shane Mackinlay. New York: Fordham University Press, 2008.

Rorty, Richard. *Achieving Our Country: Leftist Thought in Twentieth-Century America*. Cambridge, MA: Harvard University Press, 1998.

———. *Philosophy and Social Hope*. London: Penguin Books, 1999.

———. "Religion as a Conversation-Stopper." In *Philosophy and Social Hope*, 168–74. London: Penguin Books, 1999.

Rose, Gillian. *The Broken Middle: Out of Our Ancient Society*. Oxford: Blackwell, 1992.

———. *Dialectic of Nihilism: Post-Structuralism and Law*. New York: Blackwell, 1984.

———. *Hegel Contra Sociology*. London: Athlone, 1981.

————. "Interview with Gillian Rose." Ed. and intro. Vincent Lloyd. *Theory, Culture and Society* 25:7–8 (December 2008): 201–18.

————. *Judaism and Modernity: Philosophical Essays.* Oxford: Blackwell, 1993.

————. *Love's Work: A Reckoning with Life.* New York: Schocken Books, 1995.

————. *Mourning Becomes the Law: Philosophy and Representation.* Cambridge: Cambridge University Press, 1996.

————. *Paradiso.* London: Menard Press, 1999.

Rosen, Gideon. "Who Makes the Rules Around Here?" *Philosophy and Phenomenological Research* 57:1 (March 1997): 167–71.

Rosset, Clément. *Joyful Cruelty: Toward a Philosophy of the Real.* Trans. David F. Bell. New York: Oxford University Press, 1993.

Schrader, Paul. *Transcendental Style in Film: Ozu, Bresson, Dreyer.* Berkeley: University of California Press, 1972.

Schmemann, Alexander. *Introduction to Liturgical Theology.* Crestwood, NY: St. Vladimir's Seminary Press, 1996.

————. *Liturgy and Tradition: Theological Reflections of Alexander Schmemann.* Ed. Thomas J. Fisch. Crestwood, NY: St. Vladimir's Seminary Press, 1990.

Schmitt, Carl. *Political Theology: Four Chapters on the Concept of Sovereignty.* Trans. George Schwab. Chicago: University of Chicago Press, 2005.

Schwartz, Regina Mara. *Sacramental Poetics at the Dawn of Secularism: When God Left the World.* Stanford, CA: Stanford University Press, 2008.

Shanks, Andrew. *Against Innocence: Gillian Rose's Reception and Gift of Faith.* London: SCM Press, 2008.

Sharlet, Jeff. "The Supreme Love and Revolutionary Funk of Dr. Cornel West, Philosopher of the Blues." *Rolling Stone,* May 28, 2009.

Shulman, George. *American Prophecy: Race and Redemption in American Political Culture.* Minneapolis: University of Minnesota Press, 2008.

Sontag, Susan. "Spiritual Style in the Films of Robert Bresson." In *Against Interpretation,* 177–95. New York: Farrar, Straus and Giroux, 1964.

Staten, Henry. *Eros in Mourning: Homer to Lacan.* Baltimore: Johns Hopkins University Press, 1995.

Stout, Jeffrey. *Democracy and Tradition.* Princeton, NJ: Princeton University Press, 2004.

————. "Modernity Without Essence." *Soundings* 74:3–4 (Fall–Winter 1991): 525–40.

Strauss, Leo. "Progress or Return?" In *Jewish Philosophy and the Crisis of Modernity: Essays and Lectures in Modern Jewish Thought,* ed. Kenneth Hart Green, 87–136. Albany: State University of New York Press, 1997.

Taylor, Charles. *A Secular Age.* Cambridge, MA: Belknap Press of Harvard University Press, 2007.

Thompson, Michael. *Life and Action: Elementary Structures of Practice and Practical Thought.* Cambridge, MA: Harvard University Press, 2008.

Turner, Victor. *The Ritual Process: Structure and Anti-Structure.* Ithaca, NY: Cornell University Press, 1977.

Tyrrell, George. "*Lex Orandi, Lex Credendi.*" In *Through Scylla and Charybdis; or, The Old Theology and the New,* 85–105. London: Longmans, Green, 1907.

Villa, Dana. *Socratic Citizenship*. Princeton, NJ: Princeton University Press, 2001.

Vlastos, Gregory. "The Individual as Object of Love in Plato." In *Platonic Studies*, 3–42. Princeton, NJ: Princeton University Press, 1973.

Wainwright, Geoffrey. *Doxology: The Praise of God in Worship, Doctrine, and Life: A Systematic Theology*. New York: Oxford University Press, 1980.

Wallace, James D. *Norms and Practices*. Ithaca, NY: Cornell University Press, 2009.

Walzer, Michael. *Exodus and Revolution*. New York: Basic Books, 1985.

———. *Interpretation and Social Criticism*. Cambridge, MA: Harvard University Press, 1993.

———. *Thick and Thin: Moral Argument at Home and Abroad*. Notre Dame, IN: University of Notre Dame Press, 1994.

Weil, Simone. *Gravity and Grace*. Trans. Emma Craufurd. London: Routledge and Kegan Paul, 1963.

———. *Letter to a Priest*. Trans. A. F. Wills. London: Routledge and Kegan Paul, 1953.

———. *Waiting for God*. Trans. Emma Craufurd. New York: Perennial, 2001.

West, Cornel. *The American Evasion of Philosophy: A Genealogy of Pragmatism*. Madison: University of Wisconsin Press, 1989.

———. *Democracy Matters: Winning the Fight Against Imperialism*. New York: Penguin Books, 2004.

———. *Prophetic Reflections: Notes on Race and Power in America*. Vol. 2 of *Beyond Eurocentrism and Multiculturalism*. Monroe, ME: Common Courage Press, 1993.

———. *Prophetic Thought in Postmodern Times*. Vol. 1 of *Beyond Eurocentrism and Multiculturalism*. Monroe, ME: Common Courage Press, 1993.

Wolin, Sheldon. *Politics and Vision*. Expanded ed. Princeton, NJ: Princeton University Press, 2004.

Zerilli, Linda M. G. *Feminism and the Abyss of Freedom*. Chicago: University of Chicago Press, 2005.

———. "Toward a Feminist Theory of Judgment." *Signs: Journal of Women in Culture and Society* 34:2 (January 2009): 295–317.

Žižek, Slavoj. "The Fundamental Perversion: Lacan, Dostoyevsky, Bouyeri." *lacanian ink* 27 (2006): 114–29.

———. *The Parallax View*. Cambridge, MA: MIT Press, 2006.

———. *The Sublime Object of Ideology*. London: Verso, 1989.

Index